Global Food Security Governance

In 2007–2008 world food prices spiked and global economic crisis set in, leaving hundreds of millions of people unable to access adequate food. The international reaction was swift. In a bid for leadership, the 123 member countries of the United Nations' Committee on World Food Security (CFS) adopted a series of reforms with the aim of becoming the foremost international, inclusive and intergovernmental platform for food security. Central to the reform was the inclusion of participants (including civil society and the private sector) across all activities of the Committee.

Drawing on data collected from policy documents, interviews and participant observation, this book examines the reorganization and functioning of a UN committee that is coming to be known as a best practice in global governance. Framed by key challenges that plague global governance, the impact and implication of increased civil society engagement are examined by tracing policy negotiations within the CFS, in particular, policy roundtables on smallholder sensitive investment and food price volatility and negotiations on the Voluntary Guidelines on the Responsible Governance of Tenure of Land, Fisheries and Forests in the Context of National Food Security, and the Global Strategic Framework for Food Security and Nutrition. The author shows that through their participation in the Committee, civil society actors are influencing policy outcomes. Yet analysis also reveals that the CFS is being undermined by other actors seeking to gain and maintain influence at the global level. By way of this analysis, this book provides empirically informed insights into increased participation in global governance processes.

Jessica Duncan is an Assistant Professor in the Rural Sociology Group, Wageningen University, The Netherlands. She has a PhD from the Centre for Food Policy, City University London, UK.

Global Food Security Governance

Civil society engagement in the reformed Committee on World Food Security

Jessica Duncan

LONDON AND NEW YORK

First published 2015
by Routledge

2 Park Square, Milton Park, Abingdon, Oxfordshire OX14 4RN
711 Third Avenue, New York, NY 10017

Routledge is an imprint of the Taylor & Francis Group, an informa business

First issued in paperback 2017

© 2015 Jessica Duncan

British Library Cataloguing-in-Publication Data
A catalogue record for this book is available from the British Library

Library of Congress Cataloging in Publication Data
Duncan, Jessica.
Global food security governance : civil society engagement in the reformed Committee on World Food Security / Jessica Duncan.
pages cm. -- (Routledge studies in food, society and environment)
Includes bibliographical references and index.
1. Food and Agriculture Organization of the United Nations. Committee on World Food Security. 2. Food security--International cooperation. 3. Nutrition policy--International cooperation. I. Title.
HD9000.6.D846 2015
338.1'9--dc23
2014035779

ISBN: 978-1-138-80252-0 (hbk)
ISBN: 978-1-138-57486-1 (pbk)

Typeset in Bembo
by Greengate Publishing Services, Tonbridge, Kent

In memory of Ken Hatt

In memory of Ken Platt

Contents

Illustrations

Figures

Tables

Acknowledgements

I am indebted to the participants of the Committee on World Food Security (CFS), especially those who engage through the International Food Security and Nutrition Civil Society Mechanism (CSM), for letting me participate in and research this process with them. My deepest gratitude and appreciation are extended to David Barling and Tim Lang at the Centre for Food Policy, City University London, for their enthusiasm, guidance, valuable suggestions and patience. This book would not have been possible without them. My parents, Janice Brown and Robert Duncan, for their support and inspiration and Thomas Blight for keeping me grounded and inspiring adventure. I acknowledge the financial contributions of City University London and the Social Science and Humanities Research Council of Canada.

Acronyms and abbreviations

AfDB	African Development Bank
AMIS	Agricultural Market Information System
APEC	Asia–Pacific Economic Cooperation
AUC	African Union Commission
BRICS	Brazil, Russia, India, China and South Africa
CAADP	Comprehensive Africa Agriculture Development Program
CAAS	Chinese Academy of Agricultural Sciences
CAD	Canadian dollar
CFA	Comprehensive Framework for Action
CFS	Committee on World Food Security
CFSAM	Crop and Food Security Assessment Mission
CGIAR	Consultative Group on International Agricultural Research
CONSEA	National Council of Food and Nutrition Security
CSM	International Food Security and Nutrition Civil Society Mechanism
CSO	civil society organization
EC	European Community
ECOSOC	United Nations Economic and Social Council
ECOWAS	Economic Community of West African States
EU	European Union
FAO	Food and Agriculture Organization of the United Nations
FIAN	FoodFirst Information and Action Network
FOC	Friends of the Chair
G8	Group of 8
G20	Group of 20
GAFSP	Global Agriculture Food Security Program
GATT	General Agreement on Trade and Tariffs
GCARD	Global Conference on Agricultural Research for Development
GDP	gross domestic product
GEF	Global Environment Facility
GFRP	Global Food Crisis Response Program
GIEWS	Global Information Early Warning System on Food and Agriculture

GMO	genetically modified organism
GSF	Global Strategic Framework for Food Security and Nutrition
HLPE	High Level Panel of Experts
HLTF	High-Level Task Force on Global Food Security
IAASTD	International Assessment of Agricultural Knowledge, Science and Technology for Development
ICARRD	International Conference on Agrarian Reform and Rural Development
IFAD	International Fund for Agricultural Development
IFC	International Finance Corporation
IFPRI	International Food Policy Research Institute
ILO	International Labour Organization
IMF	International Monetary Fund
IPC	International Planning Committee for Food Sovereignty
MDG	Millennium Development Goal
MDTF	Multi-Donor Trust Fund
MIJARC	Mouvement International de la Jeunesse Agricole et Rurale Catholique
NEPAD	New Partnership for Africa's Development
NGO	non-governmental organization
OECD	Organisation for Economic Co-operation and Development
OEWG	open-ended working group
PRAI	Principles for Responsible Agricultural Investment that Respects Rights, Livelihoods and Resources
RAI	Responsible Agricultural Investment
Rio +20	United Nations Conference on Sustainable Development, 2012
ROPPA	Le Réseau des organizations paysannes et de producteurs de l'Afrique de l'Ouest
SAP	structural adjustment program
SOFA	State of Food and Agriculture in the World (FAO annual report)
SOFI	State of Food Insecurity in the World (FAO annual report)
SUN	Scaling-Up Nutrition
UCFA	Updated Comprehensive Framework for Action
UDHR	Universal Declaration of Human Rights
UN	United Nations
UNCED	United Nations Conference on Environment and Development
UNCTAD	United Nations Conference on Trade and Development
UNDIP	United Nations Declaration on Indigenous Peoples
UNDP	United Nations Development Programme
UNECA	United Nations Economic Commission for Africa
UNEP	United Nations Environment Programme
UNESCO	United Nations Educational, Scientific and Cultural Organization

UNFCCC	United Nations Framework Convention on Climate Change
UNICEF	United Nations Children's Fund
UNIDO	United Nations Industrial Development Organization
US	United States of America
USSR	Union of Soviet Socialist Republics
VGGT	Voluntary Guidelines on the Responsible Governance of Tenure of Land, Fisheries and Forests in the Context of National Food Security
WFP	World Food Programme
WHO	World Health Organization
WSSD	World Summit on Sustainable Development
WTO	World Trade Organization

1 Introduction and overview

The world food price spikes

Introduction

From 2007–2008 world food prices spiked and global economic crisis set in. The United Nations' (UN) Food and Agriculture Organization (FAO) (2008c) declared that more than 1 billion people were going hungry. The rise of food prices heightened awareness of food insecurity and gave fresh political momentum to addressing the problem. The international community responded with a swell of activity. One important resulting initiative was the reform of the UN's Committee on World Food Security (CFS).

At the height of the crisis, the Committee's 123 member countries adopted a series of reforms with the aim of becoming the foremost international, inclusive and intergovernmental platform for food security. Central to the reform was the opening up the Committee to the participation of non-governmental actors. The mandate of the reformed CFS is ambitious; understanding how the Committee is achieving its reform objectives and the position it occupies in the changing architecture of global food security governance is the focus of this research.

The state of hunger in the world

Between 2006 and 2008 international food prices soared and an additional 200 million people were estimated to have gone hungry (DEFRA 2010:2).[1] When prices peaked, one-sixth of humanity (around 1 billion people) were estimated to be undernourished (Demeke et al. 2009; FAO 2009b, 2011a, 2012a).[2] In addition to malnutrition, 130–155 million people were pushed into poverty in 2008 because of soaring food and fuel prices (Cord et al. 2009). Rising food costs resulted in food riots and civil unrest in more than 60 countries (FAO 2011a; Zaman et al. 2008) and generated appeals for food aid from 36 countries (USA 2011). Countries that had long been considered food secure faced the threat of limited food imports as a result of protectionist export restrictions put in place by some food exporting countries (DEFRA 2010; Sharma 2010). Journalists declared the end to the era of cheap food (Arusa 2011; Cookson 2011; Elliot 2012), while the international NGO Oxfam (2012:1) accused policy makers of having "taken cheap food for granted for nearly 30 years," adding "those days are gone."

Post-crisis analysis suggests that in response to rising food prices, countries adopted different net trade positions (e.g., exporter, importer) and different policy responses to price and income shocks, leading to a broad range of outcomes (FAO 2011b:8). Larger countries were able to insulate their markets from the crisis through the implementation of restrictive trade policies and safety nets, but these policies had the negative effect of increasing prices and volatility on international markets (FAO 2011b:8). Countries most vulnerable to food swings on the international market are typically poor and net food importing. In 2008, the food import bill for low-income food-deficit countries increased by about 35 percent from 2006 (FAO 2012a). They lacked capacity to restrict exports, and had limited food reserves and inadequate funds to procure food at the higher prices (FAO 2011b:8). These countries, the majority of which are in Africa, bore "the brunt of the crisis, and staple food prices rose substantially in these countries" (FAO 2011b:8). Across the African continent, an additional 28 million people went undernourished as a result of the food price spikes (FAO 2011b). Food riots broke out in Burkina Faso, Cameroon, Côte d'Ivoire, Egypt, Mozambique and Somalia, leading governments to increase military presence and to take emergency policy measures (FAO 2008b). In East Africa, more than 17 million people faced serious food insecurity as a result of low harvests, high food prices and conflict (FAO 2008b). In West Africa, high food prices negatively affected access to food as the price of staples such as sorghum, millet, rice and maize increased. The FAO (2008c) estimates that in Southern Africa high food prices impacted over 8.7 million people. In Asia, the number of people suffering from undernourishment, while higher than the numbers suffering in Africa, has been decreasing and the impact of the 2007–2008 food price spikes did not have as great an impact.

In 2007 alone, 41 million additional people in Latin America and the Caribbean were added to the rapidly growing number of undernourished people worldwide. Prior to the food price spikes, Latin America had implemented far-reaching economic reforms geared towards trade liberalization and was:

> considered relatively stable and capable of absorbing external shocks, thanks to its higher foreign exchange liquidity; decreased public sector and external borrowing needs; exchange rate flexibility; lower exposure to currency, interest rate, and rollover risks in public sector debt portfolios; and improved access to local-currency loans.
>
> (Robles and Torero 2010:117)

Robles and Torero (2010:118) note that prior to the 2007–2008 price spikes, countries in the region were generally on track to achieve the Millennium Development Goal (MDG) of halving the proportion of hungry people by 2015. This success is no longer guaranteed. The Latin American case serves to highlight the fragility of "emerging economies" and the impact of rising food prices on vulnerable populations, as illustrated by the regression in development targets.

Buttressed amid a burgeoning global economic crisis and a rapidly expanding environmental crisis, the food price crisis of 2007–2008 challenged dominant assumptions about food security, agriculture and development, prompting many policy makers, analysts and food producers to grapple with an increasing number of variables that made up a so-called "perfect storm" (Headey et al. 2009). These variables included environmental challenges, demographic shifts, rising energy prices, demand for biofuels, depreciation of the US dollar, unfavorable weather and trade shocks, panic purchases and export restrictions (Headey et al. 2009). This storm served to illustrate the growing interconnectedness of agricultural, energy and financial markets (Wise and Murphy 2012), but also disrupted the dominant food security policy, permanently changing the public policy debate on food security (HLPE 2011:17) and ushering in an era of food price volatility.

We now live in a world where supply and demand are more closely aligned, natural resource bases are shrinking, and agricultural systems are increasingly threatened by climate change. Research indicates that food price volatility is expected to remain the norm but drivers of volatility in international markets (e.g., biofuels, speculation and climate change) have yet to be adequately addressed (FAO 2009b; G20 2011; HLPE 2011; McCreary 2011). This new context demands increased international cooperation and coordination. Things are not likely to return to what they were, and now the human, social and economic costs are higher than the cost of inaction. In response, the world food situation is being redefined (Hart 2009; Von Braun 2007).

The problem has also shifted. When the concept of food security emerged in the 1970s, it was very much framed in the context of availability: how to get enough food supply to meet growing demand. The 1980s and 1990s were marked by questions of access as it became clear that availability of food does not guarantee access (Sen 1981). However, the post-2007–2008 crisis reality is grounded where these two challenges intersect. While access remains a problem, the question of availability has re-emerged as a new challenge and will be an increasingly pressing issue due to impacts of climate change, growing demand for food (e.g., changing diets, population growth, biofuels), rising cost of petroleum, restricted availability of water, desertification and soil degradation.

Having examined some of the impacts of the food prices spikes and the resulting crises, attention now turns to a review of the main triggers of the price spikes.

Triggers of the 2007–2008 food price spikes

After decades of historic lows, the food price rise of 2007–2008 sparked a new era of higher food prices and extreme food price volatility (HLPE 2011:9).[3] While food prices peaked in the summer of 2008, they actually started to rise in late 2006 alongside rising oil prices. Some claimed that high prices presented an opportunity for producers of agricultural commodities; however, the cost of agricultural production rose at the same time due to higher energy and fertilizer prices (DEFRA 2010:9) often nullifying potential gains from increased market prices.

While several factors contributed to the food price spikes, DEFRA (2010:10) noted:

> Attributing significance to one factor or another in the price spike is very difficult (and attributing robust percentages, arguably impossible), given the complex way that the various issues combine. Take away one or other of several of these factors and it may well be that there would have been no price spike, but that does not mean then that each of these was the cause of the event.

There is general agreement that contributing factors on the supply side included increases in the cost of oil, poor harvest—especially of wheat—and decreased production due to drought (Abbott et al. 2008; Baffes and Haniotis 2010; Collins 2008; DEFRA 2010; FAO 2008a, 2008c; Gilbert 2008; Trostle 2008; Wiggins et al. 2010; Zaman et al. 2008). On the demand side, and from a financial perspective, inflation from world economic growth is a commonly accepted factor. Policies, including export bans and restrictions as well as the reduction of import tariffs, also played a role. The depreciation of the US dollar led to an increase in prices tied to the US dollar, resulting in higher costs across the food supply chain (Demeke et al. 2009; Oxfam 2012; Sharma 2010; Wiggins et al. 2010). Speculation on futures markets also played a role in the price spikes, although the significance is debated (FAO 2008a, 2011a; Gilbert 2008; Oxfam 2012; Sharma 2010; Wiggins et al. 2010).

Yet changes in supply and demand fundamentals cannot adequately explain the price spikes (Robles and Torero 2010:122). As David Barling (2012) notes, trying to categorize challenges in these terms can prove problematic in agriculture and food policy and some elements are central to both supply and demand. Barling (2012:5) uses the example of land, which is both a demand and supply factor:

> [A]s demand for good fertile land for production is often in heavily populated coasted and estuarial areas and river valleys and plains where there are residential demands. Equally, land is a prerequisite for food production while competing with a range of other demands, not least other non-food crops such as large scale production of biofuels to meet the competing demand for new energy sources.

Similarly, ad hoc trade policy interventions and excessive speculation in the commodity futures market also fall outside of a simple supply and demand equation (Robles and Torero 2010:122). Attempting to understand the reasons for these spikes through such a model inevitably frames solutions with the same perspective, reinforcing an approach which may not warrant reinforcement.

Crisis repeating: Era of food price volatility

After the food price spikes of 2007–2008, food security, and agriculture more broadly, remained on the international agenda as we shifted into the predicted era of food price volatility. And, as the name would suggest, food prices spiked again in 2010. Global figures on hunger from 2010 suggest that the number of hungry people had decreased to 925 million, in part due to economic growth and a reduction in international food prices from the 2008 highs (FAO 2012b). However, between July and September 2010, the price of wheat increased from 60 to 80 percent, a reaction to crop losses due to a period of drought in Russia and a subsequent export ban imposed by the Russian Federation (FAO 2012a). Rice and maize prices also rose during this period.

The food system remains in a state of crisis: food markets remain remarkably volatile. In the spring of 2011 international food prices were on the rise for the second time in three years. In February 2011, the World Bank Food Price Index reached its 2008 peak, after rising by 47 percent from June 2010 (World Bank 2011:i).

In 2012, in the US, a large proportion of agriculture was located in areas affected by drought. In July 2012, 88 percent of US corn, 44 percent of cattle production and 40 percent of soybean production was being grown in regions affected by drought (Oxfam 2012). Russia faced dry weather and severe flooding (in the south) that seriously reduced its grain harvests and caused damage to unpicked and stored grain (Oxfam 2012). Ukraine and Kazakhstan were also impacted by dry weather, which in turn impacted their 2013 harvests. Ukraine was the world's third largest exporter in 2011. India, which relies on monsoon rains as the main source of irrigation for 55 percent of its farmlands, received rainfall 19 percent below average (Oxfam 2012). In July 2012, maize and soybean prices reached all-time peaks, following high temperatures and lack of rainfall in the US and Eastern Europe (World Bank 2012:1). During this time, prices of wheat and rice remained below their historical peaks, but hovered at levels comparable to the 2011 spikes (World Bank 2012:1).

Food price volatility presents significant challenges for food security and has a disproportionate impact on the poor and vulnerable. The post-2008 crises had differentiated features when compared to the 2007–2008 crisis, but shared at least four similarities (World Bank 2011:1). First, global grain stocks remained low. Second, the cost of oil remained high and unrest in the Middle East and Africa added a new level of uncertainty in oil markets. Third, the US dollar continued to depreciate against other currencies.[4] Finally, financial investment in agricultural commodities remained high.

Food price volatility witnessed in 2010 and 2012 showed price increases were more widespread across agricultural commodities and production shortfalls due to poor weather were more prevalent. Policy responses had an impact on the grain price spikes in 2011, but not to the extent they did in 2008 when policy responses to grain shortages came as a surprise and greatly impacted prices and shortages

(World Bank 2011:1). The implications of ongoing food price volatility remain significant for poor and developing economies. High food prices pushed the global food import bill for 2011 over a trillion US dollars, further illustrating the failures of global food security governance and reinforcing the idea that policies guiding agricultural development and food security are deeply flawed.

The food price crisis, as it is understood and described above, was sparked by market fears linked to low world stocks. The declines were the result of several factors, including policies to reduce stock holdings, weather shocks which led to drastically reduced yield, increased demand for biofuels and increased demand for energy costs and animal products, which created increased demand for oil and animal feed. The global financial crisis shook confidence in global markets and a depreciated US dollar left many countries with tied currencies unable to afford food. Countries reacted with export restriction policies that sought to protect people but inadvertently led to more market stress, and increased food price volatility for others. Some speculators saw an opportunity to increase profits and some, as a way of securing food or increasing income, began acquiring large parcels of land in what some have called a new global land rush (Arezki et al. 2012). The impact was that millions more people were pushed into poverty and hundreds of millions added to the already appallingly high number of undernourished people worldwide (FAO 2008c). Lost faith in markets illustrates a point of rupture in the commonsense (hegemonic) ordering of the governance of food security and arguably the wider economy.

Structure of the book

This book starts from this point of rupture: a noted disjuncture in the normal ordering of the everyday world. The food price spikes and ensuing crises represent a disjuncture in the logic of the global food system and in global governance more broadly. The system failed. Reflecting the profoundly sad and problematic ordering of the global food system, what propelled this rupture was not the increase in the number of hungry and poor, but rather the significant challenges these crises presented to wealthy countries and the tenets of trade liberalization. When food exporting countries enacted protectionist measures, wealthy countries faced the realization that wealth and market rule will not always ensure access to food. As such, the reactions to the food price crisis and the corresponding changes to the architecture of global food security governance represent both a challenge to and defense of the hegemonic global project of neoliberalism.

Given this context, this book provides a window onto one aspect of the restructuring of the global architecture of food security governance: the reform of the United Nations' CFS. The reformed CFS is now recognized by the international community as the foremost platform for promoting policy coherence and discussion around food security, but the process of achieving this consensus has been hard fought and is not guaranteed. The capacity and authority of the CFS are continually challenged.

Throughout this book, the presentation and assessment of the CFS reform focuses on the inclusion of civil society organizations (CSOs) as participants and assesses their impact on policy process and outcome. The objective of the book is to understand and analyze the reorganization, operation and capacity of the CFS in its early reform years and the implications of civil society participation therein. Each chapter of the book has been written so that it can be read independently, while also contributing to the broader objective of the book.

Chapter 2 presents a theoretical framework that situates global governance theory within a context of embedded neoliberalism. The framework is introduced to help make sense of processes under way in the ever-changing architecture of global food security governance. To historicize the research, and illustrate the application of the theoretical framework, Chapter 3 outlines the evolution of food security since its entry into global policy processes in 1974. Here the focus is on food security as discourse. The international reaction to the food price spikes is then reviewed with particular focus on multilateral initiatives. This serves to map out changing architecture of global food security governance.

In Chapter 4, focus turns to the reform of the CFS as the foremost international and intergovernmental body for the discussion and coordination of food security policy at the global level. The reform is contextualized and then the reform process itself is reviewed. The roles and responsibilities of the key actors in the CFS are presented along with a review of important post-reform activities. The latter serves to illustrate not only how the reformed CFS is operating but also elucidates its capacity and potential impact.

Central to the CFS's claims for legitimacy in the new architecture of global food security governance is the inclusion of stakeholders, including CSOs, as official participants. Thus, evaluating participation is central to accessing the capacity and success of the CFS. Moreover, the CFS offers unique insight into how CSOs, traditionally on the periphery of policy making, are organizing themselves to shift towards the center. Chapter 5 explores how civil society actors have organized themselves so as to effectively engage in the work of the CFS. The chapter reviews how the Civil Society Mechanism was developed to coordinate the autonomous participation of civil society actors and to facilitate communication among them.

From there, focus turns to three case studies that provide empirical insight into how the CFS operates and moves towards achieving its reform objectives. The cases address three important events and related themes in the early reform years of the CFS. A review and comparison of policy roundtables in Chapter 6 illuminates tensions around multinational power dynamics and lend support to theories of transnational neopluralism. In Chapter 7, the negotiations of the Voluntary Guidelines on the Responsible Governance of Tenure of Land, Fisheries and Forests in the Context of National Food Security shed light on processes of developing best practices to support policy making. Finally, the analysis of the Global Strategic Framework in Chapter 8 sparks discussion on the implications and possibilities for policy cohesion and coordination in global food security governance. Importantly, the cases also illustrate the complexity of actors' positions and challenge the tendency in the literature on global food security governance to put actors into ideological boxes, assuming (wrongly) that they do not stray from these static positions. As such, the cases describe some of the ways in which actors strategize and compromise, and how coalitions are built around specific issues, not necessarily in line with traditional alliances.

More specifically, Chapter 6 presents a comparative analysis of two policy roundtables that took place at the 37th Session of the CFS: how to increase food security and smallholder-sensitive investment in agriculture; and food price volatility. A key aspect of the reform of CFS was to focus more on policy and best practices so as to support country-level plans. In line with this, the CFS has developed policy roundtables at each session with the aim of proposing policy recommendations. The comparative analysis of the policy roundtables provides: insight into the dynamics of a participatory CFS; highlights the power of new actors; illustrates the spheres of influence of new actors; provides insights into the policies being produced by the CFS; and points to where CSOs are most influential in the negotiation process.

Chapter 7 reviews and analyses the negotiations of the Voluntary Guidelines on the Responsible Governance of Tenure of Land, Fisheries and Forests in the Context of National Food Security (VGGT). The negotiations of the VGGT were a litmus test for the reformed CFS and represent the most significant accomplishment and contribution of the reformed CFS to date. The process of consultation and negotiation that shaped them is argued here to be a best practice in global governance.

Chapter 8 considers the development of the Global Strategic Framework for Food Security and Nutrition (GSF), a single, living reference document of core priorities for food security and nutrition. The GSF offers guidelines and recommendations for coherent action at the global, regional and country level by the full range of stakeholders, while emphasizing the central role of country ownership over food security programs. As such, it is fundamental to the CFS's work on policy coordination and cohesion.

Together, the three case studies provide empirical insights into the working processes of the newly reformed CFS, including how the Committee functioned in practice. The cases confirm not only the value of enhanced participation of civil society actors in policy-making processes but also how the CFS is emerging as an effective and innovative governance model to address key limitations in global governance.

Chapter 9 provides a summary of the impact of civil society participation in the CFS. The chapter reviews successful strategies employed by CSOs to advance political change. Attention then turns to the CFS more broadly and considers implications for the future of global food security governance and global governance. The limitations of global governance are revisited and reconsidered based on the reform experience of the CFS. In this final chapter it is argued that the CFS is producing the most comprehensive policies in a consultative and participatory way (i.e. democratically) but that it is also being systematically undermined by other actors. The book concludes by identifying areas for future research.

Methods

This book is the result of qualitative inquiry that employed mixed methods. Document analysis was used to establish the empirical context and to provide a map of the changing architecture of global food security governance. From there, the case study method was enhanced by ethnographic methods. Ethnographic methods provided opportunities to explore specific aspects of operation in the reformed CFS and helped establish a coherent but sufficiently expansive picture of how the CFS operates. For this research, participant observation was undertaken across key sites (i.e., listservs, consultations, meetings, working groups and informal correspondence). Participant observation began in October 2010 with the first session of the reformed CFS and continued through to July 2014. The time period covered provides a picture of a moment of transition in the ordering of food security policy at the global level and a key window into the reform and functioning of the CFS.

Conclusion

Food security is one of the more complex challenges facing the global community, yet failure to secure universal access to adequate food is a great failure of the twentieth century. The fight against hunger and the restructuring of the food system towards one that is just and sustainable remains a policy challenge that requires strong and sustained policy responses. However, there is no single international institution responsible for managing or governing food security. Responsibility for food security is distributed in a fragmented way across a number of international organizations, resulting in duplication and contradictions in rules and norms (Margulis 2010).

After the food price spikes, and in response to the fragmentation, there was "a unified call to define a new governance in the fight against world hunger" (Viatte et al. 2009:2). Contributions towards a new system of governance are being advanced by key actors through the reinforcement of existing structures, the creation of new ones, the challenging of norms, the search for alternatives and the fight for leadership. As such, global food security governance is shifting in important ways. Whether the food security policies promoted therein will also shift remains to be seen. With the proliferation of new and competing structures vying for leadership over food security, there is even more need to create harmony where there is duplication or contradiction. This book argues that the CFS is the most appropriate platform to lead the restructuring of the global architecture of food security governance.

Notes

1 The FAO (2009b) calculated an additional 115 million people were pushed into chronic hunger due to rising prices.
2 The FAO (2008c) reported that at the height of the food price spikes, 1.2 billion people were chronically undernourished. In 2012, upon the request of the CFS, the FAO

revised its methodology and enhanced its data. With these improvements the estimated number of chronically undernourished was reduced to 870 million in 2010–2012 (FAO 2012b). These are the most legitimate figures available with respect to global hunger and therefore large shifts can motivate policy makers to act. Unfortunately, these measurements remain limited. First the prevalence of an undernourishment indicator is defined solely in terms of availability of dietary energy and its distribution in the population. It does not consider other aspects of nutrition. Second, the calculations rely on minimum activity levels, whereas many poor and hungry have livelihoods that involve manual labour. Finally, the method is unable to capture the impact of short-term shocks unless they impact on longer term consumption patters (FAO 2012b).

3 It is important here to note that volatility is the normal state of agricultural markets, but what is new are the extreme highs and lows.

4 This is not clear cut. In 2008 the US dollar was trading lower than in the summer of 2012: in April 2008 it was $1.55 against the euro and $1.98 against the UK pound, while in July 2012 it was $1.23 against the euro and $1.56 against the pound (Oxfam 2012:3). The higher dollar value meant higher costs for food-importing countries, and many low-income countries are net food importers (Ng and Aksoy 2008).

References

Abbott, P., C. Hurt, and W. Tyner. 2008. *What's Driving Food Prices?*. Oak Brook, IL: Farm Foundation. Retrieved (www.farmfoundation.org/news/articlefiles/404-ExecSum8.5x11.pdf.).

Arezki, R., K. Deininger, and H. Selod. 2012. "Global Land Rush." *Finance and Development* 49(1):46–48. Retrieved (www.imf.org/external/pubs/ft/fandd/2012/03/pdf/arezki.pdf).

Arusa, K. 2011. "End of Cheap Food Era as Grain Prices Stay High." *Reuters*, January 24. Retrieved (www.guardian.co.uk/business/2012/sep/02/era-of-cheap-food-over).

Baffes, J., and T. Haniotis. 2010. *Placing the 2006/08 Commodity Price Boom into Perspective.* Policy Research Working Paper 5371. Washington, DC: World Bank.

Barling, D. 2012. "The Challenges Facing Contemporary Food Systems: Policy and Governance Pathways to Sustainable Consumption and Production." *Agronomie, Environnment et Societes* 2(1):15–25. Retrieved (www.agronomie.asso.fr/fileadmin/user_upload/Revue_AES/AES_vol1_n2_dec2011/AES_Vol1_n2_Defi_alimentaire_et_agronomie.pdf).

Collins, K. 2008. *The Role of Bio-Fuels and Other Factors in Increasing Farm and Food Prices.* Rome: K. Collins. Retrieved (http://books.google.nl/books/about/The_Role_of_Biofuels_and_Other_Factors_i.html?id=-vCutgAACAAJ&redir_esc=y).

Cookson, C. 2011. "Era of Low-Cost Food Is Over, Study Warns." *Financial Times (Global Economy)*, January 24. Retrieved (www.ft.com/cms/s/0/59130262-27df-11e0-8abc-00144feab49a.html#axzz2BisL6pTt).

Cord, L., M. Verhoeven, C. Blomquist, and B. Rijkers. 2009. *The Global Economic Crisis: Assessing Vulnerability with a Poverty Lens.* Washington DC: World Bank. Retrieved (http://siteresources.worldbank.org/NEWS/Resources/WBGVulnerableCountriesBrief.pdf).

DEFRA. 2010. *The 2007/8 Agricultural Price Spikes: Causes and Policy Implications.* London: DEFRA.

Demeke, M., G. Pangrazio, and M. Maetz. 2009. *Initiative on Soaring Food Prices Country Responses to the Food Security Crisis: Nature and Preliminary Implications of the Policies Pursued.* Rome: FAO. Retrieved (www.fao.org/fileadmin/user_upload/ISFP/pdf_for_site_Country_Response_to_the_Food_Security.pdf).

Elliot, L. 2012. "The Era of Cheap Food May Be over." *The Guardian (Economics Blog)*, September 2. Retrieved (www.guardian.co.uk/business/2012/sep/02/era-of-cheap-food-over).

FAO. 2008a. *FAO's Initiative on Soaring Food Prices Guide for Immediate Country Level Action*. Rome: FAO. Retrieved (www.fao.org/fileadmin/templates/worldfood/Reports_and_docs/IFSP_guide_immediate_action.pdf).

FAO. 2008b. *Soaring Prices Add 75 Million People to Global Hunger Rolls (Briefing Paper)*. Rome: FAO. Retrieved (www.fao.org/newsroom/common/ecg/1000923/en/hungerfigs.pdf).

FAO. 2008c. *The State of Food Insecurity in the World 2008: High Food Prices and Food Security: Threats and Opportunities*. Rome: FAO. Retrieved (www.fao.org/docrep/011/i0291e/i0291e00.htm).

FAO. 2009a. *The State of Agricultural Commodity Markets (2009): High Food Prices and the Food Crisis – Experiences and Lessons Learned*. Rome: FAO.

FAO. 2009b. *The State of Food Insecurity in the World 2009: Economic Crises- Impacts and Lessons Learned*. Rome: United Nations. Retrieved (www.fao.org/docrep/012/i0876e/i0876e00.htm).

FAO. 2011a. *High Food Prices: The Food Security Crisis of 2007-2008 and Recent Food Price Increases – Facts and Lessons*. Rome: FAO. Retrieved (www.fao.org/fileadmin/user_upload/ISFP/High_food_prices.pdf).

FAO. 2011b. *The State of Food Insecurity in the World 2011: How Does International Price Volatility Affect Domestic Economies and Food Security?* Rome: FAO. Retrieved (www.fao.org/docrep/014/i2330e/i2330e.pdf).

FAO. 2012a. "Initiative on Soaring Food Prices." Rome: FAO. Retrieved (www.fao.org/isfp/en/).

FAO. 2012b. *The State of Food Insecurity in the World: Economic Growth Is Necessary but Not Sufficient to Accelerate Reduction of Hunger and Malnutrition*. Rome: FAO.

G20. 2011. *Ministerial Declaration: Action Plan on Food Price Volatility and Agriculture*. Paris: G20.

Gilbert, C. 2008. *Commodity Speculation and Commodity Investment* Discussion Paper No. 20. Trento: Università degli studi di Trento (Economics Department).

Hart, T. 2009. *Food Security Definitions, Measurements and Recent Initiatives in South Africa and Southern Africa*. Pretoria: Human Sciences Research Council.

Headey, D., S. Malaiyandi, and F. Shenggen. 2009. *Navigating the Perfect Storm: Reflections on the Food, Energy and Financial Crises*. IFPRI Discussion Paper 0889. Retrieved (www.ifpri.org/sites/default/files/publications/ifpridp00889.pdf).

HLPE (High Level Panel of Experts). 2011. *Price Volatility and Food Security*. Rome: FAO. Retrieved (www.fao.org/fileadmin/user_upload/hlpe/hlpe_documents/HLPE-price-volatility-and-food-security-report-July-2011.pdf).

Margulis, M. E. 2010. *The Evolving Global Governance of Food Security*. Hamilton, Ontario. Retrieved (http://papers.ssrn.com/sol3/papers.cfm?abstract_id=1823453).

McCreary, I. 2011. *Protecting the Food Insecure in Volatile International Markets: Food Reserves and Other Policy Options*. Winnipeg. Retrieved (http://foodgrainsbank.ca/uploads/Food SecurityPriceVolatilityandPolicy Responses-final-25March11.pdf).

Ng, F., and M. A. Aksoy. 2008. *Who Are the Net Food Importing Countries?* Washington, DC: World Bank. Retrieved (http://elibrary.worldbank.org/docserver/download/4457.pdf?expires=1354265287&id=id&accname=guest&checksum=8744FF395DA9F7728E1544A1CF7B5879).

Oxfam. 2012. *Food Crises Doomed to Repeat until Leaders Find Courage to Fix Problems (media Advisory)*. Oxford: Oxfam. Retrieved (www.oxfam.org/sites/www.oxfam.org/files/food-price-crisis-oxfam-media-advisory-aug2012.pdf).

Robles, M., and M. Torero. 2010. "Understanding the Impact of High Food Prices in Latin America." *Economia* 10(2):117–64. Retrieved (http://nepad.org/system/files/High_Food_Prices_LAC.pdf).

Sen, A. 1981. *Poverty and Famines: An Essay on Entitlement and Deprivation*. Oxford: Clarendon Press.

Sharma, R. 2010. *Food Export Restrictions: Review of the 2007–2010 Experience and Considerations for Disciplining Restrictive Measures*. Rome: FAO. Retrieved (www.fao.org/fileadmin/templates/est/PUBLICATIONS/Comm_Working_Papers/EST-WP32.pdf).

Trostle, R. 2008. *Global Agricultural Supply and Demand: Factors Contributing to the Recent Increase in Food Commodity Prices*. Washington, DC: USDA.

USA. 2011. *Food Prices Crisis of 2007–2008: Lessons Learned*. Washington, DC. Retrieved (www.state.gov/r/pa/prs/ps/2011/03/157629.htm).

Viatte, G., J. De Graaf, M. Demeke, T. Takahatake, and M. R. de. Arce. 2009. *Responding to the food crisis: synthesis of medium-term measures proposed in inter-agency assessments*. Rome. Retrieved (www.fao.org/fileadmin/user_upload/ISFP/SR_Web.pdf).

Von Braun, J. 2007. *The World Food Situation: New Driving Forces and Required Actions*. Washington, DC: IFPRI.

Wiggins, S., J. Compton, and S. Keats. 2010. *Food Price Crisis*. New York: ODI. Retrieved (www.odi.org.uk/sites/odi.org.uk/files/odi-assets/publications-opinion-files/5727.pdf).

Wise, T., and S. Murphy. 2012. *Resolving the Food Crisis: Assessing Global Policy Reforms since 2007*. Medford: IATP. Retrieved (http://iatp.org/files/2012_01_17_ResolvingFoodCrisis_SM_TW.pdf).

World Bank. 2011. *Food Price Watch (April)*. Washington, DC: World Bank. Retrieved (www.worldbank.org/foodcrisis/foodpricewatch/april_2011.html).

World Bank. 2012. *Food Price Watch (August)*. Washington, DC: World Bank. Retrieved (http://siteresources.worldbank.org/EXTPOVERTY/Resources/336991-13119665 20397/Food-Price-Watch-August-2012.pdf).

Zaman, H., C. Delgado, D. Mitchell, and A. Revenga. 2008. *Rising Food Prices: Are There Right Policy Choices?* Washington, DC: World Bank.

2 Global governance

A framework for analysis

Introduction

To suggest that we live in a neoliberal era is both correct and incomplete given the multiplicity of definitions attributed to the term. Some have suggested that due to multiple applications more precise terms should be used (Clarke 2008; Ferguson 2009). Susan Watkins (2010:7) has proclaimed that neoliberalism "is a dismal epithet ... imprecise and overused." Jamie Peck (2010:14–15) warns against the "adjectival promiscuity" that surrounds neoliberalism. He argues that "neoliberalism seems often to be used as a sort of stand-in term for the political economic zeitgeist, as a no-more-than approximate proxy for a specific analysis of mechanisms or relations of social power, domination, exploitation, or alienation." Peck (2010:15–16) continues that "for all its doctrinal certainty, the neoliberal project is paradoxically defined by the very unattainability of its fundamental goal—frictionless market rule." It follows that clean or precise definitions of neoliberalization do not exist. Instead, Peck argues "concretely grounded accounts of the process must be chiseled out of the interstices of state/market configurations." In some respects, this research seeks to undertake such a process in the analysis of the CFS in its early reform stage.

To do this, it is important to articulate a theoretical framework to support the analysis undertaken in this book. The theoretical framework presented here situates global governance theory within a context of embedded neoliberalism. This framework helps make sense of processes under way in the ever-changing architecture of global food security governance. In what follows, the neoliberal is identified and explored in five ways, leading to a description of embedded neoliberalism and a defence of using it as a starting point for analysis. It is argued that mechanisms of global governance operate within the confines of embedded neoliberalism. Global governance is presented as both an observable phenomenon and as a political project. This is followed by a review of the challenges and critiques aimed at global governance and its related theories, including questions related to accountability, legitimacy and categorization.

The neoliberal era

The diversity of meanings of "neoliberal" reflects the different perspectives of actors trying to make sense the world as they experience it. Thus, neoliberalism is here used as a starting point and consequently will be presented in a number of ways, each one with the aim of helping to make sense of global food security policy and governance. This is by no means a novel approach. Wendy Larner (2000), for example, engages with neoliberalism as ideology, policy and governance.

In this book, the neoliberal is understood in five ways. First, it is explored as a discursive formulation with forms of reasoning and discourse enacted as neoliberalism. Second, it is reviewed as a project (the extension of liberalism) advanced to enhance trade through minimizing barriers, as made visible through trade liberalization. Third, neoliberalism is considered as a product that leads to the development, rationalization and maintenance of particular food structures. Fourth, it is examined as a process that is mediated primarily through a state complex and plays out as neoliberalization. Finally, neoliberal is considered as a strategy which is implemented through processes of governance to maintain status quo. These manifestations of the neoliberal are not discreet categories and are in fact densely interconnected, full of personal, organizational, social and/or dispersed networks.

When approached from the perspective of food governance, the inherent contradictions of the neoliberal are made obvious. The most blatant contradiction is arguably between trade liberalization which involves reducing barriers to trade (neoliberal as project) and food governance (neoliberal as strategy) which involves the regulation of trade. This tension is not new. In 1944, Karl Polanyi (2001) wrote about a "double movement" where economic forces place demands on the broader social formation in which they are located. This double movement refers to the ways in which economic forces come to dominate but are then coerced or calmed by resistance from social formations.

David Harvey (2005:2) explains that neoliberalism is a theory of political economic practice that:

> proposes that human well-being can best be advanced by liberating individual entrepreneurial freedoms and skills within an institutional framework characterized by strong private property rights, free markets and free trade. The role of the state is to create and preserve an institutional framework appropriate to such practices.

For Cerny (2010:128), the development of neoliberalism since the 1980s has led to a "complex, flexible, fungible and increasingly variegated set of discourses that have proved particularly useful to a diverse range of actors in a globalizing world." Neoliberalism reflects the current of ideas and formulations developed predominantly from US trade and foreign policy through the late twentieth century. However, Jessop (2002) reminds us that neoliberalism is only one of a number of orientations accessible to social formations. Others include neostatism, neocorporatism or neocommunitarianism. Indeed, neoliberalism should not be seen as a fully comprehensive and self-contained rational doctrine. It is, rather, a social construction that reflects political, and above all, economic forces.

Neoliberal models of government are characterized by the capacity for direct intervention by means of empowered and specialized state apparatuses and indirect techniques for leading and controlling citizens without at the same time being responsible for them (Lemke 2001:201). More broadly within neoliberal governance, the role of the state remains fundamental although not static, despite rhetoric of minimized state influence and power.

Philip Cerny (2010:129) reminds us that:

> neoliberalism is not a seamless web doctrinally and discursively. It is not only a contested concept in theoretical terms but also a highly internally differentiated one, made up of a range of politically linked but potentially discrete and freestanding subcategories and dimensions.

These categories and dimensions are manipulated in different ways by actors, resulting in "a much larger spectrum of strategic options, policy prescriptions, and de facto practices than the original conservative version would suggest" (Cerny 2010:129). The implications of this are that different actors are able to select specific aspects and try to claim this for diverse political objectives. By extension, neoliberalism, as a political rationality, tries to render the social domain economic and to link a reduction in state services to increased calls for personal responsibility. It is maintained through tensions inherent to liberal democracy: totalizing bureaucratization competes with the primacy of the individual (Cerny 2010; Mouffe 2000). Indeed, a central feature of neoliberal rationality is the search to achieve congruence between the responsible and moral individual and the rational economic actor (Lemke 2001:201). Here, the aspiration is "to construct prudent subjects whose moral quality is based on the fact that they rationally assess the costs and benefits of a certain act as opposed to other alternative acts" (Lemke 2001:201). The choice of action is made based on the free will of actors (in line with liberal logic) and the consequences of the actions are borne by the subject who is solely responsible for them. When it comes to CSO engagement in food governance, especially at the global level, we see the expectation of liberal democracy support the development of spaces to facilitate their engagement. However cynical this may sound, it is not explicitly meant to be. It should be noted that this tendency to opening up participation could be a double-edged sword. While there is the potential for transfer of responsibility, especially of implementation and monitoring onto civil society actors, as we will see throughout this book, there is also a widening of debate that has the potential to deliver stronger policy outcomes.

Neoliberalism can also be understood as a process: neoliberalization. Peck (2010:19) argues that process-focused "definitions of neoliberalization are preferable to static and taxonomic renderings of neoliberalism, since the latter tend to rely too heavily on regime-like conceptions, bracketed in time and space." "Neoliberalism," he continues, "defies explanation in terms of fixed coordinates." Neoliberalization, in turn, refers to a contradictory process of market-like rule, principally negotiated at the boundaries of the state, and occupying the ideological space defined by a (broadly) sympathetic critique of nineteenth-century laissez-faire and deep antipathies to collectivism planned and socialized modes of government, especially those associated with Keynesianism and developmentalism (Peck 2010:20).

Neoliberalism has evolved through processes of shape-shifting, and uneven open-ended mutations and cross-referential development (Peck 2010:30). As a process, neoliberalization encourages individuals to give their lives a specific capitalist form and by extension, policy makers to give their policies specific capitalist forms. Neoliberalism generalizes the scope of the economic order and in doing so successfully generalizes social activity in relation to economy and evaluates all activity by way economic analysis or with respect to market concepts (Lemke 2001:198). The existing worlds of neoliberalism are "institutionally cluttered places marked by experimental-but-flawed systems of governance, cumulative problems of social fallout and serial market failure" (Peck 2010:31).

Neoliberalism, in its current forms, represented not only a "political and ideological manifestation of economic structural change and public policy innovation at national level but also into the ideational driving force behind the politics of globalization" (Cerny 2010:129). To reflect the hegemonic nature of neoliberalism, Cerny advances the concept of embedded neoliberalism. Embedded neoliberalism provides a framework, or outlines the logic, within which processes of global governance take place. This proves useful for starting to frame analysis into global food security governance.

Embedded neoliberalism

Processes of neoliberalization have become "embedded in twenty-first century institutional behavior, political processes, discourses and understandings of socioeconomic realities" (Cerny 2010:129). Through this processes of embedding, neoliberalism has become the "shared mental model" (Roy et al. 2007) of the evolving art of governmentality (Burchell et al. 1991; Foucault 2008): the Gramscian "common sense" notion of what is expected and/or taken for granted.

Writing from within a fascist prison between 1925 and 1935, Antonio Gramsci was broadly concerned with the problem of understanding capitalist societies and the possibility of creating alternative types of states or societies based on the working class. Of prime interest to Gramsci were: the state, relationships of civil society to the state, and relationships of politics, ethics and ideology production. Concerned by the economic determinism of Marx's model, and informed by his own experiences, Gramsci (1971) developed a similar dialect to Marx, in so far as the interacting elements create a larger unity. But Gramsci introduced social relations into the level of superstructure and articulated how these relations can reinforce or undermine the material basis. At the level of superstructure, key actors (the state and civil society) engage in spheres of authority. Gramsci introduces political, ethical and ideological spheres of activity into his model.[1] The economic structure and coalitions at the level of the superstructure (social and political) form organic—implying long-term—orders for Gramsci. The caretakers of this order are the dominant class who control the economy and permeate the state, thereby maintaining hegemony over civil society.

Hegemony is perhaps most commonly used to refer to the dominance of one group over another without the threat of force. However, in the current era of late capitalism, hegemony is increasingly understood as "organizing consent to the ruling relations of capitalism" (Carroll 2006:10). Hegemony, much like neoliberalism, is a concept that has suffered from adjectival promiscuity. It is here used to describe an intricate and multifaceted process that Canadian cultural historian Ian McKay (2005:61) likens to a dance, in which the lead dancer maneuvers the partner, gently coaxing the partner to glide, turn and dip in response to the leader. With practice, the partner's actions, despite being controlled by the lead, begin to feel natural to the extent that they forget they are being led. By way of this process, the actions and language of the hegemonic group (the lead) are normalized and society (the partner) learns to follow to the extent to where followed actions are also normalized and feel natural and autonomous. Robert Cox (1993:63) uses a less subtle but equally effective metaphor to define hegemony: "Hegemony is like a pillow: it absorbs blows and sooner or later, the would-be assailant will find it comfortable to rest upon." The relational nature of hegemony recalls the similarly relational nature of power and is fundamental to understanding embedded neoliberalism.

Embedded neoliberalism reflects not only an emerging neoliberal consensus developed "as market forces and transnational interpenetration constrain institutions and actors to behave in certain ways" (Cerny 2010:148), but also a political construction, given shape in the everyday world by political actors and interest groups seeking political legitimacy. Central to this idea is the understanding that the "scope and significance of neoliberalism has been transformed not merely into the political and ideological manifestation of economic structural change and public policy innovation at national level, but also into the political driving force behind globalization itself" (Cerny 2010:3).

This is similar to what Emelie Peine and Philip McMichael (2005) have described as market rule: the act of states incorporating multilateral or bilateral protocols into national policy. This process is ideologically maintained by giving "primacy to increased investment, production and trade over social concerns," and wherein national and international spheres are represented as mutually exclusive categories in an attempt to "encourage domestic policies, such as farm subsidies, that artificially cheapen commodity process and ultimately serve agribusiness interests" (Peine and McMichael 2005:24; see also Duncan and Barling 2012; McMichael 2000).

The introduction of the idea of a "neoliberal era" advanced at the beginning of this section reflects the fact that contemporary social formations revolve around the leadership of a power structure that operates through the use of coercion and the organization of consent within a social formation. This process is by no means stable and is often the site of antagonism and resistance. A hegemonic arrangement within a population is thus in part achieved when a population comes to be dominated partly through its own consent. However, hegemony "cuts both ways" since the processes of organizing consent may also create opportunities for constructing counter-hegemonic movements and resistance (Carroll 1990:393).

With respect to food security, many farming and food social movements actively and publicly challenge the neoliberal logic that informs global institutional direction of national production and push localized peasant agricultural systems to compete in volatile global markets that do not favor smallholder producers. For example, in response to the Group of 8's (G8) proposal for a New Alliance on Food Security and Nutrition, which promotes strengthened partnerships with African governments and the private sector with an aim to increase food security, the leader of ROPPA (Le Réseau des organizations paysannes et de producteurs de l'Afrique de l'Ouest or the West African Peasant and Food Producer's Network), issued a letter to the leaders of African Union countries, which was then co-signed by 15 farming groups across the continent. He wrote:

> At the moment in which the President of the United States, acting in good faith I am sure, has decided to organize a Symposium on food security on 18–19 May 2012 in Washington on the eve of the G8 meeting in Camp David, I address myself to you, as President of the African Union, and through you to all of the African Heads of State. I ask you to explain how you could possibly justify thinking that the food security and sovereignty of Africa could be secured through international cooperation outside of the policy frameworks formulated in an inclusive fashion with the peasants and the producers of the continent ... I would simply like to recall that food security and sovereignty are the basis of our general development, as all of the African governments underline. It is a strategic challenge. This is why we must build our food policy on our own resources as is done in the other regions of the world. The G8 and the G20 can in no way be considered the appropriate fora for decisions of this nature.
>
> (Cissokho 2012)

This critique builds on theme that has been developing throughout the course of the chapter: change. A major challenge of neoliberalism within late capitalism is that by virtue of being common sense, resistance, while omnipresent, is easily thwarted, dismissed or reintegrated into the dominant model. An example of this is the shift of the organic food movement from a grassroots eco-health movement to a multinational industry now monitored and mediated by the agri-business players it originally worked to resist. Another example has already been mentioned above: increased engagement of civil society actors in global policy could serve to legitimize processes while providing a way for governments and the private sector to pass on/along key responsibilities.

It is important to note that within the framework of embedded neoliberalism, contemporary neoliberal logic at the global level embodies a structural tension left over from the Enlightenment era. Cerny (2010) identifies the two poles of this tension as institutional hierarchy and the liberal primacy of the individual. The former—the polity—involves a totalitization of modern bureaucratic institutions, and the latter—the economic component—the individuation of people via capitalism. This individuation is expressed in part through the primacy of the individual and the role of personal consciousness. This tension is visible, for example, through liberal democracy which Chantal Mouffe (2000) explains has an inherently conflictual nature: the tension of democracy and liberalism.[2] This individuation is expressed in part through the primacy of the individual and the role of personal consciousness, a process evident in the development of food security policy through a shift from global cooperation to increased production in the 1970s to a focus on individual and household livelihoods throughout the 1980s (Maxwell 1996; Maxwell and Slater 2003; Mechlem 2004; Sen 1981; Shaw 2007).

This process of authoritative direction and control at the global level is creatively managed by through the art of governmentality (Cerny 2010). Thus, the dynamic process of governmentalization, managed through the art of governmentality results in systems of global governance that "include systems of rule at all levels of human activity—from the family to the international organization—in which the pursuit of goals through the exercise of control has transnational repercussions" (Rosenau 1995:13). In this sense, global governance becomes less a process than a reference to the international superstructure of world politics (Cerny 2010:186).

Global governance

Theories of global governance furnish us with tools to assess processes that we can observe and strategies to understand complex processes as political projects. Yet using the term "global governance" is not without challenges. In an early edition of the journal *Global Governance*, Lawrence Finkelstein (1995:368) warned that "'[g]lobal governance' appears to be virtually everything" and that "we say 'governance' because we really don't know what to call what is going on." Despite the wealth of literature and analysis that has since been dedicated to the topic, there remains little consensus as to what is meant by global governance. However, rather than a paucity of definitions, we are grappling with too many (Dingwerth and Pattberg 2006; Kersbergen and Van Waarden

2004), leading one scholar to state that global governance is "contested terrain": a term that obscures more than it describes (Woods 2007:28).

To help make sense of this multifarious concept, it is useful to begin by defining governance. According to Thomas Weiss (2000:795) "[m]any academics and international practitioners employ 'governance' to connote a complex set of structures and processes, both public and private, while more popular writers tend to use it synonymously with 'government'." Similarly, Chris Brown and Kirsten Ainley (2009:129) explain that governance, originally synonymous with government, "has been pressed into service as a convenient term for the collective impact of the various disparate quasi-governmental institutions that have proliferated (internally and externally) over the last century or more" (see also Rosenau and Czempiel 1992). Yet at a time marked by "shifting boundaries, relocated authorities, weakened states, and proliferating nongovernmental organizations (NGOs) at local, provincial, national, transnational, international, and global levels of community," scholars have tended to turn to global governance as a way of starting to "confront the insufficiency of our ways of thinking, talking, and writing about government" (Rosenau 1999:287).

Tim Lang et al. (2009:75) contrast governance and government, explaining that:

> governance implies more indirect, softer forms of direction from the state than command and control, and reflects collaborative outcomes, involving a wide range of actors often from the private sector, as well as from government bureaucracy, as much as deliberate interventions by the state.

They (Lang et al. 2009: 81) argue that governance is "an interactive process of state and public laws and policy with private interests and actors."

In their book *Governance and Performance: New Perspectives*, Carolyn Heinrich and Laurence Lynn (2000:4) state that governance

> implies an arrangement of distinct but interrelated elements—statues, including policy mandates; organizational, financial, and programmatic structures; resource levels; administrative rules and guidelines; and institutionalized rules and norms—that constrains and enables the tasks, priorities, and values that are incorporated into regulatory, service production, and service delivery processes.

To summarize then, governance broadly refers to the management functions of societies—formal and informal—that are generally focused or coordinated around the state or government institutions but include diverse actors, including civil society and the private sector. It reflects two complementary dimensions: purpose (guiding and directing) and regulating (restraining, managing and controlling) while highlighting the "deeper purposes that groups and societies pursue" (Dahlberg 2001:136).

Common characteristics of governance, taken from across the literature (i.e., Cardoso 2003; Jessop 1998; Kersbergen and Van Waarden 2004; Rosenau 1999, 2002; Smouts 1998), suggest that governance implies measures of control, orderliness and manageability but at the same time is made up of inter-subjective norms, rules and principles. Moreover, governance reflects a process more than a system of rule or an activity. It appeals to accommodation over domination and is thus dependent on participation, negotiation and coordination. In lieu of formal institutions, or perhaps working in tandem with them, governance relies on continual interactions between formal and informal networks, partnerships, projects and consensus. Governance is pluricentric rather than unicentric but there is emphasis on functioning administrative capacities, accountability and responsiveness to those the regime serves and ideally, transparency. Following this, networks play an important role in governance and these networks function to organize relations between relatively autonomous but interdependent actors. Finally, within contemporary governance systems relations between actors pose risks and uncertainties and correspondingly, different sectors have developed institutions to support cooperation and reduce risk. As will be shown later, these characteristics are all present in the changing global food security policy arena.

The concept of global governance emerged alongside governance as a way of conceptualizing the rapid changes to global economics and politics brought about by processes of globalization. Such processes and resulting forces have changed the political, economic and social landscape (core principles of the international order) leading to a redistribution of "power within the international systems away from the nation-state to new international non-state actors" (Muldoon 2004:4).

There have been important efforts at developing definitions of global governance. One widely used definition was presented by the UN Commission on Global Governance in their report *Our Global Neighborhood* (Carlsson et al. 1995:7):

At the global level, governance has been viewed primarily as intergovernmental relationships, but it must now be understood as also involving nongovernmental organizations (NGOs), citizens' movements, multinational corporations, and the global capital market. Interacting with these are global mass media of dramatically enlarged influence.

This definition importantly acknowledges the role of new actors and the mass media but remains rather limited and inadequate. Yet, as Daniel Compagnon (in Overbeek et al. 2010:711) notes, "reflecting on global governance should not be a gratuitous and vain search for the 'right' definition: rather, it should become an exploration of the specific historical context—multidimensional globalisation—in which it is nested."

The term global governance is often criticized for suggesting that governance is global in scope, or that the globe is in some way governed. In an attempt to avoid these limitations, scholars have forwarded other terms such as "polyarchy" (Brown 1995), "panarchy" (Sewell and Slater 1995), "collibration" (Dunsire 1993) and "fragmentation" (Rosenau 1999), but none have been widely adopted in the global context. However, the concept of global governance is not to be equated with global rule but rather with multilevel governance, referring to multiple and interconnected levels of governance taking place at national, international, subnational, regional and local levels (Brühl and Rittberger 2001:2). As such, for example, it demands asking how World Trade Organization (WTO) rules impact specific communities and how local initiatives in turn impact national or regional or even global initiatives. Given that this book considers global-level governance, that food security aims to end hunger, and that hunger is experienced first and foremost at the individual level, a global governance approach presents a useful starting point.

Klaus Dingwerth and Philipp Pattberg's (2006) survey of the academic literature has led them to conclude that there are two dominant applications of global governance as a concept: global governance as observable phenomena and global governance as political program. These approaches to global governance are not necessarily applied exclusively and most academic applications tend to combine both approaches: analytic-institutionalism (Dingwerth and Pattberg 2006:195). However, here, an attempt will be made to qualify each approach separately, while recognizing that there is often overlap between the two.

Observable phenomena

The development of global governance is made visible through the proliferation of international organizations and their increasing influence, and the increasing interconnectedness of local and global events. Seen as an observable phenomenon, global governance tends be understood as part of a continuum: an evolution from international relations. Building on this tradition, global governance is seen to be the domain of three primary actors: government (political domain), markets (economic domain) and civil society (socio-cultural domain) (Muldoon 2004:9; UNDP 1997:14–18). These can be conceptualized as three pillars of global governance. Each pillar has distinct institutions and organizations that operate on three different levels of support (international, national and community) and in turn support the system as a whole. James Muldoon (2004:9) argues that the interaction between levels results in the integration and differentiation within and between organizations and institutions. Yet, with the onward march of globalization, and the expansion of global governance, the analytic lines that previously existed have been blurred or have started to disappear.

To help make sense of these pillars and changes we must first recognize that non-governmental and governmental mechanisms have influence on how the global system is governed. Second, there are a diverse range of actors involved in the formation of instruments of global governance. Third, global governance infers the increasing integration of the three pillars and the fragmentation of the word order as a result of transitory and contested spheres of authority (Rosenau 1997). Finally, we must recognize that the architecture of global governance operates at multiple levels and is not inherently hierarchical.

Moving on from the interactions between the actors and levels of support, James Muldoon (2004) identifies several common characteristics. First, global governance is multilayered in that it is constituted by and through the structural enmeshment of key infrastructures of governance with the national government folded in between each of the layers. These are referred to as multipolarity of power and decentralization of authority which are critical to the transformation of the international system to the global system. Second, there is no single locus of authority and political authority is fragmented. It is thus often described as polyarchic or pluralistic. A third characteristic is that the architecture of global governance has a variable geometry, meaning that the political significance and the regulatory capacity of these infrastructures vary considerably. Here, Muldoon (2004:8) highlights the role of structures: global governance requires institutions, regimes and organizations that work as intermediaries to tie together different components of social systems.

Through transformation, international organizations are likely to maintain many of the features that define them and add new features as needed to address particular demands of the global system. Part of Muldoon's rationale for this stems from what he sees as a need for stability within the global system: "governance structures only survive if they promote stability in the system" (Muldoon 2004:9). A fourth observation is that systems of global governance are structurally complex, composed of diverse agencies and networks with overlapping jurisdictions, and maintain differential power resources and competencies. Finally, within the architecture of global governance, national governments have become increasingly crucial sites for stitching together the various infrastructures of governance and legitimizing regulation beyond the state, an underlying premise of international relations as well.

Beyond common characteristics and established understandings of global governance, the literature identifies common shifts within governance structures that happen vertically, horizontally and both vertically and horizontally. Vertical shifts refer to changes—be they of power, responsibility or coordination—between nation-states and international institutions with supranational characteristics (known to as upwards shifts) or to shifting of responsibility and power from national or international bodies to subnational or regional level (referred to as downward shifts). A downward shift is related to internationalization wherein international bodies rely on local agencies to implement or enforce their regulations, thereby potentially strengthening local bodies (Kersbergen and Van Waarden 2004:153).

As Kersbergen and Van Waarden (2004:149–150) point out, horizontal shifts are part of a broader tendency of increased juridification of social relations, wherein once informal relations are becoming increasing formalised via agreements. Kersbergen and Van Waarden (2004:155) also note that these

types of shifts in governance lead to a rise in the popularity and usage of information comparison, such as benchmarking and best practices. As we will see,
this process has become quite pronounced in the reformed CFS, which promotes the sharing of case studies to support its various roles and objectives.

Network governance is a key trait of horizontal shifts in global governance.
One implication of horizontal shifts is that governance decisions are being made
through increasingly complicated networks. Network governance has two origins: international relations theory (Hasenclever, Mayer, and Rittberger 1997)
and comparative European public policy analysis (Bulmer 1998; Moravcsik
1993, 1998; Peterson and Bomberg 1994; Wallace and Wallace 1996). A network governance approach sees governance as relating to both power relations
resulting from rules and substance of policies, whereas multilevel refers to the
engagement of different levels of government (regional, national and subnational) as well as the involvement of private and public actors at these levels
(Kersbergen and Van Waarden 2004:149–150).

Brown and Ainley (2009:129) suggest that in the absence of a world government, due to the unwillingness of states to surrender their juridical status
as sovereign, among other things, efforts at ruling and the exercise of political
sovereignty have led to the creation of extensive networks of global governance. The development of these networks effectively changes the location
of decision making, policies, regulation, as well as the rules of production
and enforcement leading to shifts in governance styles (Kersbergen and Van
Waarden 2004:155). The result is increasingly complicated network structures
wherein traditional approaches of command, control and enforcement are no
longer efficient or effective (Kersbergen and Van Waarden 2004:153).

In the context of increased globalization and fragmentation, Robert
Keohane and Joseph Nye (2000:37) note that any emerging pattern of governance will have to be networked rather than hierarchical and must have
minimal rather than highly ambitious objectives. As will be explored in this
book, evidence suggests that in the shifting architecture of global food security
governance, networks are playing an increasingly important and influential
role. Kersbergen and Van Waarden (2004:149) add that the primary mode of
interaction between networks is negotiation. However, as we will see, from
the perspective of social movement, civil society and NGO networks, the
interactions tend to be based more on communication, information sharing
and strategic alignments to forward similarly held positions or shared objectives.

Up to this point, the description provided of global governance fails
to describe why it has been taken up to the degree that it has. Bob Jessop
(1998) identifies four possibilities: expansion of the governance discourse;
persistence of "governance" mechanisms in contract to markets or hierarchy; the cycle of modes of coordination; and a fundamental secular shift in
state–market–society relations. This final reason, which recalls Muldoon's
pillars of global governance, is also most visible in the relations that are of
interest to analyses of global food security governance: mainly, that there
has been a fundamental secular shift in state–market–society relations.

These imply new economic and social conditions and address related problems which cannot be managed or resolved by top-down state planning or market-mediated anarchy. As we will see however, despite the shifts towards governance models, the tendency in food security remains state centric in terms of accountability and policy making.

Political project

Having reviewed global governance as an observable phenomenon, we can now consider the implications of this phenomenon by considering global governance as a political project. There are several ways that global governance as political project is taken up, including: global governance as a way of solving the world's collective problems; global governance to re-democratize in the face of globalization; and, global governance as advancement of a neoliberal project. As this suggests, global governance is often referenced in the context of a broader vision of how we might begin to address some of the world's most pressing problems. Here language related to the coordination of multiple actors to solve economic, environmental and broad social problems is invoked. Examples can be seen throughout the series of world summits that took place throughout the 1990s. From this perspective, enhanced global governance is needed to begin to adequately address global problems. The perspective tends towards long-term projects of global integration, often modelled on the UN and the European Union (EU) (Dingwerth and Pattberg 2006; Gordenker and Weiss 1996). The approach enacts language of communal efforts often through diplomatic rallying cries. For example, in advance of the 36th Session of the CFS, the FAO Media Centre issued a statement proclaiming that "as the cornerstone of the global governance of agriculture and food security, the CFS will be more effective in facing challenges to food security" (FAO 2010). The sentiment suggests that the UN provides the appropriate and necessary space to tackle the pressing problem of food insecurity and thus proclaims its position as the leader in this process: "the CFS has been undergoing a major reform with the aim of making the Committee the most inclusive international and intergovernmental platform for all relevant stakeholders to work together to ensure food security and nutrition for all" (FAO 2010). Indeed, as we will see, this logic permeates the reform of the CFS as well as rationales for why it should be leading policy debates on global food security. The rhetoric of coming together to solve problems is also taken up by groups like the G8. Their 2012 Camp David Declaration (G8 2012: para 16) makes use of similar language:

> For over a decade, the G-8 has engaged with African partners to address the challenges and opportunities afforded by Africa's quest for inclusive and sustainable development. Our progress has been measurable, and together we have changed the lives of hundreds of millions of people.

Global governance as political project is also linked to a redemocratization of politics in the wake of a wave of globalization defined by increased corporate engagement and a shift in state responsibilities towards facilitation (be it through policies or infrastructure). As Dingwerth and Pattberg (2006:195) explain, from this perspective, it is argued—perhaps overly optimistically—that "the goal of global governance lies in regaining society's control over market forces which [have] been lost in the wake of globalizations."

The third way in which global governance can be understood as a political project is through the advancement of the neoliberal project. Consider for example the following statement from the G8 ministers of agriculture *Final Declaration on Agriculture and Food Security at the Core of the International Agenda*:

> We need to sustain the benefits of globalization and open markets, highlighting the crucial importance of rejecting protectionism and encouraging the development of local, regional and international integrated agricultural markets. We underline the importance of a rules-based international trading system for agricultural trade and we are committed to reaching a balanced, comprehensive and ambitious conclusion of the Doha Round. We wish to support the role of well functioning markets as a means for improving food security.
>
> (G8 2009)

But this market-based approach to food security faces active contestation. For example, La Via Campesina, the world's largest peasant movement, forwards a food sovereignty framework as a direct challenge to neoliberal globalization. From the perspective of La Via Campesina (2012):

> The advance of the capitalist system that has reached unprecedented dimensions in the past two decades is resulting in crises that are of equally unprecedented dimensions. The financial, food, energy and environmental crises are phases of the structural crisis of capitalism, which has no limits in its search for more profits. And, as in other structural crises, it impacts the peoples of the world and not the elites ... [T]o say that capitalism is in crisis does not mean that the system is in retreat. On the contrary, it is precisely in this moment that it advances with more intensity because the corporations take advantage of the crisis to extend their domination over territories that have not yet been conquered.

La Via Campesina is increasingly engaging in formal and informal processes of global governance and moderating their participation through a food sovereignty framework (discussed in greater detail below). La Via Campesina is an example of how global networks are seeking to redefine global governance by forwarding a framework for the re-democratization of governance systems. Their challenge to the ordering of global governance also serves to illustrate ways in which global governance as political project is also visible as a neoliberal project.

Henk Overbeek (in Overbeek et al. 2010:702) cautions that what is often referred to as global governance is in fact "*neoliberal* global governance, serving the freedom of capital to accumulate around the planet." Indeed, the pursuit and maintenance of neoliberal hegemony is not absent from global food security governance, and in fact is often a key motivating and rationalizing factor in world food security policy, arguably to the detriment of the eradication of hunger (Busch and Bain 2004; Duncan and Barling 2012; Lang et al. 2009; Lawrence et al. 2010; McMichael 2000; Pechlaner and Otero 2008; Peine and McMichael 2005). Overbeek (in Overbeek et al. 2010:702), lamenting the loss of its initial reference to a radical restructuring of the global economic order, suggests that global governance is now applied as a reformist concept to accommodate the interests of neoliberal globalization with only the most necessary reforms to keep the system running (a good example of analytic institutionalism: global governance as political project and observable phenomenon). He suggests that by presupposing common interests, instead of questioning the existence of common interests and a willingness to work together, most definitions of global governance effectively depoliticize the debate about world order. Furthermore, as Ulrich Brand (2005) illustrates, global governance, understood as a discourse, is often articulated in ways which legitimize shifts and developments so as to forward and maintain neoliberal globalization. This builds on Muldoon's (2004) concern that transformations of international organizations are likely to take place in ways that adapt to particular demands of the global system rather than provide structural change.

From this critical theory perspective, global governance is not so much an answer to state failures in the globalization process as it is a hegemonic discourse invoked to disguise the negative effects of neoliberal economic development on a global scale. In the words of Ulrich Brand (translated and cited in Pattberg 2006:43), "the discourse of Global Governance … serves as a means to deal more effectively with the crisis-prone consequences caused by [postfordist-neoliberal social transformations]." The prevailing neoliberal logic steering policy processes beyond the state are deeply embedded in a broader political trend towards reregulation of the world economy in ways that obscure the negative tendencies of late capitalism. Neoliberal approaches to global governance and the policies that result are advanced to maintain or reclaim political influence in order to stabilize the institutional landscape of world politics. Through these processes, neoliberalism becomes so deeply embedded that it emerges as an ideological companion to globalization.

Challenges and critiques to global governance

As noted above, the concept of global governance is not without critique or challenge, both in terms of scholarship and processes. For Overbeek (in Overbeek et al. 2010), given the multiplicity of uses, definitions and applications, the term global governance is not only not useful, it is also misleading. He argues that the three largest weaknesses facing applications of global governance are that analysis tends to be ahistorical, necessarily pluralist in so far as they tend to take the plurality of actors, interests and structures as essential, and apolitical in so much as power is often removed from analyses. Dingwerth and Pattberg (in Overbeek et al. 2010) agree with Overbeek on the apolitical nature of global governance scholarship and forward two other limitations: that global governance assumes globality and non-governance is ignored. However, they also argue that global governance studies present a way of examining diverse power relations at the global level. Despite structural imbalances in the distribution of power and resources in the global political economy, countries from the South have not lacked influence in transnational politics. Towards this end, Compagnon (in Overbeek et al. 2010) argues for more nuanced and fact-based assessments of global governance and the inclusion of multiple actors in global governance research.

Klaus Dingwerth and Philipp Pattberg (in Overbeek et al. 2010:708) note, in most cases, researchers evoking global governance do not extend their analysis beyond relevant steering mechanisms that exist in relation to the respective issue within the world. Correspondingly, efforts to make sense of a specific field of global governance often start by establishing a list of relevant regulatory mechanism. However, if this is the way that scholars approach global governance, then, according to Dingwerth and Pattberg (in Overbeek et al. 2010), it is important to anticipate some potential blind spots. First, there is a need to avoid the temptation of overestimating the amount of rule-based coordination that exists in the political world. Second, it follows that global governance research has a tendency to adopt a narrow focus on the rules that can be most easily identified (for example, written rules, legal texts and codes of conduct).[3] Third, global governance research is likely to concentrate on issue areas with dense formal rules resulting in a paucity of investigation into less institutionalized, but not necessarily less effective, areas of global governance. Finally, there is little clarity or consensus on what constitutes a global policy problem, how one is recognized and why some issues are constructed as global problems while others are left as domestic challenges.

With respect to food security, there is an inter-governmentally negotiated definition of what constitutes food security although understandings for why there is food insecurity and methods to achieve food security remain highly contested. Despite myriad attempts to address the problems by way of a variety of policy programs, food insecurity remains prevalent and there are clear differences and divergences in how to address the issue. Furthermore, more often than not, the proposed solutions comprise part of the problem (Holt-Giménez and Altieri 2013). This leads to concerns about global governance processes.

Marie-Claude Smouts (1998:88) argues that global governance processes are based on eirenic representations of social life and disregard situations of outright domination as well as questions arising from ungovernability. An even larger challenge stems from an underlying criterion of global governance—effectiveness—and a lack of a world government. Global governance emerges and evolves to manage an issue or a problem to be resolved by way of accommodation of mutual interest. At present, the sole regulator acting at the global level that cuts across interacting social and subsystems is the international market. Smouts (1998:88) warns that in this respect, global governance could effectively conceal "the most devious type of economic liberalism." Aware of these limitations, efforts have been made throughout this research to ensure that processes of domination are not ignored by remaining aware of the critique of social movement actors fighting for their rights, and trying to ensure that the analysis of how multilateral actors seek out effectiveness in global food security policy does not serve to mask efforts to advance neoliberal policies. Indeed, the theoretical framework developed in this chapter actively serves to uncover and critique such processes.

Before moving on, a review of dominant challenges and critiques of global governance processes and institutions is presented. These include accountability, legitimacy and categorization and are introduced so as to flag some of the key challenges that are likely to arise within the changing architecture of global food security governance.

Accountability

As new forms of governance render traditional mechanisms for checks and balances less effective, or even obsolete, new understandings and mechanisms for accountability are emerging. Questions related to accountability tend to ask which entities or actors are, or should be, accountable, to whom and how. From the perspective of food policy, it is, also important to consider what the answers to these questions mean for accountability gaps; that is where practices differ from the desired outcomes. Furthermore, there is need to consider who is accountable not just for policy development, but equally for implementation, monitoring and evaluation.

The immediate challenge is thus defining what is meant by accountability. Some define accountability as a relationship "in which an individual, group or other entity makes demands on an agent to report on his or her activities, and has the ability to impose costs on the agent" (Keohane 2002:13). For Kersbergen and Van Waarden (2004:156), accountability is linked to governability—that is, the capacity to solve urgent societal problems and to develop systems to control the exercise of power, or to hold power holders accountable—and consequently, governability and accountability need to develop together. Others argue that democratic accountability in world politics is a hypothetical system wherein the action of agents have to be reported to those people whose lives are impacted by them (Held 2002:27).

For this study, questions of accountability loom large. As the architecture of global governance shifts and opens up to include new actors, questions of who is accountable in negotiations, who is responsible for implementation, follow-up and evaluation emerge as highly sensitive and political questions. These will be addressed throughout the book.

Legitimacy

Governance, in any form, requires legitimacy. Following from James Rosenau (2003), legitimacy is understood as a relational concept, implying that the legitimacy of an actor's actions can only be understood in relation to the perception of all relevant stakeholders (see also Boström and Hallström 2010). Achieving and maintaining legitimacy requires convincing actors that there is a value-added component to the rules or policies established by the organizations (Boström and Hallström 2010:10). New regulatory arrangements which are constructed and organized around horizontal non-state relationships are subject to structural drawbacks as they cannot rely on the presumed legitimacy of the nation-state as well as traditional enforcement capacities (Bernstein and Cashore 2000; Boström and Hallström 2010).

Empirical belief in the legitimacy of an institution depends in part on the normative validity of the political order (Lipset 1960:77). There is broad agreement that in normative terms the current operation of international institutions, and global governance more broadly, does not meet democratic standards (Dahl 1999; Held 2004; Scholte 2004). Zürn (2004:260) notes that:

> [a]cknowledged democratic deficits include the lack of identifiable decision-makers who are directly accountable for wrong decisions made at the international level, as well as the inscrutability of international decision-making processes and thus the advantage the executive decision-makers have over others in terms of information.

A commonly proposed solution to this problem is the enhancement of participation. Middendorf and Busch (1997:45) argue that "a closer approximation of the 'public good' can be achieved by encouraging the participation of the fullest range of constituents." The call for public participation in policy processes is not new. For example, Carole Pateman (1970) argued that developing of the ability and desire of people to participate is crucial to democratic societies.

Participation, as it is used here, relates to the engagement of civil society actors in decision making procedures, including the multiple conceptualizations connected to this norm (Saurugger 2010:471). Participation "is a problematic and contested ground, but one with the potential to deliver real benefits to those who have hitherto been incorporated" (Parfitt 2004:538). Parfitt (2004), writing specifically about development practice, argues that when participation is viewed as a means, the power relations between those at the grassroots and decision makers are left largely untouched and consequently objectives, goals and targets remain defined by traditional authorities and espouse top–down approaches. Alternatively, approaching participation as an end suggests the potential for a transformation in power relations. As such, "[w]here as participation as a means is politically neutral insofar as it does not address such power differentials, participation as an end has an emancipatory, politically radical component in that it seeks to redress unequal power relations" (Parfitt 2004:539). Thus, while in many multilateral fora (e.g., the World Bank) participation is used as a means of improving processes, enhancing legitimacy or to enhance implementation, other fora employ participatory approaches to capture knowledge or promote empowerment (e.g., the CFS). It is important here to acknowledge that in practice processes tend to fall between the poles of means and ends.

Given the increasing influence of participatory approaches, it is not surprising that they have received a high level of attention from researchers, commentators and practitioners. Participatory approaches have been particularly challenged on the basis of providing a legitimizing discourse; another way of advancing status quo policy making while creating the impression of inclusive, participatory, and therefore legitimate, processes (Cooke and Kothari 2001). Deliberative democratic scholarship has been critiqued for being too focused on processes of deliberation, or participation, within deliberative fora and not the processes that take place around the fora of the structural features of the wider society and political system within which these deliberative fora are situated (Bartelson 2006; Chandler 2006; Joseph 2012; Pateman 2012). This is not to suggest that theorists completely ignore the institutional background but there is a tendency to leave the conventional institutional structures and political meanings of democracy and participation intact (Pateman 2012).

When it comes to food, meaningful public participation is central and "[w]hile creating opportunities for participation does not guarantee that the best possible decision will result, at least it does appear to increase the possibility of better decisions that are more responsive to the needs and desires of the broader public" (Middendorf and Busch 1997:54). The complexity of food security policy should not be used as a rationale for restricting involvement. By arguing that global food security policy is too complex to involve a diversity of players, we end up forwarding a system that encourages decision making without consideration for broader implications (Middendorf and Busch 1997:48).

Middendorf and Busch (1997) provide a rationale for public agriculture research, if we accept that all technical changes are also social changes. The arguments can be adapted and applied in support of public participation in agri-food governance and policy-making processes. First, increasing participation in decision making at the global level is compatible with the democratic principles of participating nations. Second, while not guaranteeing it, "broad public involvement in decision making will increase the chances of better decision making … because a broader range of values is likely to be represented and the probability of error may be reduce" (Middendorf and Busch 1997:46).

Within multilateral organizations where non-state actors play an active role, questions of legitimacy are inevitable. In these circumstances, non-state actors must achieve active approval from a broad group of stakeholders, including state actors (Boström and Hallström 2010). These actors are normally not democratically elected and are, in many instances, self-elected. Achieving legitimacy entails working to gain broad support for their activities, which often involves developing partnerships (Boström and Hallström 2010:10). To further complicate things, in these networks, each actor will hold a different view on legitimacy and who and what is considered to be legitimate. Furthermore, as Boström and Hallström (2010:15) remind us, legitimacy is not a stable condition but something fluid that must be repeatedly created and recreated. Kersbergen and Van Waarden (2004:158) note that multilevel governance theorists often distinguish between input legitimacy and output legitimacy, with the former relating to political systems and specific policies which are legitimated by established rules and processes (Thomassen and Schmitt 1999:255) and the latter referring to political systems and policies which are legitimated by their success.

Without a representative mechanism at the global level (and often even with these), political choices are made by unaccountable executive agencies (extra-national and national), including powerful lobbies, organizations or private subjects (such as multinational corporations) (Benvenisti and Down 2007). As a result, there is a very real risk that opinions which conform to dominant ideologies or highly influential interests will prevail over underrepresented interests. Like accountability, the legitimacy of actors—who has the legitimacy to speak on behalf of others—is an increasingly important factor as global governance opens up to new actors and as these actors stake their claim to being "legitimate" actors. This book considers what and who is considered legitimate in CFS policy negotiations.

Categorization

Multi-stakeholder organizations are, by definition, comprised of different types of actors. Within international relations theory, political strategies are stabilized through established categories (notably, national actors). However, at the transnational level, there is a need to establish new actor categories so as to distinguish among participating stakeholders (Beck 2005; Pattberg 2006). To establish these categories is a challenge in and of itself as they cannot be negotiated among stakeholders because stakeholders must first negotiate who is to be recognized as a stakeholder (Boström and Hallström 2010:7). Furthermore, categorization is an exercise in power and a process that is often invisible. Moreover, categories, once adopted, tend to be taken for granted or go uncontested (Boström and Hallström 2010:7). This is problematic insofar as power relations become embedded in organizational arrangements which can then make it easier for some stakeholders to consolidate power due to their categorization (Davis et al. 2005). There is also the issue of the symbolic implications of how categories influence stakeholders' perception of self and others and how they are in turn perceived (Boström and Hallström 2010:9). Finally, categories can restrict diversity and by grouping organizations together present problems of representation and are subject to simplifications and will inevitably group organizations together in ways that some may find problematic. These issues of categorization are further explored in the analysis of the International Food and Nutrition Civil Society Mechanism to the Committee on World Food Security (see Chapter 5), where constituencies have been developed in an attempt to develop representative categories of global civil society. This process of categorization across the CFS, and the global architecture of global food security governance more broadly, warrants consideration.

Global food security governance

This book is about the global governance of food security. Having defined global governance and understanding that these relations take place within a context mediated by a flexible and ever-changing neoliberal logic, it is important to reflect on what is meant by global food security governance. Mathias Margulis (2012:231), acknowledging the large number of international institutions active in the field of food security working alongside "numerous regional, non-governmental and private organizations," describes global food security governance as a "decentralized patchwork of institutions."

The FAO has defined it as "a mechanism that will facilitate debate, convergence of views and coordination of actions to improve food security at global but also at regional and national levels" (FAO 2009:1). The UN's High Level Task Force on the Global Food Security Crisis proposes that good governance of food and nutrition security "is fundamentally about national governments prioritizing policies, plans, programs and funding to tackle hunger, malnutrition, and food insecurity in the most vulnerable populations, whether it be through humanitarian or development assistance, nationally, bilaterally or multilaterally" (High Level Task Force on the Global Food Security Crisis 2010:3). One definition that has garnered a bit more traction, and also emphasizes national responsibility, was advanced by the FAO who noted that food security governance "relates to formal and informal rules and processes through which interests are articulated, and decisions relevant to food security in a country are made, implemented and enforced on behalf of members of a society" (FAO 2011:17). Following a detailed literature review, Candel proposes the following definition of food security governance: "The formal and informal interactions across scaled between public and/or private entities ultimately aiming at the realization of food availability, food access, and food utilization, and their stability over time" (Candel 2014:598). Candel also identifies seven themes that cut across the growing body of literature on food security governance:

1   Governance is both a challenge and solution to food security.
2   The governance of food security is characterized by a high degree of complexity.
3   There are failures in the current architecture of food security governance.
4   New players are moving to the forefront of governance.
5   There is need for greater coherence and coordination across multiple scales of governance.
6   There is variation and conflict in how key issues are understood.
7   There are calls for adequate resources and integration of democratic values in food security governance.

Pascal Lamy, former Director-General of the WTO (Lamy 2012:721), notes that "part of the difficulty in thinking global governance lies in the gap between theory and practice." Indeed, a review of policies promoted across the transnational policy space in response to the food price crisis revealed a different set of themes. More specifically, a framework analysis of key policy recommendations emerging from the food price spikes of 2007–2008 uncovers eight dominant and repeating themes that mark the post-crisis response and frame international reactions:

1   immediate relief;
2   increased production;
3   improved markets;
4   financing and funding;
5   country-led plans;
6   policy cohesion;
7   cooperation; and
8   sustainability.

These themes do not represent concrete categories and often policies objectives and actions overlap and transcend multiple themes. Figure 2.1 provides examples of words that illustrate of how these themes are enacted in the policy documents.

These themes are reflected in key policies that have come to influence the transnational space occupied by the changing architecture of global food security governance. It is important to recognize that the actors engaged in multilateral fora at the global level are not ideologically bound to concrete or singular decisions. Analyses of global food security policies must acknowledge the complexity and political nature of negotiation and decision making. The policies that have been advanced in response to the food price crisis are certainly informed by the subjectivities and perspective of participating individuals. However, they are also the product of highly negotiated processes which more often than not are the result of give and take, and above all compromise.

Alongside the key themes outlined above, there is growing awareness and commitment to acknowledging and supporting small-scale farmers and women alongside recognition of the importance of agricultural development and food production in developing countries. There has been a clear discursive shift, followed by various levels of activity related to engagement of multiple stakeholders, including civil society (Duncan and Barling 2012; Lang and Barling 2012; McKeon 2009a, 2009b). Yet actors overwhelmingly maintain a commitment to market-oriented strategies that conform to neoliberal objectives.

Conclusion

The analysis undertaken in this book starts from the notion that processes of global governance take place within the boundaries of embedded neoliberalism. Such an approach valuably theorizes how formulations and enactments of

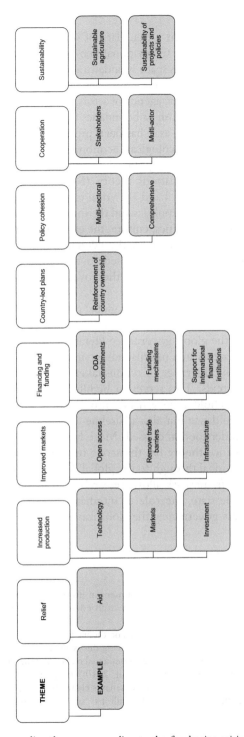

Figure 2.1 Dominant policy themes responding to the food price crisis (2007–8)

the "neoliberal" come to form a boundary of sorts—rigid but not imperme-
able—within the context of a transnational neo-plural space defined by global
governance (Cerny 2008). This space is understood to be organized in ways that
facilitate the objectives of economic actors over all other priorities. Importantly,
the approach makes space for the agency of actors, including those who resist and
act against neoliberalism and push its boundaries from within and from outside.

Global governance theory, as it has been presented in this chapter, recognizes fundamental political, ecological, economic, technological and cultural
dynamics that engage social and political theory while also moving beyond
conventional international relations theory (Muldoon 2004). As such, the
framework provides conceptual and analytical tools to critically assess the rapidly changing terrain of global politics and the interactions of the various actors
as they respond to shifts in politics, culture, the environment and the economy.
The theory provides explanations for the evolution and impact of emerging
modes of governance and can be applied to inquiries into multilateral and
global governance processes, especially the governance of complex problems
such as food security.

It is also acknowledged that insofar as global governance theory is far reaching, it fails to identify clear boundaries within which to frame and limit the
scope of study. Yet the global governance literature supports theorizing about
the organization of actors in a multilateral environment, while also providing
guidance for grouping the range of actions taken by these actors across different geopolitical contexts. This serves to highlight issues likely to emerge in
studies of multi-stakeholder governance processes. As such, the framework
provides not only guidance but also a baseline against which emerging global
processes can be understood and assed. More broadly, a framework drawing
from global governance theory has the scope to explore social relations from
the level of the individual through to the global. Importantly, within a context
of globalization, the framework allows researchers to identify key shifts in the
transformation of the state, the role of international institutions, multilateral
arrangements, private governance, the globalization of civil society and myriad
related interactions.

Notes

1 Gramsci (1971) fails to account for environment in his model of spheres of activity. The
   inclusion of the environment into this approach could prove valuable for food policy
   research.
2 Mouffe (2000) critiques deliberative democratic theory for attempting to reconcile the liberal tradition with the democratic tradition, seeing this as an attempt to erase the tension in a
   way that leaves them unable to address the conflictual reality of democratic politics.
3 Dingwerth and Pattberg (in Overbeek et al. 2010:708) point out that the method of
   "inventorization" runs in opposition to Rosenau's claim that global governance research
   is interested in examining the "literally millions" of rule systems with transboundary
   repercussions (Rosenau 1995:13).

References

Bartelson, J. 2006. "Making Sense of Global Civil Society." *European Journal of International Relations* 12(3):371–95. Retrieved (http://ejt.sagepub.com/cgi/doi/10.1177/1354066106067348).

Beck, U. 2005. *Power in the Global Age: A New Global Political Economy.* Cambridge: Polity Press.

Benvenisti, E., and G. W. Down. 2007. "The Empire's New Clothes: Political Economy and the Fragmentation of International Law." *Stanford Law Review* 60(2):595–631.

Bernstein, S., and B. Cashore. 2000. "Globalization, Four Paths of Internationalization, and Domestic Policy Change: The Case of Ecoforestry in British Columbia, Canada." *Canadian Journal of Political Science* 33:67–99.

Boström, M., and K. T. Hallström. 2010. "The Fragile Authority of Multi-Stakeholder Standard Setting." in *Re-Discovering International Organizations* (9–11 September). Stockholm: Standing Group on International Relations.

Brand, U. 2005. "Order and Regulation: Global Governance as a Hegemonic Discourse of International Politics?" *Review of International Political Economy* 1(1):155–76. Retrieved (www.glogov.org/images/doc/GG12_2_Dingwerth_Pattberg1.pdf).

Brown, C., and K. Ainley. 2009. *Understanding International Relations.* 3rd Revise. Basingstoke: Palgrave MacMillan.

Brown, S. 1995. *New Forces, Old Forces, and the Future of World Politics.* London: Harper Collins.

Brühl, T., and V. Rittberger. 2001. "From International to Global Governance: Actors, Collective Decision-Making, and the United Nations in the World of the Twenty-First Century," pp. 1–47 in *Global Governance and the United Nations System,* edited by V. Rittberger. NY: United Nations University Press.

Bulmer, S. 1998. "New Institutionalism and the Governance of the Single European Market." *Journal of European Public Policy* 5(3):365–86.

Burchell, G., C. Gordon, and P. Miller. 1991. *The Foucault Effect: Studies in Governmentality.* Chicago: University of Chicago Press.

Busch, L., and C. Bain. 2004. "New! Improved? The Transformation of the Global Agrifood System." *Rural Sociology* 60(3):321–46.

Candel, J. J. L. 2014. "Food Security Governance: A Systematic Literature Review." *Food Security* 6(4):585–601. Retrieved (http://link.springer.com/10.1007/s12571-014-0364-2).

Cardoso, F. H. 2003. *Civil Society and Global Governance: Contextual Paper Prepared by the Panel's Chairman.* Retrieved (www.unece.org/fileadmin/DAM/env/pp/ppif/Civil Society and Global Governance paper by Cardoso.htm).

Carlsson, I., S. Ramphal, A. Alatas, and H. Dahlgren. 1995. *Our Global Neighbourhood: The Report of the Commission on Global Governance.* Oxford: Oxford University Press.

Carroll, W. K. 1990. "Restructuring Capital, Reorganizing Consent: Gramsci, Political Economy and Canada." *Canadian Review of Sociology and Anthropology* 27: 390–416.

Carroll, W. K. 2006. "Hegemony, Counter-Hegemony, Anti-Hegemony." Keynote Address to the Annual Meeting of the Society for Socialist Studies, York University, Toronto.

Cerny, P. 2008. "Embedding Neoliberalism: The Evolution of a Hegemonic Paradigm." *The Journal of International Trade and Diplomacy,* 2(1), 1–46.

Cerny, P. 2010. *Rethinking World Politics: A Theory of Transnational Pluralism.* Oxford: Oxford University Press.

Chandler, D. 2006. *Empire in Denial: The Politics of State Building.* London: Pluto Press.

Cissokho, M. 2012. "Letter from African Civil Society Critical of Foreign Investment in African Agriculture at G8 Summit." Retrieved (www.foodfirst.org/en/Challenge+to+Green+Revolution+for+Africa).

Clarke, J. 2008. "Living With/in and without Neo-Liberalism." *Focal* 51:135–47.

Cooke, B., and U. Kothari. 2001. *Participation: The New Tyranny?* London: Zed Press.

Cox, R. 1993. "Gramsci, Hegemony and International Relations: An Essay in Method," pp. 49–66 in *Gramsci, Historical Materialism and International Relations*, edited by Stephen Gill. Cambridge: Cambridge University Press.

Dahl, R. A. 1999. "Can International Organizations Be Democratic? A Skeptic's View," pp. 19–36 in *Democracy's Edges*, edited by Ian Shapiro and Casiano Hacker-Cordon. Cambridge: Cambridge University Press.

Dahlberg, K. A. 2001. "Democratizing society and food systems: Or how do we transform modern structures of power?. *Agriculture and Human Values*," 18(2), 135–151.

Davis, G., D. McAdam, W. R. Scott, and M. N. Zald. 2005. *Social Movements and Organizations*. New York: Cambridge University Press.

Dingwerth, K., and P. Pattberg. 2006. "Global Governance as a Perspective on World Politics." *Global Governance* 12(2):185–203. Retrieved (www.glogov.org/images/doc/GG12_2_Dingwerth_Pattberg1.pdf).

Duncan, J., and D. Barling. 2012. "Renewal through Participation in Global Food Security Governance: Implementing the International Food Security and Nutrition Civil Society Mechanism to the Committee on World Food Security." *International Journal of Sociology of Agriculture and Food* 19:143–61.

Dunsire, A. 1993. *Manipulating Social Tensions: Collibration as an Alternative Mode of Government Intervention (MPIFG Discussion Paper 93/7)*. Köln. Retrieved (www.mpifg.de/pu/mpifg_dp/dp93-7.pdf).

FAO. 2009. *Global Governance of Food Security*. Rome: FAO.

FAO. 2010. "Towards Improved Governance of Global Food Security: Renewed Committee on World Food Security Starts Its Annual Session." *Media Centre*. Retrieved (www.fao.org/news/story/en/item/46353/icode/).

FAO. 2011. *Good Food Security Governance : The Crucial Premise to the Twin-Track Approach Background Paper*. Rome. Retrieved (www.fao.org/fileadmin/templates/righttofood/documents/other_documents/2011_good_food_security_gov/FoodSecurityGovernanceWorkshop_backgroundpaper.pdf).

Ferguson, J. 2009. "The Uses of Neoliberalism." *Antipode* 41(S1):166–84.

Finkelstein, L. S. 1995. "What Is Global Governance?" *Global Governance* 1:367–72.

Foucault, M. 2008. *The Birth of Biopolitics: Lectures at the Collège de France, 1978–1979*. London: Picador.

G8. 2009. *Final Declaration: Agriculture and Food Security at the Core of the International Agenda*. Cison di Valmarino, Italy.

G8. 2012. *Camp David Declaration*. Office of the Press Secretary - The White House, Camp David, Maryland. Retrieved (www.whitehouse.gov/the-press-office/2012/05/19/camp-david-declaration).

Gordenker, L., and T. G. Weiss. 1996. "Pluralizing Global Governance: Analytical Approaches and Dimensions," pp. 357–87 in *NGOs, the UN, and Global Governance*, edited by L. Gordenker and T. G. Weiss. Boulder: Westview.

Gramsci, A. 1971. *Selections from the Prison Notebooks*. New York: International Publishers.

Harvey, D. 2005. *A Brief History of Neoliberalism*. Oxford: Oxford University Press.

Hasenclever, A., P. Mayer, and V. Rittberger. 1997. *Theories of International Regimes*. Cambridge: Cambridge University Press.

Heinrich, C. J., and L. E. Lynn. 2000. *Governance and Performance: New Perspectives.* Washington, DC: Georgetown University Press.

Held, D. 2002. "Law of States, Law of Peoples: Three Models of Sovereignty." *Legal Theory* 8:1–44.

Held, D. 2004. "Democratic Accountability and Political Effectiveness from a Cosmopolitan Perspective." *Government and Opposition* 39(2):364–91. Retrieved (http://doi.wiley.com/10.1111/j.1477-7053.2004.00127.x).

High Level Task Force on the Global Food Security Crisis. 2010. *Updated Comprehensive Framework for Action.* New York: High Level Task Force on the Global Food Security Crisis.

Holt-Giménez, E., and M. A. Altieri. 2013. "Agroecology, Food Sovereignty and the New Green Revolution." *Journal of Sustainable Agriculture* 37(1):90–102. Retrieved (www.tandfonline.com/doi/abs/10.1080/10440046.2012.716388).

Jessop, B. 1998. "The Rise of Governance and the Risk of Failure: The Case of Economic Development." *International Social Science Journal* 50(155):29–45.

Jessop, B. 2002. "Liberalism, Neoliberalism and Urban Governance: A State-Theoretical Perspective." *Abtipode* 34(3):452–72.

Joseph, J. 2012. *The Social in the Global.* Cambridge: Cambridge University Press. Retrieved (http://ebooks.cambridge.org/ref/id/CBO9781139149143).

Keohane, R. O. 2002. *Global Governance and Democratic Accountability.* Durham. Retrieved (http://unpan1.un.org/intradoc/groups/public/documents/apcity/unpan034133.pdf).

Keohane, R. O., and J. S. Nye. 2000. "Globalization: What's New? What's Not? (And So What?)" edited by David Held and Anthony McGrew. *Foreign Policy* 118(118):104–19. Retrieved (www.jstor.org/stable/1149673?origin=crossref).

Kersbergen, K. Van, and F. Van Waarden. 2004. "'Governance' as a Bridge between Disciplines: Cross-Disciplinary Inspiration Regarding Shifts in Governance and Problems of Governability, Accountability and Legitimacy." *European Journal of Political Research* 43(2):143–71. Retrieved (http://search.ebscohost.com/login.aspx?direct=true&AuthType=ip,cookie,url,uid&db=aph&AN=12360014&site=ehost-live).

Lamy, P. 2012. "Global Governance: From Theory to Practice." *Journal of International Economic Law* 15(3):721–28.

Lang, T., and D. Barling. 2012. "Nutrition and Sustainability: An Emerging Food Policy Discourse." *The Proceedings of the Nutrition Society* (March):1–12. Retrieved (www.ncbi.nlm.nih.gov/pubmed/23217475).

Lang, T., D. Barling, and M. Caraher. 2009. *Food Policy: Integrating Health, Environment and Society.* Oxford: Oxford University Press.

Larner, W. 2000. "The Uses of Neoliberalism." *Studies in Political Economy* 63:5–25.

Lawrence, G., K. Lyons, and T. Wallington. 2010. "Introduction: Food Security, Nutrition and Sustainability in a Globalized World," pp. 1–26 in *Food Security, Nutrition and Sustainability*, edited by G. Lawrence, K. Lyons, and T. Wallington. Earthscan: London.

Lemke, T. 2001. "The Birth of Bio Politics: Michel Foucault's Lectures at the College de France on Neoliberal Governmentality." *Economy and Society* 30(2):190–207.

Lipset, S. M. 1960. *Political Man: The Social Bases of Politics.* London: Heinemann.

Margulis, M. E. 2012. "Global Food Security: The Committee on World Food Security, Comprehengive Framework for Action and the G8/G20," pp. 231–54 in *The Challenge of Food Security: International Policy and Regulatory Frameworks*, edited by R. Rayfuse and N. Weisfelt. Cheltenham: Edward Elgar.

Maxwell, S. 1996. "Food Security: A Post-Modern Perspective." *Food Policy* 21(2):155–70.

Maxwell, S., and R. Slater. 2003. "Food Policy Old and New." *Development Policy Review* 21(5/6). Retrieved (www.odi.org.uk/sites/odi.org.uk/files/odi-assets/publications-opinion-files/1862.pdf).

McKay, I. 2005. *Rebels, Reds, Radicals: Rethinking Canada's Left History.* Toronto: Between the Lines.

McKeon, N. 2009a. *The United Nations and Civil Society: Legitmating Global Governance – Whose Voice?* London: Zed Books.

McKeon, N. 2009b. "Who Speaks for Peasants ? Civil Society , Social Movements and the Global Governance of Food and Agriculture." *Interface: a journal for and about social movements* 1(2):48–82.

McMichael, M. 2000. "World-Systems Analysis, Globalization and Incorporated Comparison." *Journal of World-Systems Research* VI(3):668–99.

Mechlem, K. 2004. "Food Security and the Right to Food in the Discourse of the United Nations." *European Law Journal* 10(5):631–48.

Middendorf, G., and L. Busch. 1997. "Inquiry for the Public Good: Democratic Participation in Agricultural Research." *Agriculture and Human Values* 14:45–57.

Moravcsik, A. 1993. "Introduction: Integrating International and Domestic Theories of International Bargaining," pp. 3–42 in *Double-edged diplomacy: International bargaining and domestic politics*, edited by P.B. Evans, H.K. Jacobson, and R.D. Putnam. Berkley: University of California Press.

Moravcsik, A. 1998. *The Choice for Europe: Social Purpose and State Power from Messina to Maastricht.* London: University of California Press.

Mouffe, C. 2000. *Deliberative Democracy or Agonistic Pluralism.* Political Science Series no. 72. Rotterdam: IHS. Retrieved (www.ihs.ac.at/publications/pol/pw_72.pdf).

Muldoon, J. P. 2004. *The Architecture of Global Governance: An Introduction to the Study of International Organizations.* Boulder: Westview Press.

Overbeek, H., K. Dingwerth, P. Pattberg, and D. Compagnon. 2010. "Forum: Global Governance: Decline of Maturation of an Academic Concept?" *International Studies Review* 12(4):696–719.

Parfitt, T. 2004. "The Ambiguity of Participation." *Third World Quarterly* 25(3):537–56.

Pateman, C. 1970. *Participation and Democratic Theory.* Cambridge: Cambridge University Press.

Pateman, C. 2012. "Participatory Democracy Revisited." *Perspective on Politics* 10(1):7–19.

Pattberg, P. 2006. *Global Governance: Reconstructing a Contested Social Science Concept. GARNET Working Paper: No 04/06.* Warwick: Warwick University. Retrieved (http://www2.warwick.ac.uk/fac/soc/garnet/workingpapers/0406.pdf).

Pechlaner, G., and G. Otero. 2008. "The Third Food Regime: Neoliberal Globalism and Agricultural Biotechnology in North America." *Sociologia Ruralis* 48(4):351–71.

Peck, J. 2010. *Constructions of Neoliberal Reason.* Oxford: Oxford University Press.

Peine, E., and M. McMichael. 2005. "Globalization and Global Governance," pp. 19–33 in *Agriculture Governance: Globalization and the New Politics of Regulation*, edited by V. Higgins and G. Lawrence. New York: Routledge.

Peterson, J., and E. Bomberg. 1994. *Decision-Making in the European Union.* New York: St Martin's Press.

Polanyi, K. 2001. *The Great Transformation: The Political and Economic Origins of Our Time.* Boston: Beacon Press.

Rosenau, J. 1995. "Governance in the Twenty-First Century." *Global Governance* 1:13–43.

Rosenau, J. 1997. *Along the Domestic-Foreign Frontier: Exploring Governance in a Turbulent World.* Cambridge: Cambridge University Press.

Rosenau, J. 1999. "Towards an Ontology of Global Governance," pp. 295–96 in *Approaches to Global Governance Theory*, edited by H. Hewson and T. Sinclair. Albany: SUNY Press.

Rosenau, J. 2002. *Globalization and Governance: Sustainability: Between Fragmentation and Integration*. Washington, DC: The George Washington University.

Rosenau, J. 2003. *Distant Proximities: Dynamics Beyond Globalisation*. Princeton: Princeton University Press.

Rosenau, J., and E. Czempiel. 1992. *Governance without Government: Order and Change in World*. Cambridge: Cambridge University Press.

Roy, R. K., A. Denzau, and T. D. Willett. 2007. *Neoliberalism: National and Regional Experiments with Global Ideas*. London: Routledge.

Saurugger, S. 2010. "The Social Construction of the Participatory Turn: The Emergence of a Norm in the European Union." *European Journal of Political Research* 49(4):471–95. Retrieved (http://doi.wiley.com/10.1111/j.1475-6765.2009.01905.x).

Scholte, J. A. 2004. "Civil Society and Democratically Accountable Global Governance." *Government and Opposition* 39(2):211–33. Retrieved (http://doi.wiley.com/10.1111/j.1477-7053.2004.00121.x).

Sen, A. 1981. *Poverty and Famines: An Essay on Entitlement and Deprivation*. Oxford: Clarendon Press.

Sewell, J. P., and M. B. Slater. 1995. "Panarchy and Other Norms for Global Governance: Boutros-Ghali, Rosenau, and Beyond." *Global Governance* 1(3):373–82.

Shaw, D. J. 2007. *World Food Security: A History since 1945*. New York: Palgrave Macmillan.

Smouts, M.-C. 1998. "The Proper Use of Governance in International Relations." *International Social Science Journal* 50(155):81–89. Retrieved (http://doi.wiley.com/10.1111/1468-2451.00111).

Thomassen, J., and H. Schmitt. 1999. "In Conclusion: Political Representation and Legitimacy in the European Union," pp. 255–273 in *Political Representation and Legitimacy in the European Union* edited by Hermann Schmitt and Jacques Thomassen. Oxford: Oxford University Press.

UNDP. 1997. *Reconceptualising Governance: Discussion Paper 2*. New York: UNDP.

Via Campesina. 2012. "Rio+20: International Campaign of Struggles: People of the World against the Commodification of Nature (May 8)." La Via Campesina.

Wallace, H., and W. Wallace. 1996. *Policy Making in the European Union*. 3rd ed. Oxford: Oxford University Press.

Watkins, S. 2010. "Shifting Sands." *New Left Review* 61: 5–27.

Weiss, T. 2000. "Governance, Good Governance and Global Governance: Conceptual and Actual Challenges." *Third World Quarterly* 21(5):795–814.

Woods, N. 2007. "Multilateralism and Building Stronger International Institutions," pp. 27–44 in *Global Accountabilities: Participation, Pluralism, and Public Ethics* edited by Alnoor Ebrahim and Edward Weisband. Cambridge: Cambridge University Press.

Zürn, M. 2004. "Global Governance and Legitimacy Problems." *Government and Opposition* 39(2):260–87. Retrieved (http://doi.wiley.com/10.1111/j.1477-7053.2004.00123.x).

3 The evolution of global food security policy

Introduction

Food security is a complex, contentious, contested and politically loaded term, and its usefulness as a policy approach has been called into question (Devereux and Maxwell 2001; Maxwell and Slater 2003; Shaw 2007). In spite of this, or perhaps despite it, food security, in all its forms and limitations, remains the primary frame through which hunger and nutrition are defined and addressed at the level of international policy making.

In response to the 2007–2008 food price spikes, the transnational food security policy space began to be redefined with new issues and by new actors. What emerged was a core group of multilateral organizations working with one another while simultaneously competing with one another (a key characteristic of global governance) to claim leadership over global food security governance. These actors include the World Bank, the G8, Group of 20 (G20), UN and the Rome-based agencies (including the Consultative Group on International Agricultural Research and related institutes), the Bill and Melinda Gates Foundation, and the World Economic Forum (Wise and Murphy 2012; Ahmad 2011; McKeon 2011).[1] These actors have presented policy recommendations and frameworks and implemented programs to advance of food security in different ways. Yet they have also agreed that the reformed CFS is the forum in the UN for the discussion and coordination of global food security policy.

In the previous chapter, a framework was presented with the aim of proving tools to make sense changes to the architecture of global food security governance. In this chapter, the framework is applied to the evolution of global food security policy. What follows is an overview of food security since 1974. The review focuses on food security as discourse and traces its evolution through to the food price spikes. At this point, the chronology of multilateral actions around food security is presented, illustrating not only the volume of activity (in turn pointing to the significance of the crisis), but also identifying international priorities for addressing the problem. The role of the CFS within this changing architecture is highlighted throughout the chapter.

Evolution of global food security policy

Since its introduction at the World Food Conference of 1974, the concept of food security has evolved, multiplied, diversified and left us with a term that now represents "a cornucopia of ideas" (Maxwell 1996:155).[2] This cornucopia has developed through a series of phases. By no means uncontested, phases allow us to broadly define the dominant themes that inform and rationalize status quo food security research, policy and practice at a certain moment in time. It is important to understand these phases and how they came about. It is also important to recognize that food security has been taken up by development practitioners, notably aid agencies and NGOs, in multiple ways. In this research, analysis is limited to global-level (multilateral) food security policy (as outcome) and does not explicitly tackle the various ways these policies translate into actionable programs. Neither does it detail the methodologies used to calculate or assess food security.

Simon Maxwell's (1996) tri-phased approach is a commonly cited version of the evolution of food security. The three categories presented are useful for beginning to sketch out the evolving nature of food security in global policy making and to start to piece together this contemporary cornucopia. For Maxwell, food security policy, since the 1970s, can been defined by three paradigms that represent shifts in policy outlooks: a shift from global and national level policies to the household and individual level (1975–1985); a move from a food first perspective to a livelihood perspective (1985 onwards); and a shift from objective indicators to subjective indicators (1980s onwards). Maxwell argues that collectively these shifts have brought food security theory and policy "progressively closer to 'real' food insecurity" (Maxwell 1996:156, see also Hewitt de Alcantra 1993). The evolution from a global and national policy approach to food security towards one that focuses on a livelihood perspective at the household level, in line with a greater embedding of neoliberal policies and practices. Mooney and Hunt (2009:472) note that these shifts are not as humble as Maxwell (1996) suggests and each shift "might be seen as distinct dimensions of a single shift towards an individualization that privileges a subsequent affinity with, or focus on, livelihood and subjectivity." There is less evidence at the level of global food security policy to support the third shift Maxwell identifies as a move towards subjective indicators. Instead, it is here argued, that by the mid-1980s food security had become aligned with wider neoliberal objectives and consequently food security policy merely adapted and altered to address contestation and change, in line with definitions of hegemony. This led not to new phases or paradigms but instead to variations or extensions of the same project. However, a key moment in the evolution of food security policy at the global level can be identified by the 1996 World Food Summit where the most influential and used definition of food security was negotiated.

Seven years after the publication of the three paradigms, Maxwell argued that "a preoccupation with food security is no longer sufficient" (Maxwell and Slater 2003:533) as too many "other issues" have infiltrated food security policy. Instead of focusing on food security policy, they argue we need to return to food policy, calling specifically for a focus on food policy "new."

Maxwell and Slater (2003) define "old" food policy as being focused primarily on rural populations, with concern for agriculture-based employment and food productions. The major actors in food marketing were traders (especially grain traders) and supply chains were relatively short. With respect to consumption, policy was designed to address at home consumption of food, purchased in local shops or open markets. The main nutritional concerns were under nutrition, with a focus on calories and micronutrients. The food insecure were understood to be peasants. Food shocks at the national and household level were predominantly linked to poor rainfall and other production shocks and the remedy for household food shortages was food-based relief and safety nets. "Old" food policy was focused in the ministries of agriculture and health as well as relief/rehabilitation ministries and focused on agricultural technologies, parastatal reform, supplementary feeding and food for work.

By comparison, "new" food policy is concerned mostly with urban populations. With respect to employment, the focus is no longer on agricultural jobs but rather on food manufacturing and retail with food companies emerging as main actors in food marketing. The supply chains are longer with a large number of food miles. Food policies for consumers are geared towards a population that eats a high proportion of prepared meals, including food eaten outside of the home. Nutritional policy is focused on chronic dietary diseases including obesity, heart disease and diabetes linked to higher consumption of fat sugar and salt. The food insecure are understood to be the urban and rural poor. The sources of food shocks shift from production issues to international prices and trade issues at the national level and income at the household level. "New" food policy is the domain of the ministries of trade and industry, consumer affairs, finance as well as food activist groups and NGOs. It is focused predominantly then, according to Maxwell and Slater (2003), on competition and rent-seeking, the value chain, industrial structure in retail, futures markets, waste management, advertising, health, education, and food safety. With "old" food policy the key international institutions were the FAO, World Food Programme (WFP), United Nations Children's Fund (UNICEF), World Health Organization (WHO) and the Consultative Group on International Agricultural Research (CGIAR). With "new" food policy, FAO and WHO remain key institutions but the rest are overlaid with the United Nations Industrial Development Organization (UNIDO), International Labour Organization (ILO) and the WTO.

Lang et al.'s (2009) critique of "new" food policy argues that it fails to properly historicize food security and assumes its development arises almost from thin air in the 1970s. This critique can be extended to Maxwell's three paradigms. As will be discussed below, the evolution of food security is indeed rooted in the experiences of the first half of the twentieth century and key changes in science, technology and geopolitics. The tension is that "new" food security calls for a rejection of food security policy in favor of food policy. But we can see food security policy emerging as a subsector—or a thread—of a more complex food policy. What is of interest is the way that food security policy is being developed, framed and then how it relates to food policy more broadly.

At this point, the call to abandon food security policy for food policy will be ignored. Despite the complex and expansive definitions and acknowledging the repetitive failure of policies and processes, the current high-level renewed interest in food security suggests that the term and associated policies will remain relevant for the foreseeable future and for this reason need to be further examined and analyzed.

The FAO (2006) also identify phases of food security that have evolved to reflect changes in official policy thinking, but it provides few hints as to what these changes were or how they came about. The FAO does usefully outline key eras in the development of the concept, starting in 1974 when food security was defined in terms of supply. By the 1980s focus had moved to access at the individual and household level. With the 1996 World Food Summit, the multidimensional nature of food security was acknowledged. For the FAO (2006:1), "as the link between food security, starvation and crop failure becomes a thing of the past, the analysis of food insecurity as a social and political construct has emerged."

This shift to the social and political nature of food security can be examined through an attempt to uncover the nuances and competing understandings that make up and challenge hegemonic definitions. Mooney and Hunt (2009) introduce the notions of frames and keying to articulate variations and their implications for agriculture, hunger and the organization of food security policy at the global level. They set out to analyze the process of frame elaboration by examining food security as a potent form of master frame. These master frames produce several distinct claims to ownership over food security. Mooney and Hunt (2009) are inspired by Snow and Byrd (2007:130), who articulate the process of "frame elaboration" as a means of accenting certain beliefs or issues in service of a newly articulated "alignment of events, experiences, and strands of moral codes."

Relying on Goffman's loosely musical theory, Mooney and Hunt (2009:471) build on collective action framing by considering the frames in relation to what Goffman (1974) called "keying," that is, "a process that may yield multiple interpretations within each of these collective action frames." One reason for focusing on collective action frames is that variations between and within the food security collective action frames are linked to the ways in which distinct interests align themselves in the multi-organizational field (Mooney and Hunt 2009:471).

Mooney and Hunt (2009:471) illustrate that food security frames can each carry a flat keying that "reinforces extant dominant interpretations and practices,

usually advanced by power holders" and a sharp keying "that offers interpretations and practices" which tend to offer "critical alternative interpretations and
practices usually voiced by challengers." To use language presented in Chapter
2, we can see flat keying as hegemonic and sharp keying as counter-hegemonic.
In their analysis, Mooney and Hunt (2009:470) explain that the successful elaboration of the term "food security" is "due, in part, to a resonance
that does not immediately engender oppositional claims, making it difficult
to mobilize opinion in favor of alternatives." They argue that it would be
challenging and "strategically dysfunctional" to mobilize a movement in favor
of "food insecurity" or "unsustainable development," even for those seeking
objectively insecure of unsustainable outcomes. Even in the most oppositional
discourses around food security, such as those forwarded by food sovereignty
activists, food security is rarely rejected outright and is often framed as part of
the end goal. Indeed, discourse is now very much intertwined and dependent
on food security if for nothing more than a starting point for discussion. At the
same time, producing definitions or frameworks with the capacity to mobilize
are needed to unify resistance, support the building of coalitions and guiding
the work needed to change the dominant food system (Mooney and Hunt
2009:471; Stevenson et al. 2007:51).

Mooney and Hunt (2009:470), building on the work of Gamson (1995),
argue that "nonreflexive consent to the values and objectives signified by
terms such as 'security' and 'sustainability' can be usefully conceptualized as a
'consensus frame'." They offer broad support for the idea that the goals of a
social movement can engender opposition with respect to how those goals are
translated into "action imperatives." Mooney and Hunt (2009:470) argue that
within consensus around the term "food security" there is contested ownership
and that "'food security' functions as an elaborate master frame encompassing
at least three collective action frames." It is by uncovering the diversity of collective action frames that we can "recognise the dynamic processes underlying
discursive work in the field of organization and social movements" (Mooney
and Hunt 2009:470; see also Snow and Byrd 2007). Collective action frames
"remain in a field of contested ownership of the concept, reflecting variations
in power and shifts in political opportunity structures" (Mooney and Hunt
2009:472).

Mooney and Hunt's approach is useful in terms of unveiling key motivations of actors engaged in global food security governance. At the same time,
there are limits to creating strict labels and categories for the various discourses
at play. The frame approach fails to make space for the process of negotiation
and contestation and consent at play in the global governance of food security.
Policy makers, the private sector and social movements are not static in their
position and a frame analysis can mask the complex strategies adopted by actors
in global level negotiations which often mean sacrificing key issues to gain in
other areas.

Michael Carolan (2013) presents a phased history food security derived
from an examination of the stated and implied aims of agri-food policies

since the 1940s.[3] He argues food security was originally imagined in the context of freedom from want, mirroring the proclamations of US President Roosevelt's influential four freedoms speech. Following from this so-called "original intent," Carolan identifies three overlapping and cumulative foci across food security policy. First is the calorie-ization of food security (1940s to present) where focus is on increasing agricultural output, characterized best by the Green Revolution. Second is the neoliberalization of food security (1970s to present), marked by a push for trade liberalization and market integration. The final focus is the empty calorie-ization of food security (1980s to present), where factors including foreign direct investment and the liberalization of marketing led to a proliferation of processed foods across national food systems. Carolan's (2013:6) contention is that measured against the food security yardstick of security of food (in contract to security through food), agri-food policy has been a success: "the world has never seen such abundance of cheap calories." However, the cost of these "gains" have been great and have been felt by the environment, individuals, communities, health and the sovereignty (food or otherwise) of nations.

Importantly, Carolan (2013:7) points out that "the fact that countries with clearly oversized ecological food-prints (the ecological footprint of an entire food system) are simultaneously lauded for their levels of food security is as unfortunate as it is telling." To get food security back to its original intention—freedom from want—Carolan proposes broader uptake of the Food and Human Security Index which takes into consideration indicators for individual and societal well-being, ecological sustainability, potential for food independence, nutritional well-being and freedom in the agri-food chain. For Carolan (2013:8), food security is not an end in itself, but rather "a process that ought to make people and the planet better off."

This research acknowledges the foci identified by Carolan across agri-food policy but does not mix agri-food policy with food security policy. In this research, and in slight contrast to Carolan, the concept did not emerge from a position of securing freedom from want, but rather securing grain markets. Second, and notably since the 1980s when food security policy shifted focus from global and national-level policies towards household and individual indicators and poverty reduction, it has been framed as a development discourse and has not been part of a wider agri-food strategy. In contrast to a narrowing of food security policy to the development discourse, agri-food policy was internationalizing. While both food security and agri-food policy have focused on productionist policies, they have been imagined and framed by different policy objectives that should not be conflated. That said, they are certainly worthy of comparison and inarguably developed in relation to one another and within a broader neoliberal policy environment.

Food security in its various manifestations is contentious and problematic. The paradigm shifts outlined above represent shifts in hegemonic definitions of food security informed by a productionist paradigm within an increasingly neoliberal/corporate food regime. The complexity that arises at the confluence of food, agriculture, aid, trade, labor, environment, health, nutrition, rights and justice, where food security and insecurity emerge, necessitates a sufficiently comprehensive policy process capable of a systems approach that tackles the root causes of food insecurity.

Food security: A summary of policy developments since 1945

As noted above, the term "food security" came into widespread policy use with the World Food Conference in 1974, but the beginning of modern interest in food security is often located in World War II, "which demonstrated that localized hunger and instability could escalate into problems of global significance" (McDonald 2010:12). Friedmann and McMichael (1989) and Lang and Heasman (2004) both conclude that the triumph of the mercantile–industrial food regime and the productionist paradigm, respectively, are rooted in the experience of food shortages, meal distribution and starvation that effected many countries in the early twentieth century. It is thus useful to start the analysis at the point where the international community came together to begin to address these problems.

In 1943, President Franklin D. Roosevelt hosted the United Nations Conference on Food and Agriculture in Hot Springs, Virginia. The use of "United Nations" in the conference title was reference to the 44 nations[4] that attended the conference (FAO 1981). The aims of the conference were summed up in the opening sentence of the declaration adopted by the conference:

> This Conference, meeting in the midst of the greatest war ever waged, and in full confidence of victory, has considered world problems of food and agriculture and declares its belief that the goal of freedom from want of food, suitable and adequate for the health and strength of all peoples, can be achieved.
>
> (FAO 1981)

There was clear agreement on several issues at this conference, and the foundation for the future of food security was laid down. The conference agreed that there was not, nor had there ever been, enough food to eat. They noted "at least two-thirds of its people are ill-nourished; many face periodic starvation; and this in spite of the fact that two thirds of the world's people are farmers" (UN 1947:685). Advances in science, and the promotion of scientific outcomes coupled with scientific rationalization, central to the development of the FAO. Developments in the science of nutrition led the conference to agree that access to the right kinds of food would raise levels of health and well-being. Faith in the modern science of production was also referenced as being able to "produce enough of the right kinds of foods" (UN 1947:685). There was agreement that issues of distribution must be addressed to raise the levels of consumption of those who do not have enough. The UN *Yearbook* noted that feeding the world required the prerequisite of "an expanding world economy, in which each nation will play its own part, but all will act together" and that "[o]nly by acting together can nations, in the close-knit modern world, achieve peace, prosperity and rising standards of living" (UN 1947:685). This cooperative tone is representative of the ideals of the postwar world, where nations worked together to solve problems and ensure a stable future.

On recommendation of the conference, in July 1943 the UN Interim Commission for Food and Agriculture was set up with representatives appointed by each of the governments that attended the conference. The role of the Commission was to plan for a permanent organization to deal with food, agriculture, forestry and fisheries. The Commission, financed by contributions of member governments, had the support of a small international secretariat as well as international technical committees. The Commission drafted a constitution for the UN FAO, which more than 20 governments accepted. This fulfilled the terms of the constitution and made the establishment of the FAO possible. The FAO came into being on October 16, 1945 with the signing of the constitution. This ceremony took place at the opening meeting of the first session of the conference, held in Quebec, Canada, from October 16 to November 1, 1945 (UN 1947:685).

The vision and approach of the FAO were clearly laid out in the preamble to the constitution:

> The Nations accepting this Constitution, being determined to promote the common welfare by furthering separate and collective action on their part for the purposes of raising levels of nutrition and standards of living of the peoples under their respective jurisdictions, securing improvements in the efficiency of the production and distribution of all food and agricultural products, bettering the condition of rural populations, and thus contributing toward an expanding world economy, hereby establish the Food and Agriculture Organization of the United Nations.
>
> (FAO 1945)

The focus on nutrition, improving production, securing rural livelihoods and supporting a world economy are strong threads that run through the organization and frame its work to this day.

Three years after the launch of the FAO, the right to food was formally recognized by the UN in the Universal Declaration of Human Rights (UDHR) (1948), as a part of the right to a decent standard of living. Article 25 of the UDHR Article states:

> Everyone has the right to a standard of living adequate for the health and well-being of himself and of his family, including food, clothing, housing and medical care and necessary social services, and the right to security in

the event of unemployment, sickness, disability, widowhood, old age or other lack of livelihood in circumstances beyond his control.

While the UN was adopting the UDHR, a process of decolonization was under way.[5] When the UN was founded in 1945, it was estimated that 750 million people, nearly a third of the world's population, lived in territories held by colonial powers (UN 2013). The post-colonial integration of developing countries into the global trading system, and in post-World War II development assistance programs, has been linked to the genesis of neoliberalism (Gonzalez 2007). Gonzalez (2007:7) identifies the origin of the inequities in the global trading system within the colonial division of labor that "relegated the colonized 'periphery' to the production of primary agricultural products for the benefit of the colonizing 'core'." After World War II, as many European countries lost control over their colonies, they focused on outsourcing their production to support the emerging upper classes with food products from former colonies. The implementation of new liberalized models of trade with emerging economies and market advantage through heavily subsidized agricultural production, allowed for economic domination by the West.

The 1960s reflected an era of hope. The Green Revolution was leading to exciting innovations in crop breeding, especially around new varieties of rice, and there was a great deal of confidence that advances in tropical agriculture would lead to increased self-sufficiency and productivity among the world's poorest farmers. In the 1950s and 1960s, developing countries expanded their agricultural outputs at a similar rate to developed countries (Shaw 2007:117–118). What differed were differences in rates of growth in demand (3.5 percent per annum in developing countries compared with 2.5 percent in the so-called developed world; Shaw 2007:118). However, to suggest that growth was evenly distributed across regions would be misleading. For example, while agricultural performance rose in India under the influence of the Green Revolution, agricultural productivity stagnated in sub-Saharan Africa. At this time, "the need for food imports rose markedly in developing countries at a time when their ability to purchase them on commercial terms did not increase commensurately" (Shaw 2007:118). While food production was increasing, the total number of hungry people increased (FAO 1974:55; Shaw 2007:118). Availability of food does not correspond to accessibility, a statement that holds true at the international level down to the household level. Part of the problem was that two-thirds of the developing world's population lived in countries where food outputs had risen more slowly than the demand for food. Large grain reserves (notably those held by the US, Canada and Australia) served to buffer prices and stabilize markets (Headley and Fan 2010).

By 1970, despite 400 million people estimated to be suffering from malnutrition, there remained a feeling of communal optimism that the problem of world hunger could be addressed. This all changed in the early 1970s.

As Shaw (2007:118) writes, the emergency of 1972–1974 "was the first intimation of what might become a recurring manifestation of an underlying basic imbalance." The 1970s food crisis was marked by the threat of mass starvation and half a million people were estimated to have died as a result of food shortages, high prices and inadequate emergency distribution. Many more suffered malnutrition resulting in important longer-term impacts. Not unlike the 2007–2008 food price spikes, the 1970s food crisis occurred in conjunction with a weakened US dollar, high energy prices, short-term climatic shocks, concerns over market information and growing export demand from transitioning economies (at that time, Spain, Korea and Taiwan; DEFRA 2010:12). It was also impacted by changing consumption patterns.

In a speech at the National Agricultural Outlook Conference held in Washington DC, in December 1973, Assistant Director-General to the FAO E. M. Ojala explained:

> The events of 1972/3 were very disturbing. The international community has become accustomed to personal surpluses of wheat and other grains in North America, which the two governments of this region had generously made available through two decades to poorer nations with food deficits. Not enough attention was paid to the more recent statements of these governments to the effect that North America could no longer be expected in the future to maintain what had amounted in practice to the entire world's food reserves. Meanwhile, the world's wheat consumption has risen dramatically. Thus, North American stocks which represented 10 weeks of world consumption in the early 1960s constituted only 5 weeks supply in the early 1970s. This diminution in the world's food security was only mildly noted, is at all, until it was starkly revealed by the events of 1972/1973. But wheat prices trebled. And experts estimated that it would take two years of more of good crops to replenish stocks. Meanwhile, the world's population was exposed more dangerously than in the past to the recurrence of shortage situations.
>
> (Ojala 1973:4)

While there are important natural events that contributed to low yields, as Dereck Headley and Shenggen Fan (2010:82) argue, the 1972–1974 crisis can be linked to "US production and trade conditions, especially with respect to wheat and other coarse grains." In the 1930s North America exported 5 million tons of grain, and by 1966 North American grain exports had increased twelvefold to reach nearly 60 million tons, while the Communist countries went from a 5 million ton surplus to a 4 million ton deficit. At the same time Asia moved from a 2 million ton surplus to a deficit of 34 million tons (Headley and Fan 2010:82). The US clearly dominated international grain trade and production and held the power to impact international prices and by extension, global food security. To this end, it has been argued that one of the main contributing factors to the 1970s food crisis was US policies regarding wheat production (Destler 1978; Headley and Fan 2010; Johnson 1975).

In the 1960s, due to policies that supported prices above market-clearing levels, the US Commodity Credit Corporation had accumulated a large amount of grain stocks and distributed the grain through cheap exports and food aid. However, there are important costs associated with storing grain, especially when income from selling grain does not cover those costs. Thus, in the early 1970s, the US government (along with Canada and Australia) set about to reduce the large stocks of wheat they had amassed and reduced production of wheat by one third between mid-1970 and mid-1972, effectively cutting their global share of world grain production to 10 percent from 15 percent (Headley and Fan 2010; Johnson 1975). As a result of those policies, by the 1970s grain reserves had been largely depleted and international grain markets became vulnerable to extreme fluctuations in price (Headley and Fan 2010; Hopkins and Puchala 1978), leading to an increasingly fragile trade regime for grains.

The US liberalization of grain exports to China, the Union of Soviet Socialist Republics (USSR) and Eastern Europe, and the large amount of grain purchased by the USSR in 1971, saw a further depletion of North American stocks, leading wheat export prices to jump from US$1.68 per bushel in July 1972 to US$2.40 per bushel just one month later.

World food security as a problem of global supply

This was the situation which led the General Assembly of the UN to convene the World Food Conference (1974) with an aim to develop "ways and means whereby the international community, as a whole, could take specific action to resolve the world food problem within the broader context of development and international economic co-operation" (UN 1975). The conference was important not only insofar as it led to the creation of the World Food Council and the Committee on World Food Security but also because it launched the International Undertaking on World Food Security.

At the 1974 World Food Conference, governments examined the global problem of food production and consumption, and proclaimed that "every man, woman and child has the inalienable right to be free from hunger and malnutrition in order to develop their physical and mental faculties" through the Universal Declaration on the Eradication of Hunger and Malnutrition (1974). The Declaration also clarified the responsibility of governments to work together to ensure increased production and equitable distribution, stating that food problems need to be tackled through national plans and that states must remove obstacles and provide incentives for food production. In some ways, the Declaration is more progressive than more recent declarations on hunger and food security, due to its assertion of the importance of waterways and waste prevention as well providing technical and financial assistance free from conditions to least-developed countries, conservation of natural resources and national policies to prioritize food production. Within the Universal Declaration on the Eradication of Hunger and Malnutrition there is no explicit mention of the private sector but there is a call for governments and NGOs to work together to end hunger, highlighting the important role NGOs were starting to play in food security policy.

The Declaration does not provide a definition for food security. However, Annex 1 of the final report, which outlines the International Undertaking on World Food Security, reaffirms:

> the urgent need for effective international action aimed at ensuring the availability at all times of adequate world supplies of basic foodstuffs, so as to avoid acute food shortages in the event of widespread crop failure, natural or other disasters, to sustain a steady expansion of consumption in countries with low levels of per caput intake, and offset fluctuations in production and prices.
>
> (FAO 1974: Resolution 1/64)

Food security is here defined in terms of supply and price stability of basic food-stuffs at the national and international level (FAO 2006). More specifically, we can identify three key components of an emerging definition of food security: food security as a supply problem, a global problem and a natural problem.

Hunger, which had been framed as a supply issue prior to the World Food Conference, continued to frame the discourse of food security afterwards. Throughout the 1950s and 1960s, Keynesian logic still dominated and debate focused on the transfer of goods and a strong state. By the 1970s, when the World Food Conference takes place, Keynesian theory was being replaced by neoclassical economic theories of growth which advanced a move towards microeconomics, foreshadowing a shift that would take place in food security discourse in the following decade. But in this period of transition, the emphasis for food security was clearly on "strengthening the food production base of developing countries" (FAO 1974: annex to resolution 1/64, I.2) directly in line with the productionist paradigm.

A second aspect of the emerging definition of food security was recognition of hunger as a global problem. The text makes reference to the international community and to adequate world food supplies (not national food supplies). This international community is encouraged to rally to increase production and stabilize prices. However, the solutions need to be applied at the national level and are targeted towards developing countries. Here then, food security becomes defined in terms of global and national priorities linked to availability based on objective indicators.

Finally, in that definition, the world food problem is constructed as a natural problem, echoing the Malthusian rhetoric that was dominant at the time. The framing of the food crisis as a natural problem conveniently ignores a series of policies that preceded the food crisis, including the US's policy of stock reduction, unforeseen large-scale grain imports into the USSR or the high cost of oil following supply cuts by OPEC (Organization of the Petroleum Exporting Countries) in 1973. By constructing food security as a natural problem, the emerging definition of food security skirts politics. Instead of a shift in policies affecting food production and distribution, international cooperation was needed to conquer natural problems: it was states against nature. Winning this battle required increasing production in the developing world and finding places to store the outputs in the form of international grain reserves. Achieving this meant handing over policy making to technocrats and scientists with the knowledge and skills to control nature and increase agricultural production. Thus from the get go, food security was defined apolitically and through technocratic language. Indeed, despite evidence highlighting the role of trade and stock policies on the food crisis, the political discourse faithfully maintained its allegiance to natural causes. The FAO council expressed concern at their 1974 session, "that the world food and agricultural situation, especially in respect of cereal supplies, had worsened ... mainly due to the fact that the weather had again been unfavourable in certain important producing areas" (FAO 1974: para 12). Yet as explored above, and albeit with the advantage of hindsight, the crisis was very much linked to grain and trade policies and while discussions of food security at the time did reflect this, solutions were not found.

With recovery from the 1970s world food crisis, and as a result of difficulties negotiating a new international grain agreement, focus drifted towards more national-level measures (Mechlem 2004:634). In 1979, the FAO Council adopted a Plan of Action on World Food Security urging governments to "take full advantage of the relatively ample world supply situation for cereals in order to build up stocks" and to "adopt and implement national cereal stock policies, and targets of objectives." Global food security was increasingly understood to be contingent on national-level programs and remained focused on increasing the amount of food available. Food security was still framed as a production problem defined by a lack of available food and remained disassociated from the political and economic decisions that impacted hunger and food availability. The policy responses were geared towards addressing fluctuations in the food supply and interventions were developed to buffer against fluctuation, which, in line with technological advancements and shifts in modes of labor, lent itself well to the advancement of the productionist paradigm (Lang and Heasman 2004). However, this logic was proving inadequate for dealing with new food security challenges, including periods of mass starvation and famine (e.g., Ethiopia and Bangladesh) that marked the early 1980s. This period marks the shift from Maxwell's (1996) first paradigm of food security as global- and national-level policies towards a policy focus on households and the individual.

Embedding neoliberalism in food security policy

Throughout the 1980s food security practitioners, analysts and policy makers had to grapple with the increasingly:

> complex relationships between chronic, seasonal and temporary food insecurity, peoples' coping strategies, their priorities when making choices as to how to spend overall insufficient resources, food security as part of a wider livelihoods concepts, and the relationship between household and individual food security.
>
> (Mechlem 2004:635)

At the same time, the International Monetary Fund (IMF) and World Bank were promoting structural adjustment policies by way of structural adjustment programs (SAPs). Much has been written on SAPs and the implications for food security (see for example, Fan and Rao 2003; Loewenson 1993; Uvin 1994), and they are mentioned here only to highlight the shift towards neoliberal policies at the multilateral level. SAPs had the stated goal of reducing a borrowing country's fiscal imbalance by reorienting the borrowing country's economy toward trade and export production as a way of strengthening their economy. The rationale was that open markets and strong specialized export economies would ensure food security through international cooperation and trade. Countries could ensure access to food by strengthening their economies, specializing in exporting crops and importing national foodstuffs. It was at this time that "donors developed an enthusiasm for national food security planning, partly as a 'proxy for poverty planning during the darkest years of structural adjustment'" (Maxwell and Slater 2003:532). As we will see, this focus on national food security planning will re-emerge as a policy priority after the 2007–2008 food price spikes, but with emphasis on public–private partnerships.

While SAPs are credited with improving economic growth in Asia and Latin America (Fan and Rao 2003), they proved detrimental across Africa. The evidence indicates that SAPs have been associated with increasing food insecurity and under-nutrition, rising ill-health and decreasing access to healthcare in the two-thirds or more of the population of African countries that already lived below poverty levels (Loewenson 1993:717).

In 1981, Amartya Sen, an Indian economist who later won the Nobel Prize in Economic Sciences in 1998 for his contribution to welfare economics and social choice theory, published *Poverty and Famines*, which dismantled the idea that food insecurity was due to a lack of availability of foodstuffs. Sen suggested that an individual's food security depended on their ability to access food or, in Sen's words their ability to "establish entitlement to enough food." Entitlements, for Sen (1984:497), are defined as "the set of alternative commodity bundles that a person can command in a society using the totality of rights and opportunities that he or she faces." An entitlement approach to poverty and famine works to describe all legal sources of food which Sen (1981:2) outlines through four categories: "production-based entitlement"(growing food); "trade-based entitlement" (buying food); "own-labour entitlement" (working for food); and "inheritance and transfer entitlement" (being given food by others). Starvation thus occurs when people's full entitlement set does not provide them with adequate food for subsistence. With the publication of Sen's work on entitlements, food security policy shifted focus from states securing adequate supplies of food for their populations to a focus on the household and individual having access to food.

The value of Sen's thinking, which was not new but which Sen successfully brought to the center of development thinking, was the shift away from Malthusian claims that hunger was the result of too many people and too little food and towards a focus on the inability of people to acquire food. From this perspective, food security is linked to access and food insecurity and famine can occur irrespective of food availability (Devereux 2001:246). Indeed, Sen (1981:8) showed that some of the worst famines in the world had taken place due to entitlement shifts with no significant decline in food availability per capita.

The limitations of this approach, as identified by Sen (1981:48–50), are the ambiguities in the specification of entitlements; the focus on legal rights disregards the fact that the transfer of entitlement relations can involve the violation of these rights (e.g., looting); the actual food consumption of people may fall below their entitlement; and starvation is not the same as famine. Stephen Devereux (2001:246) also points out that Sen's analytic approach is limited insofar as it appropriates a normative term like "entitlement" and strips it of all ethical and political connotations.

Despite these limitations, and with good reason, Sen's concept of entitlements gained currency as public and political focus shifted to addressing the growing famine in Africa and while UNICEF sought to put a human face to hunger (Shaw 2007). In 1983, the FAO revised the concept of food security to include a third dimension to the established dimensions of ensuring adequate food production and maximizing the availability of food supplies: "security of access to supplies on the part of all those who need them" (FAO 1983:15). This third dimension sought to balance the supply and demand side of food security (FAO 2006:1; Shaw 2007:349). This definition was later revised to include the individual and household level as well as regional and national level of aggregation in food security analysis (FAO 2006).

In 1985, the World Food Security Compact (FAO 1985; see also Mechlem 2004:635), adopted by the FAO Conference to collect principles and suggestions for action at the governmental, organizational and individual level, made reference to food security at the national, household and individual level, a clear shift from the 1974 definition of food security as the "availability at all times of adequate world food supplies." This Compact also pushed forward the link between food security and poverty, recognizing that the "achievement of the 'fundamental right over everyone to be free from hunger' depends ultimately on the abolition of poverty" (FAO 1985: para 2).

At the same time, the food security agenda expanded to include chronic hunger (Clay 1997:7; Mechlem 2004:635). The World Bank (1986:v) led the trend, placing people's needs as the starting point in their definition of food security as "access by all people at all times to enough food for an active, healthy life" (see also Mechlem 2004:635). With this definition, the focus is shifted from availability to access and also foreshadows the health discourse that will come to influence food security policy. The World Bank (1986) report *Poverty and Hunger* disregarded the availability question and reframed the debate around access in economic terms. "The world has ample food," opens the report:

> The growth of global food production has been faster than the unprecedented population growth of the past forty years ... Many countries and hundreds of millions of poor people do not share in this abundance. They suffer from a lack of food security, caused mainly by a lack of purchasing power.
>
> (World Bank 1986:1)

The report takes the complexity of Sen's argument and reduces it to a simplified discussion of purchasing power. The World Bank's report (1986:v) argued that economic growth would provide people with the income needed to acquire adequate amounts of food, illustrating absolute faith in the trickle-down theory of economics. Yet, despite rejecting the old tenant that supply is the main challenge for achieving food security, the report suggests that supply, production and trade are central to ending world hunger. *Poverty and Hunger* served to frame food security through an economic development discourse linked to income growth as a means for ending poverty.

Having established the link between famine and poverty and the need for focus to be at the household and individual level, the World Bank was then able to take the next step and link food insecurity to lack of purchasing power, again diverting the political, social, cultural and environmental factors that also contribute to food insecurity. However, this is arguably a misrepresentation of Sen's work. Sen (1981:166–7) argued while that income is relevant, especially in areas affected by famine, such an approach is inadequate. He also noted that:

> [T]he inadequacy of the income-centred view arises from the fact that, even in those circumstances in which income does provide command, it offers only a partial picture of the entitlement pattern, and staring the story with the shortage of income is to leave the tale half-told.
>
> (Sen 1981:156)

Poverty and Hunger was published at the end of a major humanitarian food crisis and at a time where SAPs were showing signs of promoting economic growth and development. The launch of the report, which built on the momentum of the Sen's work, established the World Bank as a key actor in food security and in doing so presented a challenge the FAO's unilateral authority on the issue. These developments changed status quo understandings of food security. No longer the collective responsibility of the international community, food security is now an output of economic growth and individual responsibility. This mirrors wider processes of neoliberalization under way across other sectors. From a food security perspective, this move facilitates blaming the poor as much as it facilitates a stepping away not only from international commitments, but also from international factors that aggravate food insecurity. Here again, food security is made apolitical. It is defined by technocrats who are constructed as technicians and rational decision makers, free of ideology and thus most suited to make decisions and guide policy. A further consequence is that agricultural experts (including farmers and all other food producers) are further removed from decision making.

The shift from world food supply to household access illustrates the downward focus of this era of food security policy: no longer were states responsible for solving challenges of global supply and distribution; instead, the focus was on ensuring access at the household level through poverty reduction and increasingly open and international markets. Importantly, changing how food security is defined changes who should be consulted about it. If production is no longer an issue, then agricultural specialists are no longer the authoritative voice informing policy. They must be replaced by social scientists and economists who can address issues of access and markets. This represented a challenge for the FAO which had established itself, its reputation and its legitimacy as the primary actor in food security on a foundation of research and knowledge. This challenge only amplifies with the acceleration of globalization through the 1990s into the 2000s.

World Food Summit: Food security as development

The 1990s were marked not only by a deeper embedding of neoliberal logic in international policy processes but also by a new era of globalization. The EU was formally established when the Maastricht Treaty came into force on November 1, 1993. The USA, Canada and Mexico signed a continental free trade agreement which came into force in 1994. In 1996, the WTO emerged as the result of pressure through the 1980s to formalize the General Agreement on Trade and Tariffs (GATT). The WTO, established during the Uruguay Round of GATT negotiations (1986–1994), subsumed the GATT and transformed it into a formal international organization with a broad mandate to address issues once reserved for nation-states, such as subsidies, food safety, agriculture and intellectual property. Amidst this economic reordering were a series of World Summits which added another layer to globalization: global-level problems required global solutions. At most of these Summits, poverty was forwarded as the major cause of hunger, framing food security as a development issue. A notable example was the 1992 International Conference on Nutrition. The conference:

> focused on food security at the household and community levels and helped to make more explicit the linkages between nutrition and agricultural development. FAO is promoting agricultural development to increase food consumption and provide income to reduce poverty. In light of the challenges facing countries and the international community in their efforts to obtain lasting food security for all, FAO will convene the World Food Summit in 1996, at which heads of State will deliberate the pragmatic and concrete measures needed to achieve this goal at the national, regional and global levels.
>
> (FAO 1992)

In a similar spirit, the World Food Summit was proposed by Jacques Diouf, following his election as Director-General of the FAO in 1994. The aim was to use the Summit to launch changes in FAO related to programs, structure and policies (FAO 1994b; Shaw 2007:347). Diouf took over the position of Director-General of the FAO at a time when 800 million people were without adequate food. Referencing the FAO's constitution in his proposal, Diouf reminded member states that they had "made a solemn pledge to raise levels of nutrition and standards of living and thereby contribute towards ensuring humanity's freedom from hunger" (Shaw 2007:345).

The 1996 World Food Summit resulted in a major shift in the concept of food security (Shaw 2007:348). At the Summit, consensus emerged around a new, highly negotiated definition: food security exists "when all people, at all times, have physical and economic access to sufficient, safe and nutritious food to meet their dietary needs and food preferences for an active and healthy life." It was also understood that these dimensions could be undermined by root causes of food insecurity, including: "natural disaster; war; inappropriate national policies; inadequate development; dissemination; adaptation and adoption of agricultural technologies; poverty; population and gender inequalities; and poor health" (Shaw 2007:349).

Food security was thus understood to be based on four pillars:

1   *Food availability*: The availability of sufficient quantities of food of appropriate quality, supplied through domestic production or imports (including food aid).
2   *Food access*: Access by individuals to adequate resources (entitlements) for acquiring appropriate foods for a nutritious diet. Entitlements are defined as the set of all commodity bundles over which a person can establish command given the legal, political, economic and social arrangements of the community in which they live (including traditional rights such as access to common resources).

3   *Utilization*: Utilization of food through adequate diet, clean water, sanitation and healthcare to reach a state of nutritional well-being where all physiological needs are met. This brings out the importance of non-food inputs in food security.

4   *Stability*: To be food secure, a population, household or individual must have access to adequate food at all times. They should not risk losing access to food as a consequence of sudden shocks (e.g. an economic or climatic crisis) or cyclical events (FAO 2006).

This definition has since become the "gold standard." The definition does not start anew but rather builds on the concept's evolution. The definition, which includes issues of availability, production and supply through "physical access" and "economic access," highlights Sen's contribution as well as that of the World Bank. Nutrition, preference and healthy life speak to livelihoods and hint at social access. The discourse of food security at the international level remains framed as a development issue. The inclusion of preference illustrates cultural sensitivity but fails to explain how preferences of wealthy consumers, or consumers in wealthy countries, impact the food security of others. The FAO (2006:1) argued the new definition "reinforces the multidimensional nature of food security" and "has enabled policy responses focused on the promotion and recovery of livelihood options" (FAO 2006:1). It is at this point that analysis of food security as a social and political construct begins to take hold.

While in 1992 there was fear of a growing food crisis necessitating humanitarian, political and economic engagement in North Korea and Somalia, by the time the World Food Summit came around the world food situation appeared to have stabilized. Unlike the world food crisis of the 1970s, the food problems of the 1990s were informed by a mutated version of Sen's theory and understood to be linked to poverty, purchasing power and food insecurity and consequently, a geographically concentrated problem (Shaw 2007:348). As Shaw (2007:348) highlights, by the "FAO's own assessment of the world food security situation," there had only been "a modest deterioration [in world food markets] in 1993/1994 compared with the previous year" (see FAO 1994a).

Shaw (2007:348) argues that the World Food Summit was poorly scheduled, organized at the end of a series of international conferences that dominated the first half of the decade and that there was a "distinct feeling of conference fatigue" in the lead-up to the summit. Shaw also highlights a growing concern within official circles of a saturation of institutional arrangements with too many bodies grappling with overlapping mandates and responsibilities. The World Food Summit came on the eve of the first meeting of the newly established WTO and in the midst of presidential elections in the US, while at the UN energy was focused on the election of a new secretary-general and the FAO was particularly preoccupied with an outbreak of a large-scale human-made disaster in Central Africa (Shaw 2007:348). There was also concern over the aims of the summit and in a position paper the US argued that the World Food Summit was designed to review ways of achieving food security and was not to be a venue for pledging new resources, creating new financial mechanisms, institutions or bureaucracies or re-examine previous agreements (Shaw 2007:348).

One outcome of the World Food Summit was the Plan of Action which articulated the objectives and actions around food security. The Plan of Action called on every nation to "adopt a strategy consistent with its resources and capacities to achieve its individual goals and, at the same time, cooperate regionally and internationally in order to organize collective solutions to global issues of food security" (FAO 1996: para 1). It continued that "[i]n a world of increasingly interlinked institutions, societies and economies, coordinated efforts and shared responsibilities are essential." The Plan of Action listed a series of commitments with related objectives on how to achieve food security:

> We will ensure an enabling political, social, and economic environment designed to create the best conditions for the *eradication of poverty* and for *durable peace*, based on full and equal *participation* of women and men, which is most conducive to achieving sustainable food security for all.

> We will implement policies aimed at *eradicating poverty* and inequality and improving physical and economic access by all, at all times, to sufficient, nutritionally adequate and safe food and its effective utilization.

> We will pursue *participatory and sustainable food, agriculture, fisheries, forestry and rural development policies* and practices in high and low potential areas, which are essential to adequate and reliable food supplies at the household, national, regional and global levels, and combat pests, drought and desertification, considering the multifunctional character of agriculture.

> We will strive to ensure that food, agricultural trade and overall *trade policies are conducive to fostering food security* for all through a fair and market-oriented world trade system.

> We will endeavour to *prevent and be prepared for natural disasters* and man-made emergencies and to meet transitory and emergency food requirements in ways that encourage recovery, rehabilitation, development and a capacity to satisfy future needs.

> We will promote optimal allocation and use of *public and private investments* to foster human resources, sustainable food, agriculture, fisheries and forestry systems, and rural development, in high and low potential areas.

> We will implement, monitor, and follow-up this Plan of Action at all levels in cooperation with the international community.
>
>   (FAO 1996: para 1, emphasis added)

The commitments reinforced the updated definition and drew attention to poverty eradication, participation, stronger markets and better investment.

This changes little from status quo definitions of the 1980s. What we can note is a new focus on participation. This can be traced back to the participatory turn in global governance that marked the world summits.

Global food security in an era of food price volatility: 2008–2013

As the above review of literature and policy evolution of food security illustrated, large-scale food crises have prompted shifts in the discourse of food security policy (e.g., 1974 food crisis, 1983–1985 famine, 1990 famine). The 2007–2008 crisis is no exception. At the same time, it is recognized that since the 1980s food security policies have not so much shifted ideologically as evolved alongside wider neoliberal trends. In the wake of the neoliberal turn, arguably marked by launch and subsequent influence of the World Bank's 1986 report *Poverty and Hunger*, food security policy has incorporated critique and contention but failed to systematically shift or reform in ways that would disrupt the logic of neoliberalism, despite ongoing failure of food security policy to address hunger and malnutrition and increasing evidence that these policies are in fact responsible for much of the problem (Wise 2009).

The definition of food security negotiated at the World Food Summit remains the preeminent and predominant definition. Despite the many weaknesses and limitations of the definition, it has ensured intergovernmental agreement around what is meant by food security in the context of multilateral processes. That said, causes of food insecurity and solutions remain key sites of contention and contestation.

Since 2008, food security has been a fixture on the international agenda. The nature of contemporary food systems now demands that policy makers come to terms with increased complexity including the inclusion of new actors and a push for more integration, systems approaches, inclusivity and varied knowledge systems. Critiques of food security as a concept (as a process within global governance) and as a serious problem for close to 1 billion people (as observable phenomenon within global governance) are being advanced to contest inadequate hegemonic definitions of food security in an effort to change status quo. As can be expected, and as will be illustrated throughout this book, overwhelmingly, elite actors are working to maintain status quo, while others are calling for the concept of food security to be enhanced, for example through the addition of explicit reference to nutrition (CFS 2012a). Others, like the UN's Special Rapporteur on the Right to Food and FIAN International, are fighting for it to be reframed within a human rights discourse. Still others, most notably La Via Campesina, are in favor of food sovereignty. In practice, these actors are staking claims that will certainly influence and construct the next variation of food security policy and by defining the problem they will also set out parameters for solutions. The result is a discursive turf war which is taking place amidst a restructuring of the global architecture of global food security governance. Importantly, these points of contestation are rich sites of inquiry and will help to articulate and uncover emerging trends and future directions of food security policy and governance at the global level.

The battle over the global governance of food security is reaching a climax with almost one billion hungry people, increased water scarcity, increased land-grabbing in poor nations by wealthy nations to enhance domestic food security, climatic variability and growing populations. This battle for leadership is being waged by the several key actors including the G8, G20, the UN secretary-general and the Rome-based food agencies (FAO, WFP and the International Fund for Agricultural Development, or IFAD), networks of CSOs, the private sector and philanthropic foundations. The stakes are high: the winner will decide who eats and how.

Multilateral reaction to the 2007–2008 food price crisis

Given the triggers of the 2007–2008 food price spikes, food security policy now necessitates the introduction of added layers of complexity (e.g., price volatility, commodity speculation, investment in agricultural land) to an already complex and multifaceted concept. Because of the causes and reactions to the crisis, there has also been widespread agreement on the need for improved coherence and cohesion at the global level. These changes suggest recognition of the interconnectedness of food security issues and the need for multilateral action to reduce food insecurity and start building linkages for a strengthened global policy arena, not only around food and agriculture, but also across sectors and industries.

However, despite the rekindled interest, skepticism around efficacy and political will remains warranted. Twice in the ten years leading up to the food price crisis governments of the world had come together to declared their commitment to ending world hunger, first in 1996, with the Rome Declaration on World Food Security and the World Food Summit Plan of Action they agreed to cut the number of hungry in the world in half by 2015 (paragraph 7). Four years later, in the UN Millennium Declaration, states pledged, more modestly, to halve the proportion of the hungry by 2015. Yet 870 million people remained chronically undernourished in 2010–2012 (FAO 2012a).

After 2007 actors steered away from quantifiable commitments and targets, although existing commitments were reiterated at various international meetings (e.g., Declaration of the High Level Conference on World Food Security: Challenges of Climate Change and Bioenergy, June 2008). Policy makers and development practitioners continue working towards the achievement of food security, yet few appear to be contemplating whether food security is indeed the most appropriate way to be framing the very real challenge of ensuring healthy, culturally appropriate, sustainable diets to a growing world population.

What follows is a chronological overview of multilateral activity sparked or spurred on by the sharp rise in food prices in 2007 and 2008, ongoing food price volatility or the resulting impacts of these. The presentation is not comprehensive and is focused primarily on global-level, state-led initiatives. The reasons for this is that this research is particularly interested in understanding how states are working multilaterally to address an issue that has international targets and commitments and is acknowledged to be global in scale and yet remains a national-level responsibility.

The review highlights the high-level interest, the types of reactions and the key actors involved. In doing so, this section identifies the main actors and asks what are the dominant initiatives within the changing architecture of food security governance? The answer maps out the broader transnational policy space within which the CFS operates, including not only opportunities but also challenges with respect to competition for legitimacy and leadership. What becomes clear is an obvious contradiction between the large number of meetings and overlapping mandates, all in the name of policy cohesion and cooperation.

Chronology of key events in global food security governance (October 2007–October 2012)

The review begins in October 2007 when the World Bank Group released its annual World Development Report for 2008, which focused on agriculture for development. The World Bank is an international financial institution tasked with providing loans to developing countries to support various programs. Since the onset of the food price spikes, they have played an active role in reshaping food security governance, returning to the role it played in the 1980s as a donor and coordinator for agriculture and rural development. The 2008 report, which one World Bank agricultural expert called "the most authoritative source on the Bank's position [on agriculture]" (interview, World Bank agricultural expert, March 2012, Rome), marked the first time in a quarter century that the World Bank had focused its annual research report on agriculture, highlighting an important shift in the Bank's international focus.

This focus was mirrored in January 2008 when the World Economic Forum met for its annual invitation-only meeting in Davos. At this meeting a Network of Global Agenda Councils, comprised of Councils on key topics of global economic importance, including one for food security, was established.[6] The Councils bring together experts on key themes and work to integrate outcomes of thematic discussions across the network and beyond to international decision-making fora.

A few months later, in April 2008, in Johannesburg, at the Intergovernmental Plenary Meeting of the International Assessment of Agricultural Knowledge, Science and Technology for Development (IAASTD) the results and conclusions of the project were reviewed and ratified. The IAASTD process began in 2005, when the World Bank initiated an international effort to evaluate the relevance, quality and effectiveness of agricultural knowledge, science, and technology, and the effectiveness of public and private sector

Table 3.1 Chronology of key moments in transnational food security policy

Who	What	When
World Bank Group	World Development Report on Agriculture for Development	October 2007
World Economic Forum	Annual Forum	January 2008
International Assessment of Agricultural Knowledge, Science and Technology for Development (IAASTD)	Results and conclusions ratified during the Intergovernmental Plenary Meeting	April 2008
UN	High-Level Task Force on the Global Food Security Crisis	April 2008
UN Economic and Social Council	Special Meeting on the Global Food Crisis	May 2008
FAO	High-Level Conference on Food Security and the Challenges of Bio-energy	June 2008
G8	Leaders Statement on Global Food Security	July 2008
World Bank Group	Global Food Crisis Response Program	May 2008
UN	High Level Meeting on Food Security for All	January 2009
World Bank Group	Implementing Agriculture for Development, World Bank Group Agriculture Action Plan: FY2010–2011	July 2009
G8	L'Aquila Joint Statement on Food Security	July 2009
Rome-based Food Agencies	Joint Food Security Strategy	July 2009
G20	Pittsburgh Summit: Proposal for Global Agriculture and Food Security Program (GAFSP)	September 2009
UN + US	Partnering for Food Security	September 2009
FAO	High-Level Expert Forum, How to Feed the World in 2050	October 2009
Committee on World Food Security	35th Session: Agreement to reform	October 2009
People's Food Sovereignty Forum	Mobilization around CFS reform and civil society mechanism	November 2009
FAO	World Summit on Food Security	November 2009
World Bank (Sustainable Development Network)	Framework Document for GAFSP	December 2009
FAO	Summit of World's Regions on Food Security	January 2010
FAO, IFAD, United Nations Conference on Trade and Development (UNCTAD), World Bank	Principles for Responsible Agricultural Investment that Respects Rights, Livelihoods and Resources	January 2010
Global Forum for Agricultural Research	First Global Conference on Agricultural Research for Development	March 2010

Table 3.1 Chronology of key moments in transnational food security policy, *continued*

Who	What	When
Scaling-Up Nutrition	Framework for Action to Scale-Up Nutrition	April 2010
Concern Worldwide, High-Level Task Force and the Government of Ireland	Consultation on the Comprehensive Framework for Action	May 2010
High Level Plenary Meeting of the UN General Assembly	Outcome Document promoting national food security strategies	September 2010
Scaling-Up Nutrition (SUN) Movement	A Road Map for SUN	September 2010
CSO Forum for the Civil Society Mechanism (CSM)	Approval of the CSM	October 2010
Committee on World Food Security	36th Session, first of the reformed CFS	October 2010
Asia-Pacific Economic Cooperation (APEC)	Ministerial Meeting on Food Security	October 2010
G20	Multi-Year Action Plan on Development	November 2010
Special Rapporteur on the Right to Food	Agroecology and the right to food	March 2011
G20 agriculture ministers	Action Plan on Food Price Volatility	June 2011
Chinese Academy of Agricultural Sciences and the International Food Policy Research Institute	International Conference on Climate Change and Food Security	July 2011
FAO	Regional Conferences	March/April 2011
Committee on World Food Security	Extraordinary 38th Session to endorse the Voluntary Guidelines on the Responsible Governance of Tenure of Land, Fisheries and Forests in the Context of National Food Security	May 2012
G8	New Alliance for Food Security and Nutrition	May 2012
United Nations Department of Economic and Social Affairs	UN Conference on Sustainable Development	June 2012
FAO	High-level forum on food insecurity in protracted crisis	September 2012
Committee on World Food Security	39th Session, adoption of the First Version of the Global Strategic Framework for Food Security and Nutrition	October 2012

policies and institutional arrangements. The IAASTD was launched as an intergovernmental process, under the co-sponsorship of the FAO, Global Environment Facility (GEF), UN Development Programme (UNDP), UN Environment Programme (UNEP), UN Educational, Scientific and Cultural Organization (UNESCO), the World Bank and WHO. It was composed of one global assessment and five sub-global assessments based on the same frameworks which assess the impacts agricultural knowledge, science, and technology on hunger, poverty, nutrition, human health, and environmental and social sustainability in the past and the future. The global and sub-global assessments were peer-reviewed by governments and experts, and approved by the panel of participating governments. The process included a global consultative process involving 900 participants and 110 countries from all regions of the world. The executive summary of the Synthesis Report was approved by 58 countries.

Also in April 2008, UN Secretary-General Ban Ki-moon, in accordance with the UN Chief Executives Board, named a High-Level Task Force on the Global Food Security Crisis (HLTF), bringing together the 22 UN agencies, the World Bank, IMF, WTO and the Organisation for Economic Co-operation and Development (OECD). Civil society was notably absent from the Task Force. Assistant Secretary-General David Nabarro was charged with leading the task force and soon became the special representative for Food Security and Nutrition. After some concern about the limited role of the FAO on the Task Force, the director general of the FAO was made vice-chairman of Task Force. The HLTF's main role was to develop a Comprehensive Framework for Action (CFA), "designed to encourage concerted responses to the food price crisis with actions to respond to the immediate needs of vulnerable populations and contribute to longer-term resilience" (High Level Task Force on the Global Food Security Crisis 2010:xi). The HLTF aims to achieve its objectives through improved coordination at the international and country level without creating any bureaucratic structures or intergovernmental layers. Initially, the Rome-based agencies[7] supported the HLTF as a short-term mechanism for raising awareness, resources and improving collaboration and efficiency and provided staff and material assistance.

In May, the UN Economic and Social Council (ECOSOC) hosted a Special Meeting on the Global Food Crisis in New York to respond to the growing calls for immediate action. The president of ECOSOC released an official statement on the occasion of the special meeting of the Council on the global food crisis in June 2008 to the General Assembly of the UN outlining "the basic elements that constitute the basis for effective and sustained global action" (ECOSOC 2008:2).

In June 2008, the FAO hosted the High-Level Conference on Food Security and the Challenges of Bio-energy, which resulted in a Declaration on the Challenges of Climate Change and Bioenergy. Here a draft of the UN's HLTF's CFA was also presented for comments, with the caveat the CFA represents the consensus view of the HLTF but it is not an intergovernmental document. The aim of presenting the CFA at the conference was for it to be a catalyst for action as well as a synthesis of policies and priorities.

In July 2008, at the height of the food crisis, G8 leaders meeting in Hokkaido Toyako, Japan issued a Leaders Statement on Global Food Security. The G8 is a forum for eight of the world's most industrialized nations. The presidency of the G8 rotates through member states in the following order: France, US, UK, Russia, Germany, Japan, Italy and Canada. The EU is represented within the G8 but cannot chair or host summits. G8 can refer to collection of these states and the annual summit meetings of the heads of government, as well as thematic meetings of G8 ministers.

The G8 has no headquarters, no budget and no permanent staff. The G8 is often criticized for their promotion of neoliberal globalization and for representing the interests of an elite group of industrialized nations to the detriment of poorer countries. Fast-growing economies such as India, China and Brazil are not represented and there are no African or Latin American members.[8] Since the financial crisis, the annual summits have tended to focus on stabilizing the world economy and stimulating economic growth, however they have also addressed food security and consequently the G8 is now a key actor in the developing architecture of global food security governance. Since 2008, food security has been on the agenda of each annual summit.

In the Leaders Statement on Global Food Security, G8 leaders expressed their ongoing commitment to pursue all possible measures to ensure global food security, noting that since January 2008, they had committed over US$10 billion to support food measures to increase agricultural outputs in affected countries. The statement emphasized the urgency of short-term needs (e.g., access of smallholder farmers to fertilizers), a commitment to increase food aid and investment and recognized the coordinating role of the UN through their support for the HLTF. They also encouraged countries with surplus to released food stocks and called for the removal of export restrictions (G8 2008).

In their statement the G8 made reference to the development of a Global Partnership:

> we will work with the international community in forming a Global Partnership on agriculture and food, involving all relevant actors, including developing country governments, the private sector, civil society, donors, and international institutions. This partnership, strengthening and building on existing UN and other international institutions, could provide efficient and effective support for country-led processes and institutions and for local leadership, draw on the expertise in existing international organizations and, in particular, ensure monitoring and assessment on progress. The UN should facilitate and provide coordination. As part of this partnership, a global network of high-level experts on food and agriculture would provide science-based analysis, and highlight needs and future risks.
>
> (G8 2008: para 4)

Importantly, the G8 here states that the UN is the appropriate forum for facilitation and coordination of such an initiative and that the partnership should build on existing institutions.

In May 2008, the World Bank established the Global Food Crisis Response Program (GFRP) to provide immediate support to countries significantly impacted by rising food prices. The GFRP used the World Development Report as its framework and implemented processes to expedite the funding of projects up to an initial US$1.2 billion, so as to ensure timely a response. By April 2009, the World Bank had increased funding to the GFRP to US$2 billion. When food prices continued to rise through the summer of 2011, the Board of the Fund extended accelerated processing to June 2012, specifically targeting projects aimed at feeding children and other vulnerable groups, nutritional supplements to pregnant women, lactating mothers, infants and small children, meeting additional expenses of food imports and buying seeds (World Bank 2011). Beyond the GFRP, the World Bank has made funding available through external-funded trust funds. Specifically, a "Multi-Donor Trust Fund (MDTF) has received contributions of AUD 50 million from the Australian government, €80 million from the government of Spain, 7.6 billion Korean Won from the Republic of Korea, CAD 30 million from the government of Canada, and $0.15 million from International Finance Corporation (IFC)" (World Bank 2011). As of September 2011, the GFRP had approved US$1.5025 billion of funding for various projects. According to the World Bank, through the GFRP, nearly 40 million vulnerable people in 44 countries have been helped (World Bank 2011). Yet, the Bank's proposals continue to push for a productionist paradigm based on neoliberal principles of increased market access and improved technology, suggesting a lack of critical reflection on not only the causes of the 2007–2008 food price crisis, but also with respect to integrated solutions for improving food security.

In January 2009, Secretary-General Ban Ki-moon and Spanish Prime Minister Rodriguez Zapatero convened the High Level Meeting on Food Security for All in Madrid, Spain, to follow up on the FAO High-Level Conference. The aim of this meeting was to assess progress made since the High-Level Conference on Food Security and the challenges of bio-energy, as well as to establish priorities and commitments for moving forward. There was also emphasis on establishing a framework for the Global Partnership for agriculture and food security. The aim of this Global Partnership for food security was to bring together governments, regional bodies, international agencies, civil society, development banks and donors and businesses to develop coherent strategies against food insecurity.

The meeting was well attended, with almost 60 ministers present, the European Community, as well as heads of all Rome-based agencies (FAO, IFAD, WFP), UNICEF, representatives from the World Bank, regional banks, donors and bilateral agencies, farmer organizations, civil society, the private sector and philanthropic organizations including the Bill and Melinda Gates Foundation and the Rockefeller Foundation.

At the meeting there was agreement on the importance of an inclusive and broad process of consultation on options leading to the establishment of a Global Partnership for Agriculture, Food Security and Nutrition and that consultations should be open to the full range of stakeholders. It was agreed that states have a primary responsibility to promote the right to adequate food, especially for children under five years of age, women and other vulnerable groups. There was agreement on the need to identify financing gaps and the additional resources needed for existing anti-famine mechanisms, including for food and nutrition assistance and social protection programs, and for supporting smallholder agriculture. There was acknowledgement that such programs would only be effective if led by countries and included broad participation of stakeholders, including civil society.

Expanding on the productionist discourse, the meeting acknowledged that to address food security is to go beyond increasing production and to look at the development of social protection systems and competition-distorting subsidies so as to promote fair agricultural trade. Far from radical, these outcomes do bring forward the more progressive discursive themes such as inclusion, cooperation and a fair playing field. This is in many ways due to the different forum within which discussions were taking place. A UN-led meeting is open to all UN member countries, not just the economic elite. There are clear rules around transparency, consultation and participation, ensuring that policy objectives of developing countries are included in the debate, and are not simply the subject of debate.

At this meeting, there was widespread support from countries for the CFA's twin-track approach. There was consensus on the immediate need for better coordination of resources and agreement around the value of expanded engagement of all stakeholders, including civil society. However, as we will see, there is often a division between rhetoric and action.

The FAO, the Latin America government regional grouping and CSOs were clear that any process to establish the Global Partnership must be driven by the newly reformed and strengthened Rome-based agencies (FAO, IFAD, WFP). Moreover, these actors demanded commitment to a UN principle of "one country, one vote," as well as broad consultation and participation of organizations of small-scale food producers.

July 2009 was a big month for food security. The World Bank released its Agricultural Action Plan: Implementing Agriculture for Development FY2010–11. At their summit in L'Aquila Italy, the G8 issued the L'Aquila Joint Statement on Food Security that expressed ongoing concern "about global food security, the impact of the global financial and economic crisis and last year's spike in food prices on the countries least able to respond to increased hunger and poverty" (G8 2009: para 1). The statement identified the role of "longstanding underinvestment in agriculture and food security, price trends and the economic crisis" (G8 2009: para 1) in increasing poverty and hunger and noted the urgent need for decisive action.

That same month, the three UN Rome-based Food Agencies developed a Joint Food Security Strategy with four pillars of cooperation so as to better address the outcomes of the food price crisis. The pillars are: policy advice, knowledge and monitoring; operations; advocacy and communication; and administrative collaboration. Through this plan, they agreed to take joint action at the global, regional, national and local levels with a focus on enhanced collaboration to support transition from relief to development in selected countries, joint advocacy to support the MDGs and alignment of early warning and monitoring information to improve food security reporting. Central to the Joint Food Security Strategy was coordination around the €1 billion EU Food Facility and addressing overlaps so as to become more efficient.

In September 2009, G20 leaders came together at the Pittsburgh Summit and backed the G8's L'Aquila Food Security Initiative. They also called on the World Bank to establish the GAFSP to facilitate disbursements (G20 2009). The G20 emerged in 1999 when the finance ministers and central bank governors of advanced and emerging countries met in Berlin, Germany, for an informal dialogue on key issues for global economic stability. The meeting was in response to the financial crises of the 1990s with growing recognition that some key countries were not adequately represented in global economic discussion and governance. From 1999 to 2008, the G20 finance ministers maintained annual meetings. During the 2008 financial crisis, US President George W. Bush convened a meeting of G20 Leaders (i.e., heads of states) in Washington DC. Here, the leaders agreed to implement an Action Plan with three main objectives: restoring global growth; strengthening the international financial system; and reforming international financial institutions.

Since the first Leaders' Summit, the G20 has strengthened its position as a forum for international cooperation around the international economic and financial agenda and brings together the world's major advanced and emerging economies. The G20 is made up of 19 member countries and the EU. Informal and leader-driven, the G8 is focused on building political consensus between 19 country leaders and the European Union. At the 2009 Pittsburgh Summit, G20 leaders agreed that the G20 would be the foremost forum for their international economic cooperation, effectively positioning the G20 ahead of the G8 in terms of coordinating bodies. However, the G8 has continued to move ahead with new initiatives, such as the New Alliance, with no link to the G20.

The G20 Pittsburgh Summit drew attention to an important trend: the rise in prominence of philanthropic and private sector actors in food security, agriculture and development. The G20 Statement states that their approach "is to use development assistance to explore synergies with private philanthropy and private sector actors" (G20 2009:2). The Gates Foundation, Rockefeller Foundation, Hewlett Foundation, Rabobank foundation, World Economic Forum and the Initiative for Global Development are listed as key partners.

That same month (September 2009), at the 64th Session of the UN General Assembly, UN Secretary-General Ban Ki-Moon and US Secretary of State Hillary Clinton co-hosted the side-event called "Partnering for Food Security" to focus on the five principles of the G8's L'Aquila Initiative.

In October 2009, the High-Level Expert Forum, How to Feed the World in 2050, was held in Rome in advance of the World Food Summit. The goal of the Forum was to examine policy options that governments should consider adopting to ensure that when (or if) the world population reaches the estimated 9.2 billion by 2050, people will be fed. There was agreement on the part of participants that there is enough food to feed everyone in the world and yet, in line with a seemingly blind commitment to production-ism, the debate remained focused on issues of production, failing to address key structural issues such as consumption, distribution and access. While production is important as the population is set to grow to a number we certainly cannot currently feed, such discussions are in vein if issues related to production, distribution and ecological capacity are not addressed. It is thus not surprising that there was disappointment at the failure of the Forum to address the root causes of the food crisis, including the structure of markets and climate change.

That same month, at its 35th Session, the CFS agreed on a wide-ranging reform to make the CFS the foremost inclusive international and intergovern-mental platform dealing with food security and nutrition. The reform was a deliberate effort to position the CFS as a central actor in the emerging Global Partnership for Agriculture, Food Security and Nutrition.

One month later, in November 2009, CSOs gathered in Rome for the People's Food Sovereignty Forum. The Forum sought to engage people in new possibilities for engagement made possible through the reform of the CFS and to coordinate actions around World Summit on Food Security. The following week, world leaders gathered in Rome for the World Summit on Food Security. At the Summit, FAO Director-General Jacques Diouf reflected on the global food system, calling it "our tragic achievement in these modern days." He went on to stress the need to focus efforts and production where the poor and hungry live and to increase agricultural investments in these regions. At the Summit the international community adopted the Declaration of the World Summit on Food Security (FAO 2009: para 1), pledging to "undertake all necessary actions required at national, regional and global levels and by all States and Governments to halt immediately the increase in—and to significantly reduce—the number of people suffering from hunger and food insecurity." The Declaration also pledged renewed commitment to eradicate hunger in a sustainable and timely way. Countries agreed to reverse the downward trend in agricultural funding at the domestic and international level and to promote investment in the sector. They also agreed to improve global food governance in partnership with relevant actors and to address the challenges of climate change to food security. At this meeting, FAO member countries also endorsed the reform of the CFS.

In January 2010, the FAO hosted the Summit of the World's Regions on Food Security in Dakar, bringing together representatives from local authori-ties, national governments and international organizations to propose innovative solutions to tackle food insecurity. The Summit was organized on the basis of a questionnaire sent to the world's regions to collect information on food-related issues. The aim was to identify specific areas where cooperation between regions could provide added value to national and international initiatives.

The same month (January 2010), FAO, IFAD, UNCTAD and the World Bank released a rather controversial discussion note: Principles for Responsible Agricultural Investment that Respects Rights, Livelihoods and Resources. The Principles were based on preliminary evidence from empirical evidence collected by the World Bank in 2009 through in-depth studies—Large-Scale Acquisition of Land Rights for Agricultural or Natural Resource-Based Use—in 20 countries, as well as the experience of a broad set of experts.

The seven principles can be summarized as follows:

- Principle 1: Existing rights to land and associated natural resources are recognized and respected.
- Principle 2: Investments do not jeopardize food security but rather strengthen it.
- Principle 3: Processes for accessing land and other resources and then making associated investments are transparent, monitored and ensure accountability by all stakeholders, within a proper business, legal and regulatory environment.
- Principle 4: All those materially affected are consulted, and agreements from consultations are recorded and enforced.
- Principle 5: Investors ensure that projects respect the rule of law, reflect industry best practice, are viable economically and result in durable shared value.
- Principle 6: Investments generate desirable social and distributional impacts and do not increase vulnerability.
- Principle 7: Environmental impacts due to a project are quantified and measures taken to encourage sustainable resource use while minimizing the risk/magnitude of negative impacts and mitigating them.

(FAO et al. 2010)

March 2010 saw the First Global Conference on Agricultural Research for Development organized by the Global Forum for Agricultural Research in collaboration with CGIAR among others. The Conference sought to provide a global action plan and strategy for improving agricultural research in order to maximize the impact on development, especially of the poor. This plan and strategy was to be established through consultations with representatives from a wide range of agricultural research stakeholders around the world.

In April 2010, a Framework for Action to Scale-Up Nutrition was released and endorsed by more than one hundred entities including national governments, the UN system, civil society organizations, development agencies, academia, philanthropic bodies and the private sector. Throughout 2009 and 2010, a group of stakeholders from governments, donor agencies, civil society, the research community, the private sector, intergovernmental organizations and development banks met at intervals to develop the Framework. In June 2010, the mayor of Rome and the WFP hosted a meeting to endorse the Framework.

In May 2010, Concern Worldwide, the UN's High-Level Task Force and the government of Ireland co-hosted a two-day meeting in Dublin to provide an opportunity to exchange views on the changes required to better reflect the current context of food and nutrition insecurity and to consult on the CFA. The result was an Updated CFA.

In September 2010, the High-Level Plenary Meeting of the UN General Assembly produced an outcome document that promoted national food security strategies that strengthen support for smallholder farmers and contribute to poverty eradication. That same month, the Scaling-Up Nutrition (SUN) Road Map Task Team released the first edition of *A Road Map for Scaling-Up Nutrition*. The Road Map emerged from the May 2010 World Health Assembly Resolution 63.23 on infant and young child nutrition and based on guiding principles developed by the Standing Committee on Nutrition in 2009 in Brussels. Framed as a movement, SUN brings together national leaders who prioritize efforts to address malnutrition. The aim is for states, organizations and individuals working to scale-up nutrition while recognizing the multiple causes of malnutrition.

In October, in advance of the 36th Session of the Committee on World Food Security, CSOs met to adopt the autonomous International Civil Society Mechanism for Food Security and Nutrition to facilitate engagement in the reformed CFS. The following week the 36th Session of the CFS took place. It was the Committee's first session as a reformed body.

On the last day of the CFS Session, the first Asia-Pacific Economic Cooperation (APEC) Ministerial Meeting on Food Security was hosted and resulted in the Niigata Declaration on APEC Food Security. The overlap suggests a disregard for the CFS process. The Declaration instructed APEC senior officials to monitor the implementation of the APEC Action Plan on Food Security, to report progress on its implementation to APEC ministers on an annual basis, and to compile an assessment report on overall achievements following the completion of the Action Plan.

In November, 2010, G20 leaders met in Seoul, where, under the leadership of French President Sarkozy, the G20 developed a Multi-Year Action Plan on Development with work to be undertaken by the Development Working Group, also charged with monitoring and reporting on the progress. Here, the G20's food security agenda was more clearly fleshed out.

In March 2011, the Special Rapporteur on the Right to Food presented the *Agro-ecology and the Right to Food* report before the UN Human Rights Council. The report demonstrates by way of an extensive review of recent scientific literature that agro-ecology, if appropriately supported, can double food production in regions within ten years while mitigating climate change and alleviating rural poverty. The report called on states to undertake a fundamental shift towards agro-ecology and was widely supported by CSOs.

In June 2011, G20 agriculture ministers met for the first time and issued an Action Plan on Food Price Volatility. As will be explored in Chapter 6, this Action Plan had an important influence on the policy processes that took place in October 2011 at the 37th Session of the CFS. The following month the

Chinese Academy of Agricultural Sciences (CAAS) and the International Food Policy Research Institute (IFPRI) jointly hosted the International Conference on Climate Change and Food Security (ICCCFS) in Beijing, China. The conference resulted in a series of recommendations from leading scientists in the BRICS countries (Brazil, Russia, India, China and South Africa), Indonesia and the US for the UN Framework Convention on Climate Change (UNFCCC) delegates meeting in Durban at the end of 2011. Recommendations were focused around a need to strengthen agricultural research and increase availability of spatial data.

The FAO Regional Conferences are held every two years and are the highest governing body and forum of the FAO in the regions. The round of conferences held in 2012 marked an important change in the structure and impact of the conferences insofar as the priorities set by the countries at the spring conferences would now be included on the agenda of the technical and political governing bodies of the FAO at the global level. Regional conferences would no longer be technical and advisory in nature, but now their decisions would guide FAO actions as part of an effort to decentralize power at the FAO.

Importantly, the Latin America and Caribbean meeting requested that the FAO "organize a wide-ranging and dynamic debate with the participation of civil society and academia to discuss the concept of food sovereignty, whose meaning had not been agreed by FAO Member Countries or the United Nations System" (FAO 2012b: para 25). This call to discuss food sovereignty within the FAO and the CFS remains controversial but suggests the growing awareness and acceptance of a term that emerged from a peasant social movement in opposition to neoliberal hegemony.

In May 2012, the CFS met for an extraordinary session (38th) to endorse the Voluntary Guidelines on the Responsible Governance of Tenure of Land, Fisheries and Forests in the Context of National Food Security. That same month, the G8 announced the launch of the New Alliance for Food Security and Nutrition, a partnership program between African governments, members of the G8, and the private sector to work together to accelerate investments in agriculture to improve productivity, livelihoods and food security for smallholder farmers. This New Alliance aims to raise 50 million people out of poverty over the next ten years through sustained and inclusive agricultural growth. Commitments to coordinate through the G20 had evidently been pushed aside along with a commitment of developing a Global Partnership coordinated within the UN and inclusive of a wide range of stakeholders. President Barack Obama unveiled plans for the New Alliance for Food Security and Nutrition at a time when only half of the L'Aquila pledges had been disbursed. With regard to the L'Aquila commitments, the New Alliance noted that since the L'Aquila Summit, they had increased their bilateral and multilateral investments in food security and changed the way they do business, consistent with core principles of aid effectiveness. Based on the findings of the 2012 G8 Accountability Report and consistent with the Rome Principles on Sustainable Global Food Security, the G8 had agreed to promptly fulfil outstanding L'Aquila financial pledges and seek to maintain strong support to address current and future global food security challenges, including through bilateral and multilateral assistance (Office of the Press Secretary 2012).

In June 2012, the UN Conference on Sustainable Development (Earth Summit or Rio +20) was held in Rio de Janeiro, Brazil. The conference was organized in pursuance of General Assembly Resolution 64/236 (A/RES/64/236). It marked the 20th anniversary of the 1992 United Nations Conference on Environment and Development (UNCED), in Rio de Janeiro, and the 10th anniversary of the 2002 World Summit on Sustainable Development (WSSD) in Johannesburg. The conference was organized around two main themes: a green economy in the context of sustainable development poverty eradication; and the institutional framework for sustainable development. In preparation for the Conference, seven priority areas were identified: decent jobs, energy, sustainable cities, food security and sustainable agriculture, water, oceans and disaster readiness. The Conference produced a report and an outcome document called *The Future We Want*. The document recognized "that farmers, including small-scale farmers and fisherfolk, pastoralists and foresters, can make important contributions to sustainable development through production activities that are environmentally sound, enhance food security and the livelihood of the poor and invigorate production and sustained economic growth" (UN General Assembly 2012: para 52). The right to adequate food as a fundamental right was recognized and governments reaffirmed their commitment to enhancing food security and access to adequate, safe and nutritious food for present and future generations in line with the Five Rome Principles for Sustainable Global Food Security (UN General Assembly 2012: para 105). They also reaffirmed the important work and inclusive nature of the CFS, "including through its role in facilitating country-initiated assessments on sustainable food production and food security," and encouraged "countries to give due consideration to implementing the Committee on World Food Security Voluntary Guidelines on the Responsible Governance of Tenure of Land, Fisheries and Forests in the Context of National Food Security" (UN General Assembly 2012: para 115). They took note of the discussions on responsible agricultural investment in the framework of the CFS, as well as the principles for responsible agricultural investment.

In September 2012, the FAO held a High-Level Forum on Food Insecurity in Protracted Crisis. The Forum provided a space for consultation and policy dialogue to increase understanding and strengthen collaborative efforts among stakeholders. A key outcome of the Forum was establishing the basic elements of an Agenda for Action for Addressing Food Insecurity in Protracted Crises (CFS 2012b). The elements of an Agenda for Action and a plan for consultations and negotiations on the Agenda were then presented at the 39th Session of the Committee on World Food Security in October 2009. At the 39th Session, the Committee considered a presentation on the State of Food Insecurity in the World 2012 (SOFI), entitled "Economic Growth is Necessary but not Sufficient to Accelerate Reduction of Hunger and Malnutrition" and welcomed the new methodology for estimating hunger. The Committee considered an in-depth review and discussions of the meaning and different uses of the terms "food security," "food security and nutrition," "food and nutrition security" and "nutrition security" but came to no conclusions on which terms to use. Importantly, the CFS adopted the First Version of the Global Strategic Framework for Food Security and Nutrition, an overarching but non-binding framework and a single reference document with practical guidance on core recommendations for food security and nutrition strategies, policies and actions validated by the wide ownership, participation and consultation of the CFS.

The number of international meetings dedicated to addressing food security in the wake of the food price spikes illustrates the importance governments placed on rising food insecurity. New actors and old have been actively reshaping the architecture of global food security governance. However, policy discussion and high-level declarations do not necessarily amount to action. As the chronology of events illustrates, there is overwhelming overlap both in terms of actors and policies. Of central importance is that the CFS was approved by governments to be the foremost platform for discussions on food security and yet post-reform, actors continue to host discussions in alternate fora thereby undermining the CFS.[9]

Interconnection of multilateral actors in global food security policy

Reflecting on the interconnectedness of the main multilateral actors in global food security policy can be summed up as follows. The G8 developed the five L'Aquila Principles which were adopted as the five Rome Principles for Sustainable Global Food Security at the FAO hosted World Food Summit. At the L'Aquila Summit countries also made pledges to increase funding for food security and agriculture programs. The G20 proposed a Fund (GAFSP) to manage the pledges made by the G8. The World Bank was made the trustee of the GAFSP. The World Food Summit reinforced the reform of the CFS as the forum for discussion about food security in the UN. The UN secretary-general launched a HLTF and tasked them with developing a CFA to guide countries on food security policies. The World Bank is a member of the HLTF. The updated CFA later informed the CFS's Global Strategic Framework. The CFS included the Standing Committee on Nutrition as a member of the Advisory Group where the World Bank was already a member along with civil society actors, the private sector and the Bill and Melinda Gates Foundation. This summary illustrates a level of coherence and cooperation, but it also highlights a great deal of overlap, inefficiency and a process of decentralizing influence and focus, even after countries agreed on the function and responsibility of the reformed CFS.

Taking this analysis a step further, a careful review of key multilateral policy documents and initiatives developed by these actors to address food insecurity after the 2007–2008 food price spikes helps to map out the contemporary policy landscape. The picture that emerges is one of tensions and fragmentation:

far from the unanimous calls for improved coordination and cohesion. For example, the FAO promotes increased agricultural production while the G8 is concerned with financial markets, notably market growth. The G20 provides a broader perspective and extends beyond, or at the very least dampens, the market-driven imperialism of the G8, showing greater awareness of and for the challenges of emerging markets, highlighting the need for not just investment but also financial support in their policy proposals and directives. The World Bank is focused on poverty, presenting agriculture and food security as a way of reducing poverty. Following from this, it is noted that across the transnational policy space, the means and the ends of the policy frameworks differ. For the World Bank agriculture and food security are the means to reducing poverty. For the G8, food security supports stable markets while in turn stable markets support food security.

Understanding the various ways that food security is understood and enacted at the global level provides insight into the future direction of food security and allows for better understanding of the current phase or era in policy development. What it also illustrates is that when compared to other actors seeking leadership of global food security governance, CFS stands apart. The structure of the reformed Committee and the commitment of actors opens up spaces for new ideas which is in turn supported by a wide acceptance of "learning by doing." The CFS's commitment to discussion and the inclusive nature of these discussions, opens up the dialogue and provides space for contestation of assumptions and the introduction of alternatives.

Conclusion

Since the mid-1980s food security has been deeply embedded within a neoliberal logic. Prior to the 2007–2008 food price and financial crises, it was perhaps more easily argued that food security and price stability could be assured by way of trade liberalization. However, the price spikes illustrated the inelasticity of the market and its capacity to adapt when challenged. In practice, the 2007–2008 food price crisis placed the global food and financial system under pressure and the poor ended up being the release valves. The large number of high-level meetings devoted to addressing food security in the wake of the food price spikes suggests that governments and international organizations have an interest in food security. Moreover, the outcomes of these meetings point to a shift in "business as usual." Alongside the key themes outlined above, there is growing awareness and commitment to acknowledging and supporting small-scale farmers and women alongside recognition of the importance of agricultural development and food production in developing countries. There has been a clear discursive shift, followed by various levels of activity related to engagement of multiple stakeholders, including civil society (Duncan and Barling 2012; Lang and Barling 2012; McKeon 2009a, 2009b). Yet the most powerful actors maintain a commitment to market-oriented strategies that protect neoliberal objectives.

Examining the international reaction to the food price spikes, it becomes clear that there has not been a shift to a new era of food security and nor has there been an emergence of a new paradigm. However, food security policy discourse is increasingly contested terrain and multiple actors are now seeking out ways to redefine it. Reflecting back on the theoretical framework, some (notably the G8 and the World Bank) are seeking to maintain status quo while offering up small concessions (e.g., gender-sensitive approaches, a focus on smallholders, public–private investment programs). Others (e.g., food social movements) are pushing for structural-level changes and challenging neoliberal assumptions. As the following chapters will show, the CFS is one location where these debates are playing out. Through an examination of the reformed CFS, we can ask whether the inclusion of new actors provides new ways to meaningfully challenge hegemony, or is the reformed CFS an example of a concession: a minor course diversion to accommodate critique, like a ship that alters its course to avoid rough waters, never losing sight of its destination?

Notes

1 Note that this is not a complete list of actors engaged in the entire spectrum of the food security cycle, especially the involvement of the private sector (Ahmad 2011:2).
2 More than 200 definitions and at least 450 indicators for food security have been presented (Mechlem 2004; Sage 2002; Maxwell 1996).
3 To be historically accurate, the focus here is on "modern" food policy discourse on food security. Arguably, Western debate begins at a serious level with Joseph Malthus's (1798) essay on the *Principle of Population*. James Vernon (2007) goes back even further in his review.
4 The countries were: Australia, Belgium, Bolivia, Brazil, Canada, Chile, China, Colombia, Costa Rica, Cuba, Czechoslovakia, Dominican Republic, Ecuador, Egypt, El Salvador, Ethiopia, France, Great Britain, Greece, Guatemala, Haiti, Honduras, Iceland, India, Iran, Iraq, Liberia, Luxembourg, Mexico, Netherlands, New Zealand, Nicaragua, Norway, Panama, Paraguay, Peru, Philippines, Poland, Union of South Africa, Union of Soviet Socialist Republics, United States of America, Uruguay, Venezuela and Yugoslavia. In addition, an official from Denmark was present in a personal capacity (FAO 1981).
5 Remarkably, discussions of decolonization are absent in the bulk of the literature on food security, but are referenced in food regime literature (e.g. Friedmann and McMichael 1989).
6 The council is made up of familiar individuals such as David Nabarro, chair of the UN High Level Task Force on the Food Crisis; Jane Kakuru, president of the Alliance for a Green Revolution in Africa; Kanayo Nwanze, president of the International Fund for Agricultural Development; Shenggen Fan, Director-General of the International Food Policy Research Institute; Kavita Prakash-Mani, head of Food Security, Syngenta.
7 The Rome-based agencies are the three UN food-related agencies headquartered in Rome: FAO, IFAD and WFP. These three organizations have a history of collaborating on projects that share their overlapping mandate of working towards eliminating hunger and poverty. Together, the Rome-based Agencies coordinate over 400 activities involving more than 70 countries. During serious food emergencies, FAO and the WFP jointly carry out Crop and Food Security Assessment Missions (CFSAMs) that aim to distribute reliable information to inform policy and action. When food prices started to rise, the FAO and WFP began collaborating on a Global Information Early Warning System on

Food and Agriculture (GIEWS), with the intension of ensuring continuous review of the world food situation, to share information to this effect and to provide early warning of possible food crises at the country level.

8 As explained below, this is somewhat addressed with the strengthening of the G20.

9 Given the large number of actors, meetings, initiatives and policy outcomes to emerge in reaction to the food price spikes, a decision was made to focus on multilateral actors. This research thus concentrated on the policies of the following actors: HLTF, the World Bank Group, the G8, the G20, FAO and CFS.

References

Ahmad, M. 2011. *Improving the International Governance of Food Security and Trade* (Issue paper). Geneva: ICTSD. Retrieved from (http://ictsd.org/i/publications/114288/).

Carolan, M. S. 2013. *Reclaiming Food Security.* New York: Routledge.

CFS. 2012a. *Coming to Terms with Terminology (revised Draft 25 July).* Rome: CFS.

CFS. 2012b. *High Level Expert Forum on Addressing Food Insecurity in Protracted Crises.* Rome: CFS. Retrieved (www.fao.org/fileadmin/templates/cfs_high_level_forum/documents/REPORT_HLEF.pdf).

Clay, E. 1997. *Food Security: A Staus Review of the Literature.* Research Report No. R5911. London: ESCOR.

DEFRA. 2010. *The 2007/8 Agricultural Price Spikes: Causes and Policy Implications.* London: DEFRA.

Destler, I. M. 1978. "United States Food Policy 1972–1976: Reconciling Domestic and International Objectives." *International Organization* 32(3):617–653.

Devereux, S. 2001. "Sen's Entitlement Approach: Critiques and Counter-Critiques." *Oxford Development Studies* 29(3):245–63.

Devereux, S., and S. Maxwell. 2001. *Food Security in Sub-Saharan Africa.* London: ITDG.

Duncan, J., and D. Barling. 2012. "Renewal through Participation in Global Food Security Governance: Implementing the International Food Security and Nutrition Civil Society Mechanism to the Committee on World Food Security." *International Journal of Sociology of Agriculture and Food* 19:143–61.

ECOSOC. 2008. *Statement of the President of the Economic and Social Council on the Occasion of the Special Meeting of the Council on the Global Food Crisis.* New York: ECOSOC. Retrieved (http://daccess-dds-ny.un.org/doc/UNDOC/GEN/N08/374/74/PDF/N0837474.pdf?OpenElement).

Fan, S., and N. Rao. 2003. *Public Spending in Developing in Developing Countries: Trends, Determination and Impact.* EPTD Discussion Paper No. 99. Retrieved (http://people.umass.edu/econ797f/Syllabus and Readings/Readings/Gender/govspending.strcadj.pdf).

FAO. 1945. *Constitution of the United Nations Food and Agriculture Organization.* Quebec: FAO. Retrieved (www.jus.uio.no/english/services/library/treaties/14/14-01/food-organization.xml).

FAO. 1974. *Report of the 64th Session of the Council of the FAO.* Rome: FAO. Retrieved (www.fao.org/docrep/meeting/007/F5340E/F5340E03.htm).

FAO. 1981. *FAO: Its Origins, Formation and Evolution 1945–1981.* Rome: FAO. Retrieved (www.fao.org/docrep/009/p4228e/p4228e00.htm).

FAO. 1983. *Resolution 2/83 on World Food Security: Report of the Conference of the FAO, Twenty Second Session (5–23 November).* Rome: FAO.

FAO. 1985. *Report of the Tenth Session of the Committee on World Food Security.* Rome: FAO. Retrieved (www.fao.org/docrep/meeting/011/ag411e/AG411E03.htm#fn5).

FAO. 1992. *World Declaration on Nutrition*. Rome: FAO. Retrieved (ftp://ftp.fao.org/es/esn/nutrition/ICN/ICNCONTS.HTM).

FAO. 1994a. *Assessment of the Current World Food Situation and Recent Policy Developments*. Rome: FAO.

FAO. 1994b. *Director General's Statement to the One Hundred and Sixth Session of the Council*. Rome: FAO.

FAO. 1996. *World Food Summit Plan of Action*. Rome: FAO. Retrieved (www.fao.org/docrep/003/w3613e/w3613e00.htm).

FAO. 2006. *Food Security: Policy Brief*. Rome: FAO. Retrieved (ftp://ftp.fao.org/es/ESA/policybriefs/pb_02.pdf).

FAO. 2009. *Declaration of the World Summit on Food Security*. Rome: FAO.

FAO. 2012a. *The State of Food Insecurity in the World 2012: Key Messages*. Rome: FAO.

FAO. 2012b. *Thirty-Second FAO Regional Conference for Latin America and the Caribbean*. Buenos Aires: FAO.

FAO, IFAD, UNCTAD and World Bank. 2010. *Principles for Responsible Agricultural Investment That Respects Rights, Livelihoods and Resources: Extended Version (January 25)*. Rome. Retrieved (http://siteresources.worldbank.org/INTARD/214574-1111138388661/22453321/Principles_Extended.pdf).

Friedmann, H., and P. McMichael. 1989. "Agriculture and the State System: The Rise and Fall of National Agricultures, 1870 to the Present." *Sociologia Ruralis* 29(2):93–117.

G8. 2008. *G8 Leaders Statement on Global Food Security*. L'Aquila: G8.

G8. 2009. *"L'Aquila" Joint Statement on Global Food Security*. L'Aquila: G8. Retrieved (www.g8italia2009.it/static/G8_Allegato/LAquila_Joint_Statement_on_Global_Food_Security[1],0.pdf).

G20. 2009. *The Pittsburgh Summit: Partnering on Food Security*. Pittsburgh: G20. Retrieved (www.whitehouse.gov/files/documents/g20/Pittsburgh_Fact_Sheet_Food_Security.pdf).

Gamson, W. A. 1995. "Constructing Social Protest," pp. 85–106 in vol. 4, *Social Movements and Culture: Social Movements, Protest and Contention*, edited by H. Johnston and B. Klandermans. Minneapolis, MN: University of Minnesota Press.

Goffman, E. 1974. *Frame Analysis: An Essay on the Organization of Experience*. New York: Harper Colophon Books.

Gonzalez, C. 2007. *Markets, Monocultures, and Malnutrition: Agricultural Trade Policy through an Environmental Justice Lens*. Washington DC. Retrieved (www.progressivereform.net/articles/Gonzalez_702.pdf).

Headley, D., and S. Fan. 2010. *Reflections on the Global Food Crisis: How Did It Happen? How Has It Hurt? How Can We Prevent the next One?* Retrieved (www.ifpri.org/sites/default/files/publications/rr165.pdf).

Hewitt de Alcantra, C. 1993. *Real Markets: Social and Political Issues of Food Policy Reform*. London: Routledge.

High Level Task Force on the Global Food Security Crisis. 2010. *Updated Comprehensive Framework for Action*. New York: United Nations.

Hopkins, R. F., and D. Puchala. 1978. "Perspectives on the International Relations of Food." *International Organization* 32(3):581–616.

Johnson, D. G. 1975. "World Agriculture, Commodity Policy, and Price Variability." *American Journal of Agricultural Economics* 57:823–28.

Lang, T., and D. Barling. 2012. "Nutrition and Sustainability: An Emerging Food Policy Discourse." *The Proceedings of the Nutrition Society* (March):1–12. Retrieved (www.ncbi.nlm.nih.gov/pubmed/23217475).

Lang, T., and M. Heasman. 2004. *Food Wars: Public Health and the Battle for Mouths, Minds and Markets.* London: Earthscan.

Lang, T., D. Barling, and M. Caraher. 2009. *Food Policy: Integrating Health, Environment and Society.* Oxford: Oxford University Press.

Loewenson, R. 1993. "Structural Adjustment and Health Policy in Africa." *International Journal of Health Services* 23(4):717–30.

Malthus, J. 1798. *An Essay on the Principle of Population.* London: J. Johnson (Liberty Fund). Retrieved (www.econlib.org/library/Malthus/malPop.html).

Maxwell, S. 1996. "Food Security: A Post-Modern Perspective." *Food Policy* 21(2):155–70.

Maxwell, S., and R. Slater. 2003. "Food Policy Old and New." *Development Policy Review* 21(5/6). Retrieved (www.odi.org.uk/sites/odi.org.uk/files/odi-assets/publications-opinion-files/1862.pdf).

McDonald, B. L. 2010. *Food Security.* Cambridge: Polity.

McKeon, N. 2009a. *The United Nations and Civil Society: Legitmating Global Governance – Whose Voice?* London: Zed Books.

McKeon, N. 2009b. "Who Speaks for Peasants? Civil Society , Social Movements and the Global Governance of Food and Agriculture." *Interface* 1(2):48–82.

McKeon, N. 2011. *Global Governance for World Food Security: A Scorecard Four Years After the Eruption of the "Food Crisis."* Berlin: Heinrich-Böll-Stiftung.

Mechlem, K. 2004. "Food Security and the Right to Food in the Discourse of the United Nations." *European Law Journal* 10(5):631–48.

Mooney, P., and S. Hunt. 2009. "Food Security: The Elaboration of Contested Claims to a Consensus Frame." *Rural Sociology* 74(4):469–97.

Office of the Press Secretary. 2012. *Fact Sheet: G-8 Action on Food Security and Nutrition.* Washington DC. Retrieved (www.whitehouse.gov/the-press-office/2012/05/18/fact-sheet-g-8-action-food-security-and-nutrition).

Ojala, E. M. 1973. "World Food Security," p. 7 in *National Agricultural Outlook Conference, Washington, DC (USA), 17–19 Dec.* Rome.

Sage, C. 2002. "Food Security." pp. 128–53 in *Human Security and the Environment—International Comparisons*, edited by E. Page and M. Redcliff. Northampton, MA: Edward Elgar.

Sen, A. 1981. *Poverty and Famines: An Essay on Entitlement and Deprivation.* Oxford: Clarendon Press.

Sen, A. 1984. *Resources, Values and Developments.* Oxford: Basil Blackwell.

Shaw, D. J. 2007. *World Food Security: A History since 1945.* New York: Palgrave Macmillan.

Snow, D. A., and S. C. Byrd. 2007. "Ideology, Framing Process, and Islamic Terrorist Movement." *Mobilization: An International Quarterly Review* 12(1):119–36.

Stevenson, G. W., K. Ruhf, S. Lezberg, and K. Clancy. 2007. "Warrier, Builder, and Weaver Work," pp. 33–64 in *Remaking the North American Food System: Strategies for Sustainability*, edited by C. C. Hinrichs and T. A. Lyson. Lincoln, NE: University of Nebraska Press.

UN. 1947. "The Food and Agriculture Organization of the United Nations," in *Yearbook of the United Nations.* New York: United Nations. Retrieved (http://unyearbook.un.org/1946-47YUN/1946-47_P2_CH2.pdf).

UN. 1975. *Report of the World Food Conference (November 5–16).* New York: UN.

UN. 2013. "Decolonization." *Global Issues.* Retrieved (www.un.org/en/globalissues/decolonization/).

UN General Assembly. 2012. *The Future We Want (A/RES/66/288*).* New York: UN.

Uvin, P. 1994. *The International Organization of Hunger.* London: Kegan Paul International.

Vernon, J. 2007. *Hunger*. Cambridge, MA: Harvard University Press.

Wise, T. A. 2009. "Promise or Pitfall? The Limited Gains from Agricultural Trade Liberalisation for Developing Countries." *Journal of Peasant Studies* 36(4):855–70. Retrieved (www.tandfonline.com/doi/abs/10.1080/03066150903354056).

Wise, T. and S. Murphy. 2012. *Resolving the Food Crisis: Assessing Global Policy Reforms Since 2007*. Medford, MA: Global Development and Environment Institute (GDEI). Retrieved (http://iatp.org/files/2012_01_17_ResolvingFoodCrisis_SM_TW.pdf).

World Bank. 1986. *Poverty and Hunger: Issues and Options for Food Security in Developing Countries*. Washington DC: World Bank.

World Bank. 2011. *Food Crisis: What the World Bank Is Doing*. Washington DC: World Bank. Retrieved (www.worldbank.org/foodcrisis/bankinitiatives.htm).

4 The reform of the Committee on World Food Security

Introduction

In October 2009, Jacques Diouf, then Director-General of the FAO, declared that "[t]he food crisis of 2007–2008 highlighted the inadequacy of current governance of world food security" (CFS 2009b:12). His comments reflected growing consensus: amid all the changes and new initiatives launched in response to the 2007–2008 food price crisis, there was widespread recognition of the need for enhanced governance and coordination around global food security policy (CFS 2009b, 2012b; De Schutter 2012; Duncan and Barling 2012; European Commission 2010; FAO 2009b, 2012; G20 2009; G8 2008, 2009; IFPRI 2013; Macmillan and de Haen 2010; McKeon 2011). There was no consensus however on what form this coordination should take. Two approaches emerged as the most likely contenders: a new Global Partnership for Agriculture, Food Security and Nutrition; and the reformed CFS.

The idea for a Global Partnership was presented in June 2008 at the High-Level Conference on World Food Security at the FAO in Rome. Here, the president of the French Republic proposed the idea of a Global Partnership for Agriculture, Food Security and Nutrition based on three pillars: governance, knowledge and finance. The Global Partnership, it was argued, would insure "coherence among policies that have an impact on food security, mobilising expertise and research to ensure food security and reversing the downward trend of food security funding" (République Française 2010:3).

The idea was refined and presented to the Madrid High-Level Meeting on Food Security for All (January 2009). At the meeting participants "agreed on the importance of an inclusive and broad process of consultation on options leading to the establishment of a Global Partnership for Agriculture, Food Security and Nutrition, which starts at the Madrid High Level Meeting" (UN 2009). The High-Level Meeting in Madrid represented a break between, on the one hand, the G8/G20 and UN in New York pushing to have the HLTF as the primary body to address the crisis, and on the other hand, the FAO and other Rome-based food agencies, acting with the support of some states and civil society, pushing for participatory processes and the reform of existing organizations.

In a statement at the closing plenary, CSOs expressed their opposition to the Global Partnership, citing the lack of consultation and consensus. Many CSOs rejected the entire process and saw it as a strategic move by wealthy countries and private interests to usurp power and legitimacy from a parallel process of reforming the UN CFS. There was also concern that the Global Partnership did not build on existing institutions but instead created new ones: a move that contradicted calls to improve coordination and coherence. This sentiment was evident in a statement made to the plenary by Louis Michel, the EC development commissioner: "We should not reinvent the wheel: we do not need new mechanisms."

Seven months later, in July 2009, at their Summit in L'Aquila, Italy, the G8 pledged to advance "the implementation of the Global Partnership for Agriculture and Food Security" consistent with their "other actions aimed at an improved global governance for food security" (G8 2009: para 9). They continued that the mission of the Global Partnership would include "enhancing cooperation in achieving global food security, promoting better coordination at the country level and ensuring that local and regional interests are duly voiced and considered" (G8 2009: para 9). It is interesting to note that "nutrition" had been dropped from the title of the Global Partnership.

In the Declaration of the World Summit on Food Security (November 2009), delegates voiced support for the G8's initiative with a decision to join "efforts and expertise to work in the Global Partnership for Agriculture, Food Security and Nutrition—building on existing structures to enhance governance and cooperation—promote better coordination at global, regional and national levels and ensure that national and regional interests are duly voiced and considered" (FAO 2009a: para 7.2). However, many continued to reject the Global Partnership and pushed instead for the international community to do what the Global Partnership was claiming it wanted to do and make use of existing institutions, notably, the CFS.

The CFS is a forum in the UN System for review and follow-up of food security policies. Weeks prior to the World Summit on Food Security, intergovernmental agreement among the 123 member states had been reached: the CFS would reform to position itself as the foremost international forum for dealing with food security and nutrition. The Committee had adopted a Reform Document that aimed to restructure the CFS so that it could "fully play its vital role in the area of food security and nutrition, including international coordination" (CFS 2009b: Appendix H, para 2).

The reform was risky as the FAO, and by extension related committees, were already struggling to prove their relevance in a changing world. The Independent External Evaluation of the FAO had noted that the FAO's role in global governance had been reduced in part due to "the entry of new institutional actors and the rise in competition, as well as an ascendant tendency of the political work of the UN (UN New York) over the more technocratic specialized agency fora" (FAO 2007: para 689). This was before the Director-General of the FAO declared that one of the main reasons why "the CFS has been unable to fully accomplish its mission of monitoring food security" was due to a lack of "authority to evaluate and coordinate policies affecting world food security, in particular as regards production, agroindustry, trade, social safety nets and financing" (CFS 2009b:12).

In a bid to remain relevant, the new vision of the CFS was reframed around participation, coordination, and being a key player in the emerging architecture of global food security governance:

> The reformed CFS as a central component of the evolving Global Partnership for Agriculture, Food Security and Nutrition will constitute the foremost inclusive international and intergovernmental platform for a broad range of committed stakeholders to work together in a coordinated manner and in support of country-led processes towards the elimination of hunger and ensuring food security and nutrition for all human beings.
>
> (CFS 2009b: para 4)

Declaring the ambition of the reformed CFS to constitute "the" foremost platform was a highly political move. As one negotiator from a G20 country explained:

> The negotiations between "the" and "a"—"the foremost" or "a foremost"—was huge and [some countries] couldn't accept "the," never. Perhaps they are now saying "the" just in their speech, but we have moved beyond that, because what other platform is there? There is no alternative unless we work with the institutions we have.
>
> (Interview, October 2011, Rome)

The role of the CFS and its level of influence remain contested, but there is growing recognition that the reformed CFS is *the* international platform for the discussion and coordination of food security policy. The G8 stated its support for the "fundamental" reform process in the 'L'Aquila' Joint Statement on Global Food Security. The Declaration from the first meeting of G20 agriculture ministers expressed a commitment to work closely with the CFS to promote greater policy convergence and strengthen policy linkages at the global level (G20 2011). The UN Conference on Sustainable Development (Rio+20) negotiated outcome document, *The Future We Want*, reaffirmed: "the important work and inclusive nature of the Committee on World Food Security (CFS), including through its role in facilitating country-initiated assessments on sustainable food production and food security" (UN General Assembly 2012b: para 115). At the 67th Session of the General Assembly (December 2012), in the report on *Agriculture Development and Food Security*, the General Assembly recognized "the important role and inclusive nature of the Committee on World Food Security as a key organ in addressing the issue of global food security, including in the context of the global partnership for food security" (UN General Assembly 2012a: para 26). While admittedly a "key organ" falls short of the reform vision of being the foremost platform, the quotes above suggest that at least rhetorically, and procedurally perhaps, the CFS is increasingly recognized as the intergovernmental and international platform for coordinating international food security policies.

Despite this recognition, to say that the CFS won the battle for leadership over varied attempts (explicit and implicit) by other actors to usurp authority would be misleading and even naïve. The Global Partnership has somewhat faded from the political agenda only to be reimagined and relaunched in several different ways, for example through the G8's New Alliance for Food Security and Nutrition. A report published by the French government noted that "[m]ore can be done to modernize global food security governance" and that the "CFS reform decided in 2009 is only one step" (République Française 2010:5).

In what follows, the history and evolution of the CFS is reviewed, from its inception at the 1974 World Food Conference through to its reform. The rationale for the reform and the process of consultation and planning that led to the reform are then presented in detail. Following this, the organization of the reformed CFS is discussed with particular attention given to the actors that make up the Committee, including the roles and responsibilities secured by new categories of participants. To conclude, a review of key post-reform activities sheds light onto the operation of the reformed CFS.

History of the Committee on World Food Security

Original structure and mandate: Pre-reform (1974–2008)

The early 1970s were hit by world food crisis that prompted the organiza-tion of the 1974 World Food Conference. Upon recommendation of that Conference, the following year the CFS was established as a Committee of the Council at the Eighteenth Session of the FAO Conference (1975, Resolution 21/75). At the Conference member states:

> agreed on the need to establish a Committee on World Food Security as a standing committee of the Council, in order to provide a forum for regular intergovernmental consultations and to carry out the functions proposed by the World Food Conference ... The new Committee should, inter alia, keep under review the progress achieved towards an effective international grains arrangement and the degree to which it was likely to accelerate implementa-tion of the principles of the Undertaking. The Conference also recommended that at its first session the Committee on World Food Security review the actions being taken by interested governments to implement the Undertaking [on World Food Security] as well as the further steps required.
> (FAO 1975:IV.43)

The CFS was thus originally envisioned not only as a forum for consultation but was also tasked with a monitoring function through the review of the international grains arrangement, as well as policies supporting the International Undertaking on World Food Security including: current and prospective demand; supply and stock position for basic foodstuffs; periodically evaluating the adequacy of current and prospective stock levels in exporting and importing countries; and reviewing steps taken by governments to implement the Undertaking.

The constitution of the FAO further described the role of the CFS as being to assist the FAO conference. While the Terms of Reference and composition of the CFS were also to be governed by the FAO Conference, the CFS was to be to report to the FAO Conference and to the UN General Assembly, through ECOSOC (Article III.9). The reporting to the UN General Assembly is important as it extends the mandate and reach of the CFS beyond the FAO. However, although the CFS reports to the FAO Conference through the FAO Council, it is not a technical committee of the Council (FAO 2007:170).

At its inception, the CFS was designed as a Category 1 governing and statutory body, meaning that it hosts intergovernmental meetings to which member governments send official delegations. The Terms of Reference of the Committee are outlined in Rule XXXIII of the General Rules of the Organization. The points that make up the rule were laid out in 1976.[1] The Rule clarified that the CFS would be open to all member nations of the FAO and UN and states wishing to become members of the CFS needed to notify the Director-General in writing of their intention to participate in the work of the Committee. Rule XXXIII also stipulates that consultants may be used by FAO to assist the Secretariat in various ways, including the introduction of agenda items. In accordance with the General Rules of the FAO and with the "Principles" set out in Volume II of the Basic Texts, meetings of the CFS could be attended by observers from member nations, non-member nations and international intergovernmental organizations and NGOs having established relations with the FAO.

In 1997, in an attempt to modernize its Terms of Reference and respond to changes in the institutional organization of the UN system, the Committee amended its General Rules of the Organization. For example, the 1975 version notes that:

> 5. The Committee shall: a) Keep the current and prospective demand, supply and stock position for basic foodstuffs under continuous review, in the context of world food security, and disseminate timely information on developments; b) Make periodic evaluations of the adequacy of current and prospective stock levels, in aggregate, in exporting end 'importing countries, in order to assure a regular flow of basic foodstuffs to meet requirements in domestic and world markets, including food aid requirements, in time of short crops and serious crop failure; c) Review the steps taken by governments to implement the international Undertaking on World Food Security; and d) Recommend such short-term and longer-term policy action as may be considered necessary to remedy any difficulty foreseen in assuring adequate cereal supplies for minimum world food security.
>
> (FAO 1975: para 351)

This changed in 1997 to read:

> 5. The Committee shall contribute to promoting the objective of world food security with the aim of ensuring that all people, at all times, have physical and economic access to sufficient, safe and nutritious food to meet their dietary needs and food preferences for an active and healthy life.
>
> (FAO 1997: Rule XXXIII.5)

In the revised Rules, the monitoring and evaluation functions of the Committee were dropped along with requirements to report to the World Food Council and to encourage the participation of the International Wheat Council. Instead the CSF was to provide regular reports to ECOSOC, to work more closely with the other Rome-based food agencies and "invite relevant international organizations to participate in the work of the Committee and the preparation of meeting documents on matters within their respective mandates in collaboration with the secretariat of the Committee" (FAO 1997: Rule XXXIII.12).

Other changes to the Rule placed emphasis on the CFS:

> as a forum in the United Nations system for review and follow-up of policies concerning world food security [that will] in particular examine major problems and issues affecting the world food situation, examine the implications for world food security relating to the supply and demand of basic food stuffs and food aid and recommend such action as may be appropriate to promote the goal of world food security.
>
> (FAO 1997: Rule XXXIII.6)

Whereas the CFS was originally meant review the steps taken by governments to implement the International Undertaking on World Food Security, after 1996 the focus of the Committee shifted to monitoring the implementation of the Plan of Action adopted by the World Food Summit in accordance with the relevant commitment of the Summit.

Reforming the CFS

Until the reform, the CFS played a relatively minor role in international politics and was generally ineffective and inactive due to a lack of interest and buy-in from member states and an insufficient budget (Shaw 2007). The *Report of the Independent External Evaluation of the FAO* warned that the:

> monitoring process through the Committee on World Food Security (CFS) and the Flagship publication, the "State of Food Insecurity in the World," served to maintain some focus on the subject, although the direct monitoring process in the CFS is beginning to lose impetus.
>
> (FAO 2007:82)

Echoing these sentiments and going a step further, the Director-General of the FAO noted that despite "its intergovernmental nature as a forum of sovereign States, its universal composition and its neutrality" (CFS 2009b:13), there were at least five reasons why the CFS failed in its mission to monitor food security:

1   The Committee lacked a high-level international policy-making body in the sectors of international cooperation and of food and agriculture;
2   It did not have an integrated framework for short, medium, or long-term scientific advice;
3   It lacked the authority to evaluate and coordinate policies affecting world food security, notably with regards to production, agroindustry, trade, social safety nets and financing;
4   The Committee lacked an effective mechanism to follow-up on food security decisions and actions taken at national and regional level; and,
5   It lacked the financial resources needed to carry out its mandate.

In October 2008, faced with a growing food security crisis, a history of ineffectiveness, limited authority and the threat of becoming increasingly irrelevant in a changing architecture of global food security governance, the CFS launched a reform process that would move it away from a monitoring and follow-up body and reposition it as the most inclusive international and intergovernmental platform to ensure food security and nutrition for all (CFS 2009a). The FAO Council considered "the CFS reform to be crucial to the governance of world food security, with a view toward exploring synergies with the emerging Global Partnership for Agriculture, Food Security and Nutrition" (FAO 2009c: para 29).

When questioned about where the mandate for reforming the CFS came from, a negotiator involved in the reform process explained:

> The mandate came from the CFS itself, the previous one, after the food crisis. So the food crisis was the start, and there was talk within the EU and Sarkozy, the French President and others, about that so-called global partnership, that no one quite knew what it was, and there was ... a resistance on the part of many G77 countries, and from FAO itself. They were feeling estranged by this talk of global partnership. And they said, look, you can do a global partnership for agriculture and food security, but we have an organization called Food and Agriculture here and everything should be done inside its premises, and look we have the Committee on Food Security. So it was the first defensive answer by FAO, led by FAO and fought for the developing countries.
>
> (Interview, October 2011, Rome)

The CFS specifically referenced rising hunger, weak performance and the need to "fully play its vital role in the area of food security and nutrition, including international coordination" as key motivations (CFS 2009a: para 2). Alongside these factors, it is important to recognize that the seeds of reform had been planted well before the food price spikes. Consider that the process of reforming the CFS was further facilitated "by the fact that the member states of the FAO were just emerging from an extensive process to reform the FAO itself, and were, therefore, 'reform ready'" (Brem-Wilson 2014:5). Furthermore, as will be reviewed in Chapter 5, CSOs had spent well over a decade lobbying for reform.[2]

When the decision was made to reform the CFS, a Contact Group was established by the CFS Bureau and tasked with developing a Reform Document. The Contact Group was structured in such a way so as to give full participation rights to CSOs. This meant that in practice CSOs had the right to table and respond to reform proposals through the Contact Group's website and to attend and intervene at meetings. Thus, from the very start, civil society participated in the reform process.

The distinction between stakeholders and participants may appear semantic but there are important political implications associated with each of these terms. Many CSOs engaged in the CFS reject the use of the term "stakeholder" for example, as it assumes everyone has an equal stake. It is argued that the stakes of peasant farmers and multinational corporations are not the same and to call them both stakeholders depoliticizes important differences and differentiations of power. These sentiments are captured in the response of one NGO actor when asked if the engagement of civil society and private sector actors in CFS could be a model for enhanced participation in other multilateral organizations:

> I don't think that it can be taken as automatically a good thing. I am aware that in other contexts, like health, the use of the term multi-stakeholder forum, has come to be understood in a very negative way, meaning: a) abdication of the responsibility of the state; b) enabling businesses, and NGO-facades for businesses, to engage in processes ... Some have argued that it is better to have private sector in the room and not states parroting for the private sector. Now the private sector and the US say the same thing. It is in your face. It is obvious to everybody.
>
> There has been great value to the reform of the CFS. And it is supportive of democracy. But it needs to be done in a way that is aware of power imbalance and retain the assertion that the buck stops with the state and that the state is not just one stakeholder amongst the others. They have responsibility to their people and they should not abdicate their duties and responsibilities in the name of a stakeholder platform. You cannot just bring stakeholders together and assume this is participation. You have to recognise and address power imbalances.
>
> (Interview, June 2014, Skype)

In the organization of participation in the Contact Group and later the Advisory Group, there was recognition of these power imbalances. This is discussed in more detail below.

Work within the Contact Group was divided across four Working Groups which focused on key sections of the reform process: role and vision of the renewed CFS; membership and decision making; mechanisms and procedures; and a High Level Panel of Experts. The Contact Group met in person a total of seven times between their first meeting in April 2009 and the adoption of the Reform Document in October 2009. They also communicated online. Over these months, the Reform Document went through a number of drafts.

In October 2009, at the 35th Session of the CFS, the then 123 member countries approved the final version of the Reform Document, thereby agreeing to reform the Committee with the aim of making it:

> the foremost inclusive international and intergovernmental platform for a broad range of committed stakeholders to work together in a coordinated manner and in support of country-led processes towards the elimination of hunger and ensuring food security and nutrition for all human beings.
> (CFS 2009a: para 4)

The Reform Document outlined specific terms of reference for the Committee on World Food Security designed to roll out in two phases.[3] Phase I concerned coordination at the global level, policy convergence and support for countries and regions. The goal was to ensure that the CFS:

> provide a platform for discussion and coordination to strengthen collaborative action among Governments, regional organizations, international organizations and agencies, NGOs, CSOs, food producers' organizations, private sector organizations, philanthropic organizations and other relevant stakeholders, in a manner that is in alignment with each country's specific context and needs.
> (CFS 2009a: para 5.i)

For Phase II the CFS was to gradually take on additional roles of national and regional level coordination by serving as a "platform to promote greater coordination and alignment of actions in the field, encourage more efficient use of resources and identify resource gaps," promote accountability and share best practices at all levels; and, develop a Global Strategic Framework for Food Security and Nutrition "to improve coordination and guide synchronized action by a wide range of stakeholders" (CFS 2009a: para 6).

In practice, the phases rolled out more organically. By 2013, the CFS had begun to share best practices through plenary presentations as well as Voluntary Guidelines, and adopted a Global Strategic Framework. Debates continue within the CFS with respect to regional and national coordination, and the scope and capacity of the CFS. The CFS has been active in the FAO regional

Table 4.1 Years and CFS session number

Year	Session number
2009	35
2010	36
2011	37
2011	38*
2012	39
2013	40
2014	41

Note: * Special session to endorse the Voluntary Guidelines on the Responsible Governance of Tenure of Land, Fisheries and Forests in the Context of National Food Security.

conferences but here is also recognition that for the CFS to be effective, the policy recommendations and guidelines endorsed by the Committee will need national- and regional-level uptake.

Key actors in the reformed CFS

The reformed CFS is made up of member states, participants and observers who in turn make up the Plenary. There is also the CFS Bureau and its Advisory Group. The CFS is further supported by the independent the High Level Panel of Experts (HLPE) and a Secretariat. The functions of each of these will be explored below.

Plenary

According to the Reform Document (CFS 2009a: para 20):

> The Plenary is the central body for decision-taking, debate, coordination, lesson-learning and convergence by all stakeholders at global level on issues pertaining to food security and nutrition and on the implementation of the Voluntary Guidelines to Support the Progressive Realization of the Right to Adequate Food in the Context of National Food Security. It should focus on relevant and specific issues related to food security and nutrition in order to provide guidance and actionable recommendations to assist all stakeholders in eradicating hunger.

The Plenary meets annually in Rome but can come together for extraordinary sessions when deemed necessary. The Plenary is made up of member states, participants, including representatives of UN agencies and bodies with

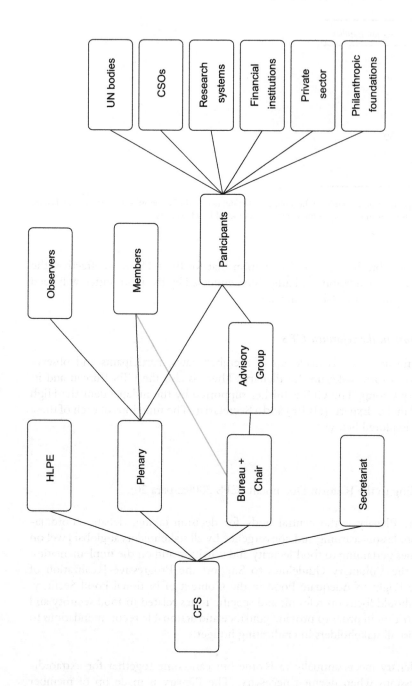

Figure 4.1 Post-reform organizational structure of the CFS

a specific mandate in the field of food security and nutrition; CSOs and their networks, with strong relevance to issues of food security and nutrition with particular attention to organizations representing smallholder family farmers, artisanal fisherfolk, herders/pastoralists, landless, urban poor, agricultural and food workers, women, youth, consumers, indigenous peoples and international NGOs; international agricultural research systems; international and regional financial institutions; and representatives of private sector associations and private philanthropic foundations active in the areas of concern to the Committee (CFS 2009a: para 11).

Member states

The membership of the Committee is open to all members states of the FAO, WFP or IFAD and non-member states of the FAO that are member states of the UN. Members of the CFS have the right to intervene in plenary and breakout discussions, approve meeting documents and agendas, submit and present documents and formal proposals and interact with the Bureau during the inter-sessional period. They also have the exclusive right to vote and take decisions, including drafting the final report of CFS Plenary sessions.

In 2013, the CFS registered 121 member states, down from 123 at the time of reform in 2009. Between 2009 and 2010, Latvia, Saint Vincent and the Grenadines and Togo left the CFS, but several countries joined, bringing the number of member nations up to 126. New countries were Central African Republic, Democratic Republic of the Condo, Djibouti, Oman, the former Yugoslav and Republic of Macedonia.

Other countries that were involved in the reform but left in the first post-reform years of the Committee were Azerbaijan, Croatia, Libyan Arab Jamahiriya, Lithuania, Mauritius, Namibia, Niger, Republic of Moldova, Serbia and Tunisia. However, many countries have joined or rejoined the CFS since 2009: Burundi, Chad, Israel, Liberia, Libya, Mauritania, Togo and Syrian Arab Republic.

Ensuring the engagement of member states is fundamental to the success of the CFS. As one leading human rights campaigner noted:

> The CFS has not demonstrated itself to be the alternative for the governments. What is the role of the CFS as a platform? It is the multiplatform space that the governments have to choose as the main mechanism to govern food security and nutrition, but if we look at the G20 and the G8 they continue to talk about the global partnership which is a process led by the private sector. The CFS needs a mandate to promote international policy coherence and they need governments to be in the seat where they can make decisions.
>
> (Interview, May 2011, Rome)

This statement was later reinforced by a representative of a large international NGO who noted "the CFS is nothing without governments" (interview, June 2012, Rome).

Member states are "encouraged to participate in Committee sessions at the highest level possible (Ministerial or cabinet level is desirable), insofar as possible representing a common, inter-ministerial governmental positions" (CFS 2009a: para 9). Ministerial engagement in the CFS has been limited but the engagement of ministers can be interpreted as a double-edged sword. While low-level political engagement in the CFS results in a host of challenges and places the CFS low on the list of political priorities, the lack of high-level engagement also gives the CFS the ability to work on more controversial issues. From observing CFS sessions it is clear that ministers come and deliver speeches, often focused on initiatives under way in their countries. This supports the CFS goal of sharing best practices but these interventions often fails to tie into the broader work under way at the CFS. These are political speeches and not contributions to discussion. The reformed CFS seeks to be a platform for discussion. Indeed, throughout the first few post-reform sessions, many diplomats presented political speeches instead of providing contributions to the discussions, however, by the 39th Session, most had begun to understand the new format and grandiose statements about local initiatives were increasingly rare. Also, negotiators reported being less able to focus on negotiations when ministers attended the CFS as priorities turned to attending to the minister.

If the CFS was to gain greater political clout it is likely that there would be increased ministerial interest and by extension, ministerial presence in Plenary. Almost paradoxically, this increased high-level interest could threaten the CFS insofar as it would likely result in a regression to political speeches, moving away from the very important, engaging and inclusive discussions that now mark Plenary. This observation and analysis was correlated by many interviews. As a negotiator from a G20 country explained:

> I think the most appropriate level for the CFS … is just under the minister level, the national secretary level that we have there [in the negotiator's country]. It's a high-level office that has the power to … these are the guys that run the government programmes. They report to their Ministers. They have a lot of capacity to sell ideas to their Ministers, if they want. They are pretty high-level, but still they don't require to be there and give general statements and that kind of thing. Whenever a Minister comes, their delegations are only worried about taking care of the Minister … so I don't think it's also healthy for it to be only the permanent representatives. I think that is also a failure. People have to come from the capital. Also, the officers involved with the policies and so on. It may be different for each country. In developing countries, maybe those who are running food security programmes. For [wealthy countries], maybe the head of the food security and development agencies.
>
> (Interview, October 2011, Rome)

When asked what role relevant ministers should play, the negotiator responded:

> The conference, the FAO conference, is political, where the ministers come. In one room, they are representing everything that comes from the sub-committees of the FAO. That is done by the same people [representing member states in the CFS]. In the other room, in the Plenary, there is scheduled of time for general statements by the ministers over the whole week.
>
> (Interview, October 2011, Rome)

Secretariat

The General Rules of the FAO (2013a: Rule XXXIII.15) note that a:

> secretary shall be appointed, in accordance with such conditions as may be established by the Committee, to serve the Committee, including the Bureau and the High-Level Panel of Experts, and to exercise liaison functions in connection with all the activities of the Committee.

The CFS Secretariat is meant to remain small and permanently located within the FAO. However, the Reform Document further stipulates:

> For the biennium 2010–2011, the Secretariat will be headed by a Secretary from FAO and include staff from the other Rome-based agencies (WFP and IFAD). Further arrangements regarding the Secretary, including possible rotation among the three Rome-based agencies, and the inclusion in the Secretariat of other UN entities directly concerned with food security and nutrition, should be decided by the CFS plenary in 2011.
>
> (CFS 2009a: para 34)

In the early post-reform years, internal discussions and letters sent to the CFS Chair suggest that the FAO was actively trying to maintain control of the Secretariat whereas the WFP was trying to gain more authority, and backing up their proposals with funding. The FAO's position, as expressed in a letter from the director general of the FAO, was that given the multidisciplinary nature of the activities of the CFS, there was a requirement of involvement from numerous FAO departments and divisions, as well as substantive and organizational contributions. Given the "exigencies of the function" of the Secretariat, the FAO argued that the secretary of the Committee be a FAO senior staff member. They further rationalized this by stating that the chair was a division director and had played a key role moving the CFS reform forward. Importantly, the FAO argued that "changing the Secretary at this juncture would be ill-advised and would not be a strategic move as it may very well jeopardize the achievements made to date" (FAO 2011).

The FAO rejected the argument for a systematic rotation of the secretary, arguing that "ownership involves primarily a common sharing of the vision and goals of the Committee, translated in common work." They continued, "a system where the Secretary would have to rotate every two years would create unnecessary discontinuity and disruption and have a negative impact on the substantive work of the Committee."

The executive director of the WFP disagreed. In her letter to the chair, she noted that the "WFP is of the opinion that the rotation of the function of the Secretary of the Committee is fully in line with the vision and the spirit of the CFS reform process."[4] She continued that the rotation of the function of CFS Secretary would "be among the next steps to complete the reform process." Noted benefits of the rotation for the WFP included further consolidation of the identity of the CFS as a central UN political platform and the addition of new perspectives to the CFS, including further emphasis on national and household food security and nutrition concerns. The WFP proposed modalities of operation for the CFS Secretariat to be reflected in a revision of the Rules of Procedures of the CFS. First, the CFS would remain physically located in FAO, as per the Reform Document, meaning that FAO would continue to provide office space. The secretary post should be full time and the WFP was willing to provide a staff member at the level of director to assume the function of the CFS secretary on a rotational basis for two years. The incumbent would be identified following WFP's internal selection procedures with the staff cost registered as in-kind contribution to the core CFS Secretariat budget. The WFP-appointed CFS secretary could manage WFP, FAO and IFAD staff who would remain the original contractual status of their respective agencies. In support of these proposals, WFP noted it was willing to increase its financial participation in the CFS to cover a third of the total CFS Secretariat operating costs, increasing their contributions from US$900,000 per biennium to around US$1.4 million for the 2012–2013 biennium.

By the 39th Session in October 2012, the CFS decided to mandate the:

> Bureau to develop the selection procedures, including the required qualifications and the terms of reference, for the position of the CFS Secretary, together with modalities and requirements for inclusion in the Secretariat of other UN entities directly concerned with food security and nutrition, with a view to submitting proposals to the Committee during its plenary session in October 2013.
>
> (CFS 2012a: para 43)

At the 40th Session (2013), the CFS endorsed the terms of reference, a revised qualifications and selection procedure for the new CFS secretary. They further endorsed the modalities and requirements for inclusion in the CFS Secretariat, through secondment of staff of other UN entities directly concerned with food security and nutrition. It was requested FAO, IFAD and WFP proceed with the process of recruiting the CFS secretary (CFS 2013b: para 61).

Bureau, Advisory Group and chair

The Bureau is the executive arm of the CFS responsible for its administration. It is made up of a chairperson and representation on the Bureau is regionally organized with members drawn from 12 member countries: two from Africa, Asia, Europe, Latin America and the Caribbean, Near East, and one from both North America and South-West Pacific.

The Advisory Group aides the Bureau to advance the objectives of the CFS, particularly to ensure linkages with stakeholders at all levels to support information exchange and provide outreach at the local level. The Advisory Group is made from representatives from UN bodies as well as four civil society representatives, one representative from international agricultural research bodies, one representative for the private sector and one representative from philanthropic bodies. Presently, the private sector is lobbying to get an equal number of seats on the Advisory Group as civil society. Their central argument has been that farmers are part of the private sector. Their attempts thus far have been unsuccessful. That CSOs were given four seats in the Advisory Group and the private sector family (i.e., private sector and philanthropic foundations) only two seats, is recognition not only of the diversity of civil society actors working on and across food security but also of the unequal distribution of power between civil society and the private sector. Recalling the discussion above about stakeholders and using CSOs to legitimize private sector participation in international fora, the distribution of seats on the Advisory Group served to reassure CSO participants that the CFS was indeed committed to it reform objective of ensuring that voices of all relevant stakeholders, particularly those most affected by food insecurity are heard in the policy debate on food and agriculture.

The role of chair has been fundamental to the success of the CFS and indeed the individuals who held the role of chair during the reform and for the first two sessions of the reformed CFS played critical roles in the evolution and success of the reformed Committee. It was the chair, alternate permanent representative of Argentina to FAO, who during the reform process, encouraged the inclusion of civil society as official participants. The chair included civil society actors in the Contact Group from the beginning. As one representative of a member state involved in the process explained:

> In the beginning of 2009 ... the new chair of the CFS ... got a mandate to reform but they didn't know where to go or what to do, and she called that meeting ... to propose to countries to create the Contact Group for the reform of the CFS ... And in the end people decided to compose this loose Contact Group that would include people from civil society, and then the precedent was set and this Contract Group moved things away from the usual bureaucracy of the FAO.
>
> (Interview, October 2011, Rome)

That chair was replaced in 2010 by an agricultural attaché and deputy permanent representative of the Republic of the Philippines, who presided over the first two sessions of the reformed CFS. This chair exemplified a deep understanding of, and respect for, process which strengthened the vulnerable Committee through its transition phase.

The importance of a strong chair was identified by many to be central to the success of the CFS, not only to ensure legitimacy but also to enhance participation. Reinforcing this observation, one diplomat noted that:

> I think finally, and most importantly, I think people are central. I think it is really, really important to have a good chair of the CFS, who not only can act as an ambassador of the CFS, but also is able to coordinate and bring these functional elements together in order so that they may work together. I think that is absolutely key ... You should have to be competent to qualify as a person who can do the job and deliver the mandate, and once to start writing out terms of reference, or a job description, you automatically start disqualifying a lot of potential candidates.
>
> (Interview, June 2012, Rome)

The chair of the first two sessions of the reformed CFS proved this. His capacity to chair was certainly enhanced by previous experiences. From 2003–2004, he served as co-chair to the Intergovernmental Working Group that formulated Voluntary Guidelines to support the progressive realization of the right to adequate food in the context of national food security. Importantly, this chair was not a diplomat or a negotiator; he was technically oriented with field experience and experience facilitating participatory processes. In 2009, he was elected to serve as the chairperson of the CFS and successfully guided the Committee through the implementation of the CFS Reform. In this capacity he enforced the new processes when members steered away and reinforced the rights of participants to engage in the process in accordance with the terms of the Reform Document.

With regards to the position of the chair, at the 39th Session of the CFS, the Committee reviewed the "Proposed Amendments to the CFS Rules of Procedure and to Rule XXXIII of the General Rules of the Organization" and proposed an amendment. By exceeding the required two-thirds majority of votes cast, the Committee approved the amendment:

> The Chairperson shall be elected for a period of two years on a rotational basis among regions and on the basis of individual qualifications and experience relevant to the mandate of CFS. He or she shall not be eligible for election for two consecutive terms in the same office. His/her term of office shall expire at the end of the Committee meeting where the elections of a new Chairperson is held.
>
> (CFS 2012a: para 41)

The results of the vote were 88 votes for, one against and zero abstentions although the member state that voted against indicated that it did so by mistake and that its intention was to vote for the amendments.

Following the new rules, a new chair was elected in 2011 at the 39th Session. The election of the ambassador and permanent representative of Nigeria to FAO as CFS chair was important insofar as it motivated many African nations to become more involved, an observation confirmed in many of the interviews. Respondents noted that country representatives are more likely to get involved in the CFS if the chair comes from their region as they feel that they will be better represented, although it is admittedly hard to substantiate this observation so early on in the process. However, when asked about participation of Asian countries in the CFS during time of the Filipino chair, a representative of an international NGO based in Rome, noted that:

> over the last few years we had a chair that was from the Philippines, so I think they [Asians] felt like they were represented. They needed … they were a bit more there, to support the chair. Now, an African is Chair and so there has been a change.
>
> (Interview, October 2012, Rome)

There was also concern, especially among CSOs, that replacing someone with technical expertise (i.e., the Filipino chair), with someone with a political mandate (i.e., the Nigerian ambassador) could threaten the fragile CFS. While it certainly shifted dynamics, the new chair did not derail or undermine the CFS. What the Nigerian chair managed to do was use diplomatic skills and rank to garner greater exposure and awareness of the CFS. In 2013, the Netherlands ambassador to the UN agencies in Rome was elected as chair.

Participants

The opening up of the CFS to include non-state actors is arguably the single most important aspect of the reform process, and indeed served to garner the most interest in the CFS. The reformed CFS is open to participants who are representatives of UN agencies and bodies with a specific mandate in the field of food security and nutrition such as FAO, IFAD, WFP, the HLTF; civil society and NGOs and their networks; international agricultural research systems; international and regional financial institutions; and representatives of private sector associations and private philanthropic foundations active in the areas of concern to the Committee.

As noted above, CSOs played an active role in the reform process and managed to secure the right to facilitate their participation in the CFS through an autonomous Civil Society Mechanism (CSM) (see Chapter 5). Their inclusion as participants on the Committee presents opportunities for more meaningful and active engagement in the procedures and debates leading up to final decision making in the CFS, while final voting authority remains with the nation-states. The term CSOs is used as an umbrella term to refer to both social movements and NGOs. NGOs are understood to be organizations that represent a specific issue or theme or the interests of certain social groups. Social movements are defined here as self-organized social actors with a shared identity that have come together to represent their own interests and in the case of the CSM live predominantly on the front line of food insecurity (Duncan and Barling 2012).[5]

The private sector also developed a mechanism outlined in a document titled *Proposal for Modalities for Private Sector Participation in the Committee for World Food Security* [sic] (CFS 2011b). The Private Sector Mechanism is open to all private sector food actors who want to participate with a particular emphasis on those active in the area of food and nutrition at any level, particularly those that represent food producers, input suppliers, agro-retailers, grain traders, food manufacturers and retailers and other actors directly involved in producing and selling.

The private sector is represented by the International Agri-Food Network, an informal coalition of international trade associations involved in the agri-food sector at the global level created in 1996. The aim of the network is to facilitate informal liaison among the professional organizations and towards international organizations in the agri-food chain at global level. Currently, one person serves as the private sector representative at the CFS. The representative has been responsible for coordinating the input business entities through the private sector mechanism, on behalf of the International Agri-food Network.

The CFS benefits from private sector engagement insofar as it demonstrates wider participation across stakeholder groups. Forty-six private sector representatives attended the 39th Session of the CFS. Yet, far from engaged in the negotiations—a responsibility delegated to the Private Sector Focal Point—they were most visible at the side events, often giving presentations.

This book is ultimately focused on the engagement of civil society actors in the CFS and not the private sector. However, it is worth noting that the private sector received support from the government of the UK for one year. In 2010, for the first session of the reformed CFS, the UK paid for the chair of the CFS to have an assistant who provided procedural support. The following year, for the 37th Session, the support to the chair was dropped in favor of a "senior private sector advisor" to the Secretariat of the CFS. The position was filled by a former consultant on private sector finance with experience working in the Trade and Markets Division of the FAO. The UK provided no support to the CSM.

However, that the UK has engaged at all in the CFS is telling. As one diplomat explained in an interview:

> The UK wasn't engaged in the CFS at all until 2010. As part of the FAO reform, [the UK] pushed very strongly for the CFS reform. And the new structure of the CFS, to be a more inclusive body, is an approach that [the UK values] a lot.
>
> (Interview, June 2012, Rome)

That said, the UK remained focused on engaging the private sector, noting that they "would like to see more contribution from the private sector." When questioned about their satisfaction with their investment, a diplomat explained:

> It was a small investment … 60,000 pounds. Yes and no. No, probably because there is a point of re-education amongst the member states to identify what the value of having the private sector there was. There is a real suspicion within the FAO of the private sector and of how to work with them, so … That was one negative. So, [the consultant] couldn't get as much traction as he wanted … But, as a positive, it put the private sector on everyone's radar.
>
> (Interview, July 2012, Rome)

The statement reflects an interesting tension within the CFS: key categories of participants believe that they experience negative bias or challenges when it comes to participating. In the above quote, the diplomat suggests that the private sector faces barriers to engagement based on perceived legitimacy. CSOs have expressed similar sentiments. Such reactions to enhanced participation are to be expected when organizational reform takes place. But the reactions also reflect the tensions that lie at the core of a hegemonic conception of embedded neoliberalism (see Chapter 2). Those advancing a neoliberal approach to food security will continue to support and push for further engagement of the private sector, while those seeking to challenge status quo may be more inclined to promote the engagement of civil society actors.

There has been widespread recognition across the CFS that because CSOs claim to represent the voices of those most affected by food insecurity, represent the largest group of food producers, and because of existing relations of power and access to resources, they should hold more seats on the CFS Advisory Group than the private sector or philanthropic foundations. However, mechanisms to enhance inclusion do not inherently ensure inclusion, both in terms of who can engage (as seen in the example of the food price volatility roundtable; see Chapter 6) but also in terms of who tries to engage. With respect to the latter, civil society and the private sector have developed mechanisms to facilitate engagement, and have been present and active in negotiations, albeit to varying degrees. The same cannot be said for philanthropic foundations.

In an interview with a diplomat it was noted:

> The last conversation I had with [a predominant Philanthropic Foundation working on Agriculture] about the CFS was very telling … They were reconsidering their engagement and assessing what the value of the CFS was. And if you have a stakeholder like [that] saying "what is the value of this body? We are not going to engage anymore," it has a political domino effect … To paraphrase their view last year, it was: "we don't need the CFS: we can do it ourselves." But their idea was that there doesn't need to be a policy coherence and coordination mechanism. Well, for them, they

think it already exists. It is an interesting way of looking at it. Also, they have got ... they attend Davos, they attend the G8, they attend the G20, and so they think there are a huge number of bodies out there trying to coordinate around agriculture, food security and nutrition and the value of the CFS only recently came out.

(Interview, July 2012, Rome)

The point is an important one and illustrates a key challenge facing the CFS: the most democratic procedures and mechanisms do not ensure highest political relevance. Indeed, when an influential actor in the global food system withdraws from the legitimate, democratic forum for discussions and sharing of best practices on food security policy, there are problems: both for the CFS, which has failed to prove its value, and with respect to the philanthropic foundation opting to ignore efforts to move towards coordinated action. Unfortunately, for reasons of time and space, this research does not delve into the complexity and changing influence of philanthropic foundations in the CFS or the multilateral transnational food security governance space. However, it recognizes that without meaningful participation from some of the world's largest donors to agriculture projects, the CFS will not be able to secure its position as the foremost inclusive platform for food security.

High Level Panel of Experts

The reform of the CFS sought to position the CFS as a decision-making committee whose decisions "gain resonance and efficiency on the ground" (HLPE 2013:1). Within intergovernmental spaces, decisions are often expected to be taken on issues where uncertainty abounds, both with respect to the knowledge base as well as the potential impacts of policies. Furthermore, with increased participation from diverse actors comes a welcomed widening of perspectives which can exacerbate already divergent positions. The Reform Document of the CFS recognized this and noted that given the multidisciplinary complexity of food security there was a need to "create synergies between world class academic/scientific knowledge, field experience, knowledge from social actors and practical application in various settings" (CFS 2009a: para 36).

Correspondingly, the CFS agreed on the need for a mechanism to provide independent, comprehensive, scientific advice. The High Level Panel of Experts for Food Security and Nutrition (HLPE) was thus created as the scientific and knowledge-based pillar of the Global Partnership for Agriculture, Food Security and Nutrition (HLPE 2013:1). It functions as the science–policy interface for the CFS.

The design of the HLPE, its rules and procedures, and the composition of the Steering Committee were decided on by the CFS. The HLPE has a two-tier structure composed of a Steering Committee of 15 internationally recognized experts in food security and nutrition-related fields. The experts were appointed by the Bureau of the CFS following a call for nominations and the review of candidatures and a proposition by an ad-hoc technical selection committee comprised of members of the FAO, WFP, IFAD, Bioversity International (for CGIAR) and a CSO representative. The Steering Committee is supported by project teams that are compiled and managed by the Steering Committee to analyze and report on specific issues. The HLPE is exclusively funded through a voluntary trust fund held in the FAO. The Fund covers the costs of the preparation of reports, Steering Committee and project team meetings, translation and publication of reports, and Secretariat support.

The themes of the reports are decided upon during the sessions of the CFS with input from all participants and the HLPE. The themes of the studies become the themes of the policy roundtables that take place during the sessions. Once the themes are decided upon, the Steering Committee compiles a project team following an open call for interest of experts, and the reports are then produced following topic and time restrictions. The work then follows clearly defined stages:

> separating the elaboration of the political question and request by the CFS, its scientific formulation by the Steering Committee, the work of the time-bound and topic-bound Project Team, external open consultations to enrich the knowledge base, and an external scientific review.
>
> (HLPE 2013:2)

The process aims to promote a scientific dialogue between the Steering Committee and project team and solicit feedback from the public throughout the project cycle. The HLPE reports to the CFS to "ensure the legitimacy and relevance of the studies undertaken, and their insertion in a concrete political agenda at international level" (HLPE 2013:2). The HLPE is independent insofar as its experts are not government appointed and their reports are not reviewed or negotiated by the CFS.

It is the unique structure of the reformed CFS governance space that allows the HLPE to operate as it does. The HLPE is a multi-actor space that addresses complex issues at the will of the CFS. The HLPE does not conduct new research. Instead, the reports are summaries of their review of existing research and knowledge with the added value of global, multisectoral and multidisciplinary analysis and recommendations. These recommendations combine the extensive literature review with grounded experience from the field. Importantly, the HLPE has a commitment to reviewing and incorporating many forms of knowledge and best practices, much of which comes from local and global experiences and best practices. This commitment extends to the Steering Committee which has a civil society representative acting as co-chairperson.

When a report is requested by the CFS, the HLPE launches a process that includes two public consultations per report. The first consultation is on the scope of the report (what the report should cover). Once a preliminary, draft version of the report (V0) is written, the HLPE again launches an online consultation.

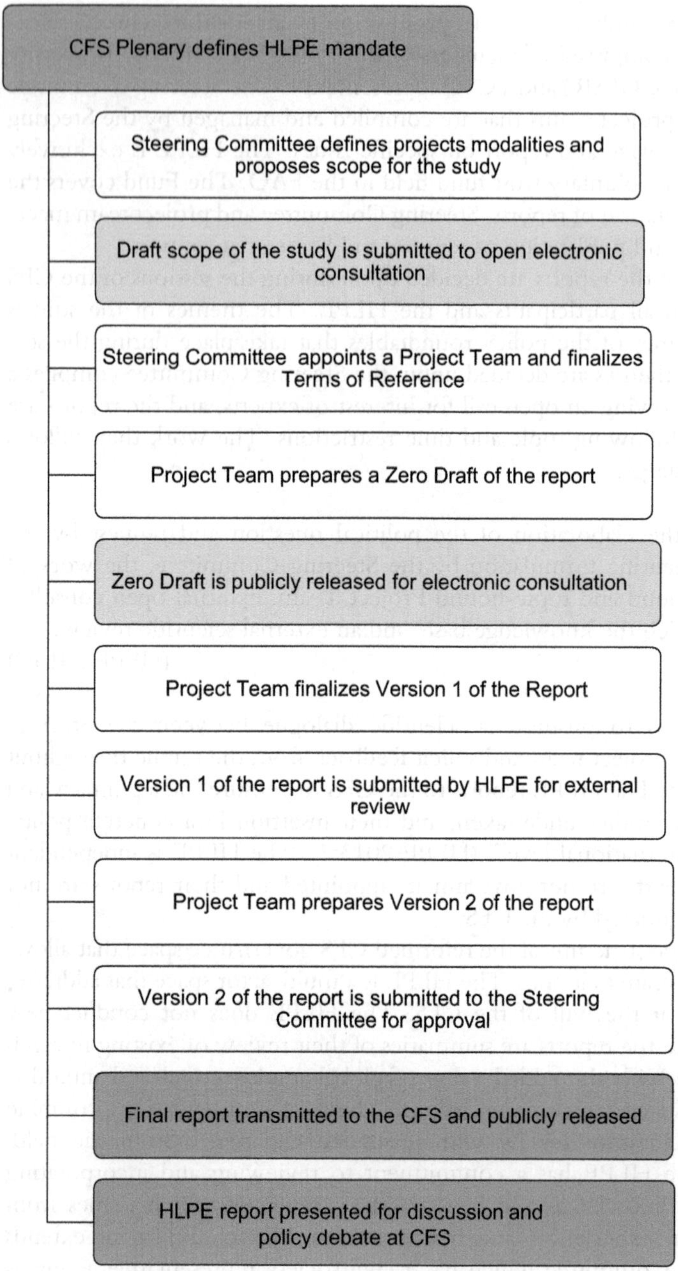

Figure 4.2 HLPE project cycle

Source: Adapted from CFS (2014)

Such processes ensure that a broader range of perspectives and knowledge-bases are taken into account in the development of the reports and contribute to the transparency and openness of the process. It is also accepted that online consultations face important limitations, most obviously that they exclude people with low literacy or non-English, French or Spanish speakers, and they exclude people who do not have access to the internet. Acknowledging these limits, given limited time and resources allotted to the HLPE, the e-consultations have served to open up the debate and the scope of scientific inquiry.

After the consultations, the HLPE Secretariat makes a summary of all input which is in turn read by the Steering Committee and the research team. Every suggestion is systematically tracked in a spreadsheet but there are no obligations for the research team to take up any of the input: the reports are not negotiated documents. The final reports are released in advance of the CFS sessions.

The reports are meant to inform policy debates and improve the quality, effectiveness and coherence of food security and nutrition policies at all levels. A member of the HLPE Steering Committee explained:

> If they [the CFS] want an effective space for global policy discussion, coordination and decision making, they need special expertise and if only left to governments to make documents, the results are very weak. The idea is that an expert panel, which is not political, may help support better decision making. This is quite unprecedented. It is not normal for a global committee to have its own expert committee and there is recognition that there are various types of expertise.
>
> (Interview, October 2010, Rome)

The HLPE has a mandate to address contentious issues. For example, on the issue of food price volatility, the CFS specifically requested that the HLPE research consider:

> All of its causes and consequences, including market distorting practices and links to financial markets, and appropriate and coherent policies, actions, tools and institutions to manage the risks linked to excessive price volatility in agriculture. This should include prevention and mitigation for vulnerable producers, and consumers, particularly the poor, women and children, that are appropriate to different levels (local, national, regional and international) and are based on a review of existing studies. The study should consider how vulnerable nations and populations can ensure access to food when volatility causes market disruptions.
>
> (HLPE 2013:9)

With respect to land tenure and international investment in agriculture, the HLPE was requested to examine the respective roles of large-scale plantations and of small-scale farming, including economic, social, gender and environmental impacts; review the existing tools allowing the mapping of available

land; and undertake a comparative analysis of tools to align large-scale investments with country food security strategies.

The HLPE is tasked with tackling contentious issues from multiple scientific
perspectives which can effectively challenge the positions of certain governments.
Correspondingly, in the first three years of the reformed CFS, the reports of the
HLPE have not always been embraced by member governments. The first indication of this came at the 37th Session when in lieu of starting from the shared
position of CFS commissioned research, the reports used in the preparation of the
background documents for the policy roundtables at the 37th Session included:

- The State of Food Insecurity in the World (SOFI) 2011 *How Does
  International Price Volatility Affect Domestic Economies and Food Security?*;
- The State of Food and Agriculture (SOFA) 2011 *Women in Agriculture:
  Closing the Gender Gap for Development*;
- The World Bank World Development Report 2012 *Gender Equality and
  Development*;
- United Nations System Standing Committee on Nutrition (2010) *Sixth
  Report on the World Nutrition Situation*;
- *Addressing High Food Prices—A Synthesis of FAO Policy Consultation at
  Regional and Sub-Regional Level*;
- *G20 Action Plan on Food Price Volatility and Agriculture*.

The inclusion of these reports as background documents can be seen in two
ways. From a positive perspective, their inclusion illustrates the scope of the
CFS and a willingness to connect with other processes advancing the CFS's
goal of improved policy cohesion. At the same time, the inclusion of non-
HLPE reports serves to devalue the work undertaken by the Committee's
own Panel of Experts and provides an example of ways in which the CFS is
undermining its own processes.

Overall, the HLPE has maintained broad support from CSOs, facilitated
in great part by the co-chair of the Steering Committee, who represents civil
society. The HLPE did however face critique by CSOs with the publication of
the report *Land Tenure and International Investment in Agriculture* (HLPE 2011)
around definitions of agro-ecology. Within Appendix 1, the report noted:

> Many processes affect crop performance, but a few have a major impact.
> They include processes helping plants use radiation, water and nutrients
> efficiently and evenly for crop growth (Monteith, 1990; Sinclair, 1990),
> those contributing to the soil water balance, and those affecting soil fer-
> tility. "Optimum growth conditions" means agro-ecological conditions
> where crops have all the water and nutrients they need for growth and
> are protected against pest, diseases and weeds. We focus on primary plant
> production as it also determines secondary animal production.
>
> (HLPE 2011:53)

The definition included in the report reflected a productionist approach and CSOs worried that the definition included in the report could be easily applied to industrial modes of production that did not uphold agro-ecological principles. In response, CSOs challenged this definition of agro-ecology, arguing instead that the definitions outlined in the *International Assessment of Agricultural Knowledge, Science and Technology for Development* (IAASTD 2009) would have been more appropriate and reflective of international consensus. They argued that the IAASTD report was the result of a global consultative process involving 900 participants and 110 countries from all regions of the world and that the Executive Summary of the Synthesis Report had been approved by 58 countries. However, the HLPE reports are not negotiated documents and respond to scientific evidence and not public pressure. Recognizing this, many CSOs opted to remain silent about the definition, worrying that creating awareness through protest was not a wise strategy.

The reformed CFS has positioned itself as an evidence-based committee and correspondingly, a strong HLPE is fundamental for a strong CFS insofar as it reinforces the reform objectives and the Committee's claims to legitimacy. Despite minor setbacks, that the HLPE reports continue to be used as the accepted point from which the CFS starts its discussion is evidence of success.

Post-reform activities (2009–2013)

In the years since its reform, the CFS has managed to implement processes that have not only served to re-energize a dormant ineffective committee, but also emerged as an example of best practice in participatory policy making at the intergovernmental level. In the years following the reform, the CFS has made great strides towards accomplishing its goals but it is also recognized that such goals are not reached in such a short period of time. It is thus not useful at this stage to assess whether or not the CFS has reached its reforms goals but rather to assess how it is moving towards them. The case studies presented in this book provide insight into this progress, specifically: engagement of civil society actors (Chapter 5); policy roundtables (Chapter 6); the negotiation and adoption of Voluntary Guidelines on the Responsible Governance of Land, Fisheries and Forests in the Context of National Food Security (Chapter 7); and the negotiation and adoption of a Global Strategic Framework (Chapter 8). Before that, it is useful to reflect on other, perhaps seemingly more minor accomplishments, which have contributed to the overall functioning and development of the CFS and served to increase its legitimacy.

From talk-shop to action output

With respect to moving from an ineffective talk-shop towards an effective, action-oriented committee, the CFS has been quite successful. In order to make the CFS more effective, the Committee understood that it needed to become active throughout the year, and not just at the annual sessions. This also meant strengthening and maintaining linkages with regional initiatives in the inter-sessional period. The CFS has established open-ended working groups (OEWGs) and task teams to advance intersession work. These OEWGs and task teams function work during the year to advance CFS outputs and they have done so with a great deal of success.

The CFS has hosted policy roundtables around central and often contentious issues, which start with scientific grounding via the HLPE report findings and lead to negotiated policy recommendations. By the 41st Session in October 2014, the HLPE had completed eight reports that informed eight of 12 policy roundtables (see Tables 4.2 and 4.3). One important indicator of success for the CFS is that despite often difficult and long negotiations, agreement was reached on policy recommendations during each of the policy roundtables. The policy recommendations derived from the negotiations have been included in the Global Strategic Framework (see Chapter 8).

The topics that the CFS chooses to address are telling. They illustrate the willingness of the CFS to address some of the more contentious issues that loom over food security policy. As a representative of a large international NGO active in the CSM noted in an interview:

> the CFS, they didn't choose necessarily the easy way and I think that they have chosen issues that were relevant. So they didn't escape the difficult debates. The member states, they didn't want to discuss food price volatility, but at the same time, the CFS is able to put issues on the agenda which are contentious.
>
> (Interview, June 2012, Rome)

Table 4.2 HLPE reports 2011–2014

Date	Report title
2011	*Price Volatility and Food Security*
2011	*Land Tenure and International Investments in Agriculture*
2012	*Food Security and Climate Change*
2012	*Social Protection for Food Security*
2013	*Biofuels and Food Security*
2013	*Investing in Smallholder Agriculture for Food Security*
2014	*Sustainable Fisheries and Aquaculture for Food Security and Nutrition*
2014	*Food Losses and Waste in the Context of Sustainable Food Systems*
2014	*Critical and Emerging Issues for Food Security and Nutrition* (concept and process note)

Table 4.3 CFS policy roundtables 2010–2014

CFS session	Policy roundtable
36 (2010)	Addressing food insecurity in protracted crises: Issues and challenges
	Land tenure and international investment in agriculture
	Managing vulnerability and risk to promote better food security and nutrition
37 (2011)	How to increase food security and smallholder-sensitive investment in agriculture
	Gender, food security and nutrition
	Food price volatility
39 (2012)	Climate change
	Social protection
40 (2013)	Investing in smallholder agriculture for food security and nutrition
	Biofuels and food security
41 (2014)	The role of sustainable fisheries and aquaculture for food security and nutrition
	Food losses and waste in the context of sustainable food systems

That issues such as social protection, food price volatility, agricultural invest-ment and biofuels make it onto the agenda is in part due to the participation of civil society actors in the advisory groups and various CFS task teams. It must be acknowledged that addressing contentious issues is just one step. Whether the recommendations developed by the Committee are taken up, implemented and then have an impact at the local level remains to be seen. Yet, that there are debates happening around these issues in the context of food security, and that negotiated policy recommendations are developed, cannot be written off.

Another key outcome of the post-reform CFS has been the decision to not endorse the Principles for Responsible Agricultural Investment that Respect Rights, Livelihoods and Resources (PRAI) developed by UNCTAD, FAO, IFAD and the World Bank upon the encouragement of the G20. Instead, it was agreed that the CFS should first negotiate and endorse Voluntary Guidelines on the governance of land tenure (see Chapter 7) and then start an inclusive process of consideration of PRAI within the CFS.

At the first meeting of the reformed CFS (2010), the Committee was pre-sented with a text for negotiation on land tenure and international investment in agriculture that requested the Committee consider:

> Endorsing the on-going elaboration of Principles for Responsible Agricultural Investment that Respect Rights, Livelihoods and Resources initiated by the

World Bank, FAO, IFAD and UNCTAD and recommending that the consultation process be pursued and include all relevant stakeholders.

(CFS 2010:1)

In the end, after an impassioned and lengthy debate, the CFS decided not only to not endorse PRAI, but also to develop their our principles. The Final Report of the 36th Session states that the CFS:

> taking note of the ongoing process of developing Principles for Responsible Agricultural Investments that Respect Rights, Livelihoods and Resources (RAI), and, in line with its role, decided to start an inclusive process of consideration of the principles within the CFS.

(Ibid.: para 26.ii)

These changes are significant in at least two ways. First, it was an example of the CFS rejecting a document developed by an influential group of international actors on the basis of it not upholding the reform principles of consultation and participation. The change in the text was evidence that the reformed CFS was willing to make political decisions to uphold its vision and objectives. Second, endorsement of PRAI within the CFS was backed and defended by the G8 countries but in the end, it was the will of less powerful countries, backed by a strong civil society presence, that won out. This reassured civil society actors, along with many member states, of the value and potential of the reformed Committee as a space where traditionally less-influential actors could have more influence and power.

In terms of follow-up, an OEWG was established, chaired by the Bureau's vice chair, who liaised with all major interested parties with a view to propose a consultation process within the CFS to prepare principles for responsible agricultural investment. CFS Responsible Agricultural Investment (CFS-rai) Principles were shared as a zero draft, which was used as the basis for regional and global consultations undertaken from September 2013 to March 2014. The outcomes of the consultations were used to develop the first draft, which in turn served as the basis for negotiation. The CFS-rai Principles, which are intended to promote investments in agriculture that contribute to food security and nutrition were endorsed by the CFS after lengthy negotiations at the 41st session of the CFS (2014). Despite active engagement in the negotiations, civil society actors involved in the CSM rejected the Principles on the basis that they were "not useful." The principles failed to address key points which were "red lines" for many CSO actors, including: not being anchored in a rights-based framework; not adequately recognizing small-scale producers and workers as the main investors in agriculture; not supporting agro-ecological production systems, and local food systems and markets; and, not prioritizing effective public policies and investment that support and defend small-scale producers, workers and local food systems. The process of negotiating the CFS-rai illustrates the political dynamics and challenges that mediate CSO engagement in the CFS. Furthermore, it reminds us that despite best practice and best efforts, political participatory processes do not always produce the outcomes desired by all participants.

Coordination and linkages within the CFS

The first role identified for the reformed CFS was to:

> [p]rovide a platform for discussion and coordination to strengthen collaborative action among governments, regional organizations, international organizations and agencies, NGOs, CSOs, food producers' organizations, private sector organizations, philanthropic organizations, and other relevant stakeholders, in a manner that is in alignment with each country's specific context and needs.
>
> (CFS 2009a: para 5.1)

First, with respect to collaboration through the reform process and propelled by efforts of new participants, the CFS has established itself as the platform for strengthened collaboration among stakeholders. Beyond collaboration, the inclusion of new participants and the active engagement of these participants is evidence that the CFS is providing space for stakeholders to have a voice and influence intergovernmental negotiations.

A second level of engagement relates to linking to other initiatives. Towards this end, at the 37th Session, there were updates on global and regional initiatives and linkages with the CFS and since the 39th Session, "Coordination and Linkages with CFS" has become a standard agenda item. The agenda item is structured as an interactive panel discussion with the objective of strengthen linkages and communication between CFS and other actors in food security governance at the global and regional levels. This agenda item supports the three roles of the CFS: coordination at global level; policy convergence; and support and advice to countries and regions. In line with the learning objectives of the CFS, at this time, participants and members are introduced to best practices and lessons learned with respect to the implementation of food security and nutrition polices at country level.

In 2012 at the 39th Session, the CFS explored the linkages between selected global and regional initiatives and CFS with an aim of establishing how such linkages can be strengthened for greater impact on food security and nutrition. The Committee received presentations on:

- *Global*: updates on the G20 Mexico Summit; Agricultural Market Information System (AMIS); Global Conference on Agricultural Research for Development (GCARD); and RIO+20.
- *Regional*: updates on the cooperation between the United Nations Economic Commission for Africa (UNECA), the African Development Bank (AfDB) and the African Union Commission (AUC); an overview of the New Alliance for Food Security and Nutrition; and the Zero Hunger Challenge and the Hunger Free Initiative for West Africa.

In 2013, the CFS examined linkages between multi-scale initiatives under the theme "Multi-stakeholder Models that Promote Food Security, Nutrition and Sustainable Agriculture: Towards the Post-2015 Development Agenda" and extended its focus to the national level.

The following initiatives were discussed:

- *Global*: Post-2015 Development Agenda.
- *Regional*: G8 Alliance for food security and nutrition in the context of the Comprehensive Africa Agriculture Development Programme.
- *National*: Country experiences and lesson learned: Brazil (the National Council of Food and Nutrition Security, CONSEA); Thailand (nutrition impact of agriculture and food systems).

For 2014, the reviewed initiatives included:

- *Global*: Food Security and Nutrition in the Post-2015 Development Agenda.
- *Regional*: Comprehensive Africa Agriculture Development Program (CAADP) and New Partnership for Africa's Development's (NEPAD) efforts to mainstream nutrition in agriculture.
- *National*: Best practices and lessons learned on implementing the Voluntary Guidelines to Support the Progressive Realization of the Right to Adequate Food in the Context of National Food Security.

Food in the Context of National Food Security. The CFS Reform Document references the need to build linkages at the regional and country level, as it is "crucial that the work of the CFS is based on the reality on the ground" (CFS 2009a: para 23). This is central to the reform strategy to increase communication and to ensure that results of deliberations of the Plenary are disseminated and relates to the fact that food security is a national responsibility and within the CFS member states remain decision makers. It is thus fundamental that the outcomes of the CFS are relevant and applicable at the national level.

The CFS has also been tasked with supporting and providing advice to countries and regions in the development, implementation, monitoring and evaluation of their nationally and regionally owned plans of action for the elimination of hunger based on the principles of participation, transparency and accountability. The CFS has produced policy recommendations designed to support policy making at the national level, and often with clear links to existing international commitments. The CFS also compiles these in the Global Strategic Framework to facilitate access and use. However, the CFS does not have the authority or the capacity to coordinate action at the national or local level. The CFS is an intergovernmental body and not a technical body. It can encourage efficient use of resources and identify resource gaps, but it has no way of ensuring these gaps are closed or that more efficient practices are put into place. It is the role of the FAO and others to support countries in the implementation of such plans and programs.

Despite the limitations on its scope, the CFS has a clear role to play in information sharing. Organized panel discussions inform and update participants and members of existing (and often competing) initiatives. Importantly, these panels bring representatives of these initiatives into the CFS, thereby also fostering awareness of the CFS.

Moving forward the CFS must reflect on how best to support the uptake of CFS policy recommendations at the national level. This must be accompanied by careful monitoring and evaluation so as to allow for the full assessment of the policy impact on national-level food security. The tensions between CFS policies and other initiatives will also remain a challenge. In some instances efforts are being made to enhance cohesion (e.g., VGGT and the African Land Policy Initiative). In other cases, actors are moving ahead with disregard for CFS processes (e.g., PRAI and the G8's New Alliance for Food Security and Nutrition).

This raises two points with respect to the CFS's role in promoting greater policy convergence and coordination. First, how can the CFS achieve this if it is being undermined by other actors? Second, in the case where multiple international frameworks are being developed, which are to be cohered to or coordinated with?

The CFS has shown that in the few years following its reform it has managed to produce evidence-based policies informed by widespread consultation and inclusive negotiations. The results are negotiated inter-governmentally and endorse policy proposals that have proven to be comprehensive and progressive in terms of addressing food security. That said, given that food security has developed in line with a wider neoliberal agenda, and the CFS itself operates within a context of embedded neoliberalism, advancing policies that stray from the dominant model is not only difficult but also challenges cohesion. Furthermore, given the nature of CFS decision making, it becomes challenging for all actors, especially nation-states, to implement CFS decisions. It is similarly difficult for the CFS to avoid giving a stamp of approval for initiatives and policies that were developed through less transparent and less participatory processes (e.g. AMIS, PRAI).

Food security in protracted crises

Extending the reach and influence of the CFS has been the work undertaken around the High-Level Expert Forum on Protracted Crises with a view of elaborating a new "Agenda for Action for Food Security in Countries in Protracted Crises" in collaboration with other specialized agencies and humanitarian partners. The preparatory work began in 2011, including a review of existing programs and initiatives and to determine the value of such an event. A concept note was prepared and submitted to the CFS Bureau and Advisory Group for consideration at the 37th Session. A policy roundtable "Addressing food insecurity in protracted crises" was organized and from these discussions the CFS requested that the possibility of organizing a High-Level Expert

Forum on Protracted Crisis no later than 2012 be explored with the aim of discussing the elaboration of a new Agenda for Action for Food Security in Countries in Protracted Crises in collaboration with other specialized agencies and humanitarian partners (CFS 2011a: para 25v). The CFS also agreed that an addendum be added to the 2010 *State of Food Insecurity Report on Food Security in Protracted Crises* that would include a revised table to include all countries and territories in protracted crisis and that the list include Palestinian territories, West Bank and Gaza strip. The addendum was later published online. The CFS was meant to endorse an "Agenda for Action for Addressing Food Insecurity in Protracted Crises" at the 41st Session but negotiations were not completed in time. Instead, at the 41st Session the Agenda was discussed and it was agreed that negotiations would continue.

Gaining legitimacy

Questions of legitimacy loom large over multilateral fora and part of the CFS's claim to legitimacy has been based on the opening up of participation within the Committee. While the Global Partnership was perceived by many to be creating a new institution behind closed doors and under the leadership of a small group of elite nations, in contrast, the CFS worked to enhance transparency and participation. This sentiment is affirmed in the Reform Document insofar as:

> the process of defining strategies and actions to be adopted by Members should be transparent and take into consideration the views of all participants and stakeholders to the fullest extent possible in order to foster ownership and full participation during implementation of these strategies and actions.
>
> (CFS 2009a: para 18)

This, along with the commitment to consensus decision making, the principle of one-country-one-vote, and the recognition of the need to support the autonomous participation of CSOs, the private sector, research bodies and philanthropic foundations, is pivotal in distinguishing the CFS from other initiatives. The language around inclusiveness, especially with reference to "those most affected by food insecurity" is important. It reflects awareness of the need for people impacted by policies to be engaged in the policy-making process. This language further reflects recognition of the historic role of CSOs in and across the work of the FAO and the CFS.

Beyond this, the CFS has an operational and increasingly influential independent HLPE producing scientifically reviewed reports that serve as the basis for policy negotiations. As such the CFS is producing policy recommendations for improving food security that are developed on the basis of independent science in a participatory way with intergovernmental agreement. Perhaps the greatest accomplishment of the reformed CFS, and also its biggest obstacle, relates to its perceived legitimacy as constituting the foremost inclusive international and intergovernmental platform for supporting countries as they work towards the elimination of hunger and ensuring food security and nutrition for all human beings.

Key to building legitimacy is ensuring accountability. Developing accountability procedures or mechanisms within the CFS is necessarily complicated insofar as governments are expected to develop and endorse mechanisms to hold themselves accountable. That said, the CFS should, as appropriate, help countries and regions assess whether their objectives are being achieved and how food insecurity and malnutrition can be reduced more quickly and effectively. This will entail developing an innovative mechanism, including the definition of common indicators, to monitor progress towards these agreed upon objectives and actions, taking into account lessons learned from previous CFS and other monitoring attempts. Comments by all CFS stakeholders will have to be taken into account.

Conclusion

When the CFS adopted the Reform Document it was setting out into unchartered territory both in terms of process and challenges. The CFS now has the legitimate function of acting as the forum in the UN System for review and follow-up of food security policies. This legitimacy is based on agreement reached by the Committee's 123 member countries and further reinforced by the participatory and transparent functioning of the reformed CFS.

In just a few years the CFS has implemented and operationalized an innovative approach to participatory policy making at the global level. The CFS has overcome its previous history of inactivity to emerge as a leading intergovernmental body that develops comprehensive food security policies through participatory processes. The reform, notably the expansion of participation in the CFS, has resulted in changes to policies that demonstrate stronger support for smallholders and prioritize food security. This is noteworthy and valuable.

As noted above, during the reform process the Director-General of the FAO (CFS 2009b:13) highlighted five key limitations that prevented the CFS achieving its mission of monitoring food security. While the reformed roles and objectives of the CFS no longer involve monitoring developments around the World Food Summit Plan of Action, it is a valuable exercise to examine how the CFS has addressed these limitations through the reform. The first challenge was the absence of a high-level international policy-making body for international cooperation and food and agriculture. In effect, this is what the CFS has sought to become and it is working towards this with the recommendations and actions of the policy roundtables, and the Global Strategic Framework and Voluntary Guidelines on the Responsible Governance of Tenure of Land Fisheries and Forests in the Context of National Food Security.

The second limitation of the pre-reformed CFS was that it lacked an integrated framework for short-, medium- and long-term sectoral scientific advice on hunger. This has been addressed again through the policy roundtables which build on the research, analysis and recommendations of the independent HLPE. This is further supported by the inclusion of a range of actors who contribute various perspectives. The third challenge was the lack of authority to evaluate and coordinate policies affecting world food security, in particular as regards production, agroindustry, trade, social safety nets and financing. As will be illustrated in the case studies (Chapters 6–8), this remains a limitation. While the capacity and legitimacy to coordinate a wide range of policies related to food security is growing, the political will to allow it to do so remains limited. Furthermore, the CFS remains weak on evaluation. The CFS has started to address issues related to monitoring, however, the nature of the Committee and diplomatic etiquette suggest that the evaluation of policies emerging from outside of the CFS will remain off-limits. In this sense the CFS, as a platform, has been partially defeatist in its outlook by agreeing not to tackle what was already agreed to in other fora, the exception being the PRAI. The extension of this way of thinking is that the CFS does not have the legitimacy to address these issues and is thus subservient to other bodies. As such, addressing issues of trade (domain of the WTO) and climate change (domain of the UNFCCC) remains a challenge. The CFS's role, however, is to address these issues as they related to food security and the Committee should not shy away from developing positions on fundamental issues for food security and nutrition.

The fourth challenge related to the lack of an effective mechanism to track food security decisions and actions at national and regional level. After the reform, the CFS began work on a mapping initiative that sought to profile actions (policies, programs, strategies, plans and projects) that support food security and nutrition objectives and to then chart the "linkages of these actions to domestic and donor resources, implementing institutions and beneficiary population groups" (CFS 2012c: para 1). The overall purpose of mapping actions was to provide policy makers and other users with better information to support decision making around national and regional policies, strategies and programs. For donors, the mapping tool could also help identify where to allocate resources. The CFS launched an Actions Mapping Task Team to advise and provide guidance. It proposed the development of a mapping tool that builds on existing tools and methods and ongoing country experiences. A demonstration web-based version of the tool was launched for the 39th Session of the CFS but is no longer functional.

The fifth constraint facing the pre-reformed CFS was a lack of financial resources to carry out its mandate. This remains a challenge. A major loss in the battle for legitimacy between Rome-based agencies and New York-based agencies was the CFS's failure to secure control over the financial arm of the restructuring of the architecture of global food security governance. Admittedly, securing a funding role would have certainly changed the reform outcomes and operations of the CFS. However a lack of funds continues to be a problem both in terms of the sustainability of the Committee and the ability to support countries with national plans to advance food security.

Finally, while it has accomplished a lot and holds a clear normative advantage, the CFS can be challenged for its inability to react quickly to emerging issues. Key to the success of the reformed CFS is that it undertakes consultation and makes decisions with the input of a full range of stakeholders. Unlike the G8 or G20, the CFS is a UN committee and is subject to the realities of highly bureaucratic processes. Yet, if the parable of the tortoise and the hare holds true for food security policy, the CFS may have the slow and steady advantage.

Given its history and the context which prompted its reform, the CFS should be seen as a benchmark, rather than a model, for participatory governance at the global level. Currently, the CFS has legitimacy and steady momentum. What it lacks in reaction time, high-level political interest and implementation capacity, it makes up for in experience, meaningful discussion and policy making, and innovative, transparent, participatory governance. However, in politics, races are not always won by steady determination. For the CFS to cross the finish line it will require more funding, the ability to broaden discussions to issues of trade and the environment, and the capacity to hold governments accountable for the decisions they make in the Committee. It will also require other actors to recognize its role and to respect its processes. This however raises the question of whether the world has the luxury of moving at a slow pace when it comes to addressing the pressing nature of food insecurity.

Notes

1 The rules were amended in 1997 after the World Food Summit and the 2009 reforms outlined in the CFS Reform Document incorporated in Part Q of Volume II of the Basic Texts of FAO (2013a).
2 These efforts were led predominantly by the International Planning Committee for Food Sovereignty (IPC). The IPC is an international network that brings together several organizations representing farmers, fisherfolk, and small- and medium-scale farmers, agricultural workers and indigenous peoples, as well as NGOs. It plays the role of facilitating the discussions between NGOs, social organizations and movements, as well as facilitating dialogue with FAO. The IPC was formalized in preparation for the June 2002 World Food Summit: Five Years Later. In January 2003, the IPC and FAO co-signed an Exchange of Letters which laid out a programme of work in follow-up to the Summit and the Forum in four priority areas: the right to food; agro-ecological approaches to food production; local access to and control of natural resources; and agricultural trade and food sovereignty. This network played a fundamental role not only in advancing the reform of the CFS but in discrediting the proposal for a Global Partnership for Agriculture, Food Security and Nutrition.
3 The phased roles of the reformed CFS mirror the Committee's 1974 objectives with expanded participation and less responsibility for monitoring. As a reminder, the original resolution established the CFS to provide a forum for regular intergovernmental consultations, review progress achieved towards an international grains agreement, while also reviewing the actions taken by states towards advancing the Undertaking on World Food Security.
4 These quotes come from internal documents that were shared with the researcher.
5 The FAO's (2013b) *Strategy for Partnerships with Civil Society Organizations* proposes different definitions. Here, social movements are defined as a category that includes "platforms,

committees, mechanisms, federations and networks of advocacy-based and policy-oriented organizations related to FAO's mandate on food security and nutrition, which promote claims or rights of specific constituencies." It then goes on to state, "FAO has collaborated with various social movements working in food security including: the Civil Society Mechanism and the International Planning Committee for Food Sovereignty." The CSM is in no way a social movement: it is a facilitation mechanism that plays a communications role to help civil society actors participate in the CFS.

References

Brem-Wilson, J. 2014. "Towards Food Sovereignty: Interrogating Peasant Voice in the UN Committee on World Food Security," in *Food Sovereignty: A Critical Dialogue*. The Hague: International Institute for Social Studies. Retrieved (www.iss.nl/fileadmin/ASSETS/iss/Research_and_projects/Research_networks/ICAS/87_Brem-Wilson.pdf).

CFS. 2009a. *Reform of the Committee on World Food Security Final Version*. Rome: FAO. Retrieved (www.fao.org/fileadmin/templates/cfs/Docs0910/ReformDoc/CFS_2009_2_Rev_2_E_K7197.pdf).

CFS. 2009b. *Report of the Thirty-Fifth Session of the Committee on World Food Security (CFS)*. Rome: FAO.

CFS. 2010. *Policy Roundtable: Land Tenure and International Investment* (CFS:2010/7). Rome: FAO. Retrieved (www.fao.org/docrep/meeting/019/k8929e.pdf).

CFS. 2011a. *Final Report Thirty-Seventh Session Committee on World Food Security*. Rome: FAO. Retrieved (www.fao.org/fileadmin/templates/cfs/Docs1011/CFS37/documents/CFS_37_Final_Report_FINAL.pdf).

CFS. 2011b. *Proposal for Modalities for Private Sector Participation in the Committee for World Food Security (CFS:2011/Inf.15)*. Rome: FAO.

CFS. 2012a. *Final Report of the Thirty-Ninth Session of the Committee on World Food Security*. Rome: FAO. Retrieved (www.fao.org/fileadmin/user_upload/bodies/CFS_sessions/39th_Session/39emerg/MF027_CFS_39_FINAL_REPORT_compiled_E.pdf).

CFS. 2012b. *Global Strategic Framework for Food Security and Nutrition (First Version)*. Rome: FAO. Retrieved (www.fao.org/docrep/meeting/026/ME498E.pdf).

CFS. 2012c. *Mapping Food Security and Nutrition Actions at Country Level*. Rome: FAO. Retrieved (www.fao.org/docrep/meeting/026/me752e.pdf).

CFS. 2013. *Report of the Fortieth Session of the Committee on World Food Security (CFS)*. Rome: FAO. Retrieved (www.fao.org/docrep/meeting/029/mi744e.pdf).

CFS. 2014. "About the HLPE." *CFS: High Level Panel of Experts*. Rome: CFS. Retrieved July 21, 2014 (www.fao.org/cfs/cfs-hlpe/about-the-hlpe/en/).

De Schutter, O. 2012. "Global Governance." Retrieved (www.srfood.org/index.php/en/areas-of-work/policy-making/global-governance).

Duncan, J., and D. Barling. 2012. "Renewal through Participation in Global Food Security Governance: Implementing the International Food Security and Nutrition Civil Society Mechanism to the Committee on World Food Security." *International Journal of Sociology of Agriculture and Food* 19:143–61.

European Commission. 2010. *Food Security Thematic Programme: Thematic Strategy Paper (update) and Multiannual Indicative Programme (2011-2013)*. Brussels: EC. Retrieved (http://ec.europa.eu/development/icenter/repository/FSTP 2011-2013_Commission adoption.pdf).

FAO. 1975. *Report of the Conference of FAO: Eighteenth Session*. Rome: FAO. Retrieved (www.fao.org/docrep/x5589e/x5589e0c.htm).

FAO. 1997. *Resolution 8/97 Report of the Conference of FAO. Twenty-Ninth Session*. Rome: FAO. Retrieved (www.fao.org/docrep/W7475e/W7475e0a.htm).

FAO. 2007. *Report of the Independent External Evaluation of the Food and Agriculture Organization of the United Nations (FAO)*. Rome: FAO. Retrieved (ftp://ftp.fao.org/docrep/fao/meeting/012/k0827erev1.pdf).

FAO. 2009a. *Declaration of the World Summit on Food Security*. Rome: FAO.

FAO. 2009b. *Global Governance of Food Security*. Rome: FAO.

FAO. 2009c. *Report of the Council of FAO: Hundred and Thirty-Sixth Session*. Rome: FAO. Retrieved (ftp://ftp.fao.org/docrep/fao/meeting/017/k4992e02.pdf).

FAO. 2011. Internal correspondence from the office of FAO Director-General Jacques Diouf (ES-DG/11/688 (05.VII. 2011).

FAO. 2012. "FAO Media Centre: FAO Calls for Strengthened Food Security Governance." Media Centre. Retrieved (www.fao.org/news/story/en/item/162391/icode/).

FAO. 2013a. *Basic Texts of the Food and Agriculture Organization of the United Nations: Volumes I and II*. Rome: FAO. Retrieved (www.fao.org/docrep/meeting/022/k8024e.pdf).

FAO. 2013b. *FAO Strategy for Partnerships with Civil Society Organizations*. Rome: FAO.

G8. 2008. *G8 Leaders Statement on Global Food Security*. L'Aquila: G8.

G8. 2009. *"L'Aquila" Joint Statement on Global Food Security*. L'Aquila: G8. Retrieved (www.g8italia2009.it/static/G8_Allegato/LAquila_Joint_Statement_on_Global_Food_Security[1],0.pdf).

G20. 2009. *The Pittsburgh Summit: Partnering on Food Security*. Pittsburgh: G20. Retrieved (www.whitehouse.gov/files/documents/g20/Pittsburgh_Fact_Sheet_Food_Security.pdf).

G20. 2011. *Action Plan on Food Price Volatility and Agriculture*. Meeting of G20 agriculture ministers, Paris, June 2011. Retrieved (http://agriculture.gouv.fr/IMG/pdf/2011-06-23_-_Action_Plan_-_VFinale.pdf).

HLPE. 2011. *Land Tenure and International Investments in Agriculture*. Rome: FAO. Retrieved (www.fao.org/fileadmin/user_upload/hlpe/hlpe_documents/HLPE-Land-tenure-and-international-investments-in-agriculture-2011.pdf).

HLPE. 2013. *The High Level Panel of Experts on Food Security and Nutrition (HLPE): Key Elements*. Rome: FAO. Retrieved (http://typo3.fao.org/fileadmin/user_upload/hlpe/hlpe_documents/Official_Docs/HLPE-Key-elements-Online.pdf).

IAASTD. 2009. *Synthesis Report of the International Assessment of Agricultural Knowledge, Science and Technology for Development*. Washington DC: IAASTD. Retrieved (www.unep.org/dewa/agassessment/reports/IAASTD/EN/Agriculture at a Crossroads_Executive Summary of the Synthesis Report (English).pdf).

IFPRI. 2013. "Global Governance for Agriculture, Food and Nutrition." Retrieved (www.ifpri.org/book-22/node/5107).

Macmillan, A., and H. de Haen. 2010. "Towards Global Governance of Food Security." *Rural 21: Focus* 44(5):6–10. Retrieved (www.rural21.com/uploads/media/R21_towards_golbal_governance_03.pdf).

McKeon, N. 2011. *Global Governance for World Food Security: A Scorecard Four Years After the Eruption of the "Food Crisis."* Berlin: Heinrich-Böll-Stiftung.

Monteith, J.L. 1990. "Conservative Behaviour in the Response of Crops to Water and Light," pp. 3–16 in *Theoretical Production Ecology: Reflections and Prospects. Simulation*

Monograph 34, edited by R. Rabbinge, J. Goudriaan, H. van Keulen, F. W. T. Penning de Vries and H. H. van Laar. Pudoc: Wageningen.

République Française. 2010. *The Global Partnership for Food Security*. Paris: Government of France. Retrieved (www.diplomatie.gouv.fr/fr/IMG/pdf/Securite_alimentaire_v_anglaise_web-2_cle04224b.pdf).

Shaw, D. J. 2007. *World Food Security: A History since 1945*. New York: Palgrave Macmillan.

Sinclair, T.R. 1990. "Nitrogen Influence on the Physiology of Crop Yield," pp. 41–55 in *Theoretical Production Ecology: Reflections and Prospects. Simulation Monograph 34*, edited by R. Rabbinge, J. Goudriaan, H. van Keulen, F. W. T. Penning de Vries and H. H. van Laar. Pudoc: Wageningen.

UN. 2009. *Statement of the Madrid High-Level Meeting on Food Security for All*. Madrid: UN. Retrieved (www.fanrpan.org/documents/d00641/).

UN General Assembly. 2012a. *Agriculture Development and Food Security: Report of the Second Committee. Sixty-Seventh Session (Agenda Item 26)*. New York: UN.

UN General Assembly. 2012b. *The Future We Want (A/RES/66/288*)*. New York: UN.

5   Participation in global governance

Coordinating "the voices of those most affected by food insecurity"

Introduction

In the reform document of the UN's CFS, it states that while the CFS is an intergovernmental Committee:

> [i]t will be composed of members, participants and observers and will seek to achieve a balance between inclusiveness and effectiveness. Its composition will ensure that the voices of all relevant stakeholders—particularly those most affected by food insecurity—are heard.
>
> (CFS 2009: para 2)

Towards this end, member states agreed that CSOs had the right to "autonomously establish a global mechanism for food security and nutrition which will function as a facilitating body for CSO/NGOs consultation and participation in the CFS" (CFS 2009: para 7).

Developing a mechanism capable of facilitating the participation of the voices of civil society, particularly of "those most affected by food insecurity," is a daunting task to say the least. However, as one leader of a European farming social movement explained:

> We have fought of the autonomous and independent organization of civil society. The identified constituencies and geographically distant demographics, to have their voice here in Rome implies a great deal of work based on respect, understanding of difference, working together. This is a complicated process but the biggest challenge we are facing is to show the governments that we are capable of self-organizing even if they are 198 and we are 198,000.
>
> (Field notes, October 2010, Rome)

This chapter reviews the rationale for, and development of, the International Food Security and Nutrition Civil Society Mechanism (CSM). This is done by first presenting the broader institutional evolution that provided the context for the reform. From there, the process of designing the Mechanism is presented, followed by an overview of the Mechanism itself. In recognition of the fact that the CSM is still "learning-while-doing," key challenges are identified and discussed with the aim of providing insight into potentially instructive practices. Further contributing to instructive practices, implications and opportunities for scaling-out the CSM model are presented. The chapter concludes by arguing that despite growing pains, the CSM has managed to effectively coordinate the participation of a broad range of civil society actors in a transparent and efficient manner while also strengthening CSO networks.

Institutional evolution towards the participatory turn

Participation in policy making has been referred to as the new orthodoxy (Henkel and Stirrat 2001:168), while others speak of a participatory turn (Duncan and Barling 2012; Saurugger 2010). Jonathan Joseph (2012) argues that the promotion of participation is central to the post-Washington consensus, with advocates at the local level, across multilateral agencies and increasingly across the private sector (often framed by language of partnership).[1] Valuable elements of participatory approaches include: the interrelated capacities, skills and characteristics of individuals with forms of authority structure; the democratization of democracy through changes that will provide opportunities for greater participation of people in decision making in daily lives and in the wider political system; the development of a more participatory society; and key structural changes that reform undemocratic authority structures (Pateman 2012:10).

As discussed above, a key aspect of the CFS reform was the inclusion of nonstate actors as participants in the Committee. Across global governance arenas participation is an increasingly accepted norm, but what constitutes meaningful participation remains vague. Furthermore, while the construction of the participatory imperative is fact, the implementation of mechanisms to ensure participation remains partial (Saurugger 2010:489). In most instances, participation remains dependent on the activities of a coherent set of actors with multiple capacities that allow them to engage. As such, the participatory turn that marks the CFS reform can be dismissed as being less radical than it perhaps was.

Understanding the way in which actors participate in the CFS is important to better understanding participatory policy making. Recent literature on food security debates at the multilateral level (e.g., Holt-Giménez and Altieri 2013; Hospes 2013) has captured the participatory shift but has failed to fully capture the complexity and multiple dimensions of the debates. This research contributes to this growing body of literature by examining the actions of actors. In turn, this reinforces the view that actors cannot be placed into ideological boxes. Instead, while their subjectivity, ethics, training and/or mandate may suggest a predisposition to a specific approach, the complexity and scope of discussion, the diversity of perspectives and the consensus model of decision making make ideological inflexibility not only difficult, but politically disadvantageous at times insofar as those actors opt out of the give and take—the compromise—that is politics.

A study of CFS negotiations provides insight into and examples of the value of consultation and inclusive negotiation processes. CSOs participate at all stages of development and have been effective in raising awareness throughout the discussions about the real-life issues facing them and their communities. Their engagement extends to the development and advancement of concrete proposals, many of which were incorporated into endorsed texts. Importantly, the reformed CFS can be seen as an experimental mechanism for participatory policy making. Furthermore, given the unique context within which it operates, the reformed CFS should be seen as a benchmark, rather than model for participatory governance at the global level.

Pateman (2012) warns that much of the contemporary focus on participatory or deliberative forms of democracy has been "political theory-led enterprise," with little focus on 30 years of participatory promotion. To address this critique what follows is a review of the process of securing enhanced civil society participation in the Committee in the years leading up to the reform. The review serves to highlight that the inclusion of non-state actors, including CSOs, was part of a historical trajectory.

A decade before the reform, when the CFS amended its Rules, members of the CFS remained interested FAO or UN member states. However, reference was made to inviting "relevant international organizations to participate in the work of the Committee and the preparation of meeting documents on matters within their respective mandates in collaboration with the secretariat of the Committee" (FAO 1997: rule V.2). At this time, CSOs attending the CFS had observer status, and their ability to engage in processes lay with the discretion of the chair.

In 1998, the CFS was provided with an information note on "Possible Modalities for NGO Participation in the Work of the Committee on World Food Security" (CFS 1998). At this time, nothing was decided but the Committee did recognize and circulate a proposal for enhancing civil society participation in the CFS drafted by a group of NGOs on the basis of their discussions at the 23rd Session of the CFS. During the 25th Session, the CFS made broader participation of civil society and other partners a main agenda item. A background paper provided suggestions for broadening the participation of CSOs in the work of the CFS and the World Food Summit implementation process (CFS 1999: para 5.1). The proposals included enhanced information exchange, contributions to technical documents, participation in CFS meetings and enhanced dialogue. It also provided possibilities for enhanced CSO engagement in the CFS, including having the chair ask CSOs to appoint designated spokespersons to intervene in debates; grant CSOs the right to make one intervention per topic; and allow CSOs to present consolidated reports of their conclusions and findings on achievements and lessons learned.

The outcomes of the discussions held at this session were key to the future of civil society engagement in the Committee. First, in this session the Committee reflected on terminology and acknowledged that the term CSO was broader than that of NGO but that the term required clarification, which was a matter to be dealt with at the UN level. This discussion on language extends beyond semantics and is highly political. The expansion of language beyond NGOs to include CSOs is central to the broader political struggle for participation.[2] NGOs are understood to be collections of professionals paid to work on specific issues or on behalf of others. Social movement actors and community and farming leaders may not conform to the definition of NGO but speak from experience and often have the legitimacy to represent local perspectives and people.

In their discussion, the Committee acknowledged the importance of the work of NGOs and CSOs in food security and encouraged further collaboration with governments in national follow-up actions to the World Food Summit recommendations. There was a recommendation on the part of some delegations for all delegations to include NGOs and CSOs in their delegations to CFS, and to facilitate participation of NGOs and CSOs from developing countries (CFS 1999: para 38). The proposal was dismissed with questions of how to fund such participation.

During the discussion, some delegates raised the issue of CSO participation in drafting sessions and the majority of delegate argued that this would be inappropriate given the intergovernmental nature of the meetings. However, during the debate on relations between the CFS and NGOs/CSOs, the Committee opened the floor without restriction for any CSO representative who wished to speak, so long as they followed prevailing rules and regulations. The CFS also stressed that this right to speak was limited to the particular discussion and did not create a precedent for any other meeting of CFS or FAO governing bodies (CFS 1999: para 38). It did however foreshadow the process that would be adapted in the reform a decade later.

During this meeting, no conclusion was reached on the number or type of representatives that should be allowed to participate in the CFS but a suggestion was made that CSOs determine the method by which their spokespeople be selected. This was a key issue for CSOs who were adamant that their participation was to be autonomously coordinated. Some delegates noted the importance of FAO collaboration with the private sector, notably in the field program and resource mobilization. The discussion that took place at the 25th Session of the CFS pointed to the possibility of stronger engagement of CSOs within the CFS, but following this meeting attention to the issue waned.

It was not until the 32nd Session of the CFS (2006) when the issue came up again. At this time, various stakeholders, including CSOs, engaged in a dialogue on progress made towards attaining the World Food Summit goals. CSOs were proving themselves to be useful allies of Committee members who, in the wake of the World Food Summit, had been tasked with monitoring the implementation of the resulting Plan of Action. Yet, beyond the role of observers, CSO engagement continued to be needs based or subject to sympathetic chairs. At this point, some members of the CFS "requested that options for continued engagement of multi-stakeholders in future years be discussed at the next Session of the CFS" (FAO 2006: para 31).

The following year, the CFS Secretariat followed up by providing background information on current practices of multi-stakeholder engagement and highlighted four potential options for the continued engagement of CSOs including: interventions by observers, CSO reports on the World Food Summit Follow-Up to be presented at the CFS sessions, multi-stakeholder dialogues with the chair, and informal panels (CFS 2008: para 3). The Committee requested the Secretariat to prepare a document outlining these and other possible options to be discussed at the 34th Session of the CFS.

The resulting paper—*Participation of Civil Society/Non-Governmental Organizations (CSOs/NGOs)*—listed best practices adopted in other FAO bodies and a suggestion that they could be applied to the CFS. These practices included allowing CSOs to organize side events; seeking CSO input into documents; encouraging CSO caucusing; permitting CSO presence during the drafting of outcomes; promoting direct dialogue between governments and CSOs; and formalizing and communicating procedures for engagement (CFS 2008: para 18). Principles of participation were also outlined along with specific measures to improve interactions between the CFS and CSOs. However, before as was discussed in Chapter 4, the actual reform process proved much more radical than the Secretariat had envisioned.

Beyond sessional work, CSOs played an active role in the work of the CFS in the monitoring the implementation of the resulting World Food Summit's Plan of Action. They also played a central role in the development of the Voluntary Guidelines to support the progressive realization of the right to adequate food in the context of national food security. In the Declaration adopted at the World Food Summit: Five Years Later, the heads of state and government reaffirmed "the right of everyone to have access to safe and nutritious food" and asked the "FAO, in close collaboration with relevant treaty bodies, agencies and programmes of the UN system, to assist the Intergovernmental Working Group, which shall report on its work to the Committee on World Food Security" (FAO 2002: para 10). The Guidelines were endorsed at the 30th Session of the CFS.

This review has served to illustrate that far from spontaneous, the reform of the CFS towards enhanced participation was shaped by a history of active CSO engagement. However, as explained in Chapter 4, it is also important to note that the formalization of participation rights within the reformed CFS was supported by other factors beyond history. Factors included the supportive individuals with power and influence, the urgency presented by the food price crisis, the resulting competition for leadership over global food security governance, and a post-evaluation change culture at the FAO.

Because of the combination of these factors and the context within which the reform was taking place, CSOs were able to play a key role in the design of the reform process and secure full and autonomous participation rights in:

> the foremost inclusive international and intergovernmental platform for a broad range of committed stakeholders to work together in a coordinated manner and in support of country-led processes towards the elimination of hunger and ensuring food security and nutrition for all human beings.
>
> (CFS 2009: para 4)

With that right secured, they then faced the challenge of developing a mechanism that would allow for coordinated participation of civil society actors from around the world.

Designing the International Food Security and Nutrition Civil Society Mechanism for relation with CFS

The reform document of the CFS invited CSOs to autonomously establish a global mechanism to facilitate their participation in the CFS (2009: para 16). Several groups submitted proposals in a bid for leadership of the process but the successful proposal was one jointly written and submitted by the Governance Working Group of the IPC, Oxfam and Action Aid International, with the support of a Methodology Group made of reference people. Discussions with actors in the CFS and FAO revealed that the reason this proposal was chosen over the others was because it extended beyond the interests of the coordinating organizations, had principles to ensure transparency and sought to be globally inclusive. It was, overall, the most sophisticated mechanism proposed.

The process and design of the Mechanism drew from and built on the extensive experience and networks of CSOs across a range of policy areas as well as from existing mechanisms, notably the IPC, the Farmers' Forum and the Permanent Forum on Indigenous Issues. For example, the IPC had experience promoting the autonomous representation of constituencies of small-scale farmers, food and agriculture workers, pastoralists, fisherfolk, women, youth and indigenous peoples.

Despite existing models, the process of drafting the Mechanism took time. A core group, led by the organizations that had submitted the successful proposal, distributed a Zero Draft in March 2010 through their networks. A First Draft, building on the feedback on the Zero Draft was distributed in July 2010 and a Second Draft was written up by the end of August. A Final Draft was released on September 15, 2010, and aimed to include all compatible recommendations collected during the consultations.[3]

Many of the people active in developing the Mechanism came to form the "Methodology Group" that provided de facto leadership while the CSM was developing. Within the Methodology Group there was a high level of reflexivity and awareness of the need for an eventual handover of power to the CSM Coordination Committee. As one member of the Group explained:

> So I was involved in the Methodology Group, which was also kind of uneasy, because it had no real mandate but at the same time it was taking important decisions in terms of programming. But now, with the new Coordinating Committee, well, I think roles are clear, so there is no methodology group anymore.
>
> (Interview, Rome, June 2012)

This was also made visible not only in the way that the CSM was structured but also in the way that CSM meetings were coordinated.

At the Civil Society Consultation held in Rome in October 2010, the chair of a Plenary Session presented those in attendance with the Final Draft of the Mechanism and encouraged the delegates to endorse the Mechanism. On a methodological note, the meeting was open to all CSOs but delegates had to be nominated from constituencies and sub-regions. In selecting delegates, balance was sought across constituencies, regions and gender. At the Consultation, decision-making processes were to be consensus-driven where possible, but only delegates had decision-making authority. This meant observers could participate but did not have decision-making authority. Facilitators sought to maintain an open forum for discussion and open processes for clarification and discussion. Everyone was asked to speak slowly and to be concise to facilitate interpretation and translation. This was particularly important as the Final Draft of the Mechanism had not been translated into French and Spanish, the two other working languages of the CSM. This in turn limited who could fully comprehend and assess the Mechanism, and in particular excluded social movement actors, especially those attending from West Africa and Latin America. Organizers of the consultation expressed frustration that the FAO had failed to provide timely support with respect to translation.

Despite these challenges, at the Consultation many delegates stood and expressed their support for the CSM as a positive first step and highlighted changes and considerations to made over the next year. Many spoke in favor of the organizing principles and the structure the mechanism which took into account inclusiveness, transparency and openness. Others drew attention to potential limitations. Some noted that the inclusivity and accountability mechanisms still needed work. Related to this, there was a call to clarify the decision-making processes within the Mechanism, for example, by defining what was meant by consensus in this context. People requested for all documents to be translated in advance of meetings, which in turn raised questions of resources. Finally, there was a call to ensure that work continued at the national and regional levels and that the CSM not be restricted to what happened in Rome. Many of these potential limitations were addressed or ironed out within the first few years of operation. However, as will be discussed below, the issues of accountability and decision making were not adequately dealt with and remain a challenge.

Despite limitations, the CSM was widely supported and approved by the CSO delegates and later acknowledged by the CFS. As a leading human rights campaigner, noted:

> The drafting team knows this is not a perfect document because it would be impossible with such restrictions ... time and money. A great effort was made. There has never been an attempt to draft this type of document: with this type of work, it is one step forward ... This mechanism isn't aimed at representing involved organizations. The goal is to facilitate involvement in decision-making processes. This ensures this is an independent process that cannot be interfered with by power interest.
>
> (Field notes, October 2010, Rome)

Over the first three years of operation, the CSM was committed to a process of learning-while-doing. However, challenges inevitably popped up as the CSM became operational, notably with regards to how to organize the executive, how to ensure appropriate decision making, how to address tensions between communication and representation, how to respond to time pressures, when to work towards consensus and when to respect diversity, how to address linguistic challenges and finally, how to best ensure that the voices of those most affected by food insecurity are heard. Before reflecting on each of those challenges, the organizational structure of the CSM is presented.

Organizational structure of the CSM

The CSM is open to all CSOs working on issues related to food security. It is made up of the general membership, a Coordination Committee, working groups and a Secretariat.

CSM executive

The Coordination Committee acts as the executive of the CSM. The Mechanism is designed to have 41 Coordination Committee members from 17 sub-regions and 11 constituencies (see Table 5.1). There are seats for one focal point per sub-region and two focal points per constituency, with the exception of smallholder farmers who have four seats in recognition of the fact that farmers produce a large proportion of the world's food but are disproportionately food insecure. It was argued that in line with the reform vision, focusing on farmers would help to ensure that those most affected by food insecurity were engaged in CFS processes. The farmer focus also reflects the political objectives of powerful actors in the CSM who advance a food sovereignty framework which claims explicit rights for peasant and small-scale food producers. The structure of the Coordination Committee ensures that any person working on food security issues is represented by at least three people (one regionally and two constituently).

The processes through which each sub-region and constituency select the focal points to the Coordination Committee is determined by each group in recognition of the diversity of histories, realities and experiences. This means that there are intended to be 28 autonomous and transparent processes to select focal points.

The Terms of Reference outline key roles and responsibilities for Coordination Committee members. First, the Coordination Committee is to ensure that the functions of the CSM are carried out as effectively as possible and according to the organizing principles contained in the CSM proposal. These principles include: inclusivity; diversity; pluralism, autonomy and self-organization; gender and regional balance; and cooperation. Another key organizing principle is for "self-organized groups to speak for themselves in the CSM and have a greater representation in the mechanism" (CFS 2010: FN 2).

Table 5.1 Constituencies and sub-regions within the CSM Coordination Committee

Sub-regions
Total of 17 members (1 member per sub-region)

North America	South-East Asia
Central America and Caribbean	Central Asia
Andean Region	Oceania
Southern Cone	Southern Africa
Western Europe	West Africa
Eastern Europe	East Africa
West Asia	Central Africa
South Asia	North Africa
Pacifica	

Constituencies
Total of 24 members (2 members per constituency, smallholder farmers have 4)

Agricultural and food workers	Pastoralists
Artisanal fisherfolk	Smallholder farmers
Consumers	Urban poor
Indigenous peoples	Women
Landless	Youth
NGOs	

In practice, this means prioritizing the voices of social movement actors. Officially, the Coordination Committee has the role of facilitating participation of CSOs in CFS processes, including overseeing the work of civil society members of the CFS Advisory Group, as well as ensuring accountability of finances of the Mechanism. In practices, the accountability of finances falls under the responsibility of the finance and administrative sub-working group of the Coordination Committee. The Coordination Committee is also meant to ensure, to the best of their ability, effective two-way communication with CSM members and broader networks. With respect to decision making, the Coordination Committee is responsible for clarifying criteria for participation in the Mechanism, quotas for participation (including speaking) at the CFS Plenary,[4] selecting civil society members for the Advisory Group, providing support to these Advisory Group members, and assisting in the organization of the civil society meetings related to the CFS. In practice, things function differently. For example, the Secretariat has taken on the role of organizing CSO meetings. Other examples will be discussed below. The Coordination Committee is responsible for communicating the range of divergent positions held by participants in the Mechanism when providing views to the CFS and at the Advisory Group. In the original Terms of Reference the Coordination Committee also had the responsibility to dialogue with the CFS Bureau regarding the allocation of civil society seats and speaking slots in the annual CFS Plenary sessions.

At the CSO Consultation in October 2010, delegates began to plan the selection processes for the first Coordination Committee focal points, working first by region and then by constituency. Some regions opted to join together. A Latin American regional group was formed, as was an African group. There was a joint South and South-East Asian group, and Europe and North America also formed a group. The sub-regions themselves opted for these groupings because of low numbers and in many cases they were already working together at a regional level and their situations were comparable. Groups were assigned a list of questions asking for reflection on the context, key actors to be involved, strengths, weaknesses and barriers, and available resources. Groups were then encouraged to developed processes for the selection of the focal point. After the sub-regional discussions, the constituencies met and worked on the same task with the same questions. The aim of the work session was not to select Focal Points, although some groups did. Rather the purpose was to establish a clear, transparent and open process with people identified to move the process forward. This was important as many individuals and delegates were unable to attend the consultation due to barriers or inabilities to get visas or tickets on time.

Undertaking the selection process and the validation of the process by the Methodology Group took time but an initial group of selected focal points became the Coordination Committee. They held the function for 12 months during the interim period of 2010–2011 after which focal points were selected for a period of two years (2011–2013), although many remained in their position.

CSO Advisory Group members

Civil society actors have four seats on the Advisory Group to the CFS's Bureau. The CSM facilitates the selection of civil society actors from the Coordination Committee to sit on this Advisory Group. It is the responsibility of the CSO Advisory Group members to ensure that the views of civil society are heard by facilitating two-way communication between civil society and the CFS Bureau.

The original CSO Advisory Group members were representatives from ROPPA, the IPC, Oxfam International and the Mouvement International de la Jeunesse Agricole et Rurale Catholique (MIJARC). Under this arrangement they would serve for one year (2009–2010) and new Focal Points would be chosen from and by the Coordination Committee once it was more operational. However, at the Coordination Committee meeting in May 2011, it was decided that the CSO Advisory Group members would continue in their roles until October 2011, at which point new Advisory Group members were selected. This was, in part, in recognition of the role the original Advisory Group members had played in the process and because it was deemed important that the CSO Advisory Group members be able to work with the restrictions of limited

Table 5.2 Make-up of the Coordination Committee Advisory Group members as of September 2013

Advisory Group members 2010–2011	Advisory Group members 2011–2013
• NGO Coordination Committee Member (Oxfam then FoodFirst Information and Action Network (FIAN)) (male then female) • Small-Scale Farmer Coordination Committee member (male) • IPC representative (female) • Youth Coordination Committee member (male)	• Indigenous Coordination Committee member (2011–2012) (male) • Fisherfolk Coordination Committee member (2011–2012) (female) • Pastoralist Coordination Committee member (2011–2012) (male) • Two Youth Coordination Committee members (2011–2012 and 2012-13) (male and female) • Agricultural Workers Coordination member (2012–2013) (female) • Small-Scale Farmer Coordination Committee member (2012-2013) (male) • Latin American Coordination Committee member (2012-2013) (female)

time and resources, and be highly attuned to the politically sensitive nature of the work while maintaining a high degree of knowledge and political fluency. It also reflected challenges faced by the CSM in establishing the Coordination Committee. Whereas the first CSO Advisory Group members had legitimacy and trust based on their historical participation, in October 2011, eight new members were elected by and from the Coordination Committee for a period of two years on a rotational basis, with the acknowledgment that the eight CSO Advisory Group members would share responsibility and participation in the meetings. This was in part because of the difficulty of making a representative selection with only four people. This also reflects the fact that many of the actors selected to hold the Advisory Group seats are unable to travel at certain times because of existing commitments (e.g., harvest). The newly elected Advisory Group members had legitimacy based on their being elected, however, they lacked the historical experience and knowledge of their predecessors. They did, though, represent a far more diverse set of interests although, again, their function is not meant to be representation but rather facilitation.

These Advisory Group members are accountable to the Coordination Committee but in practice have taken on a stronger leadership role, for example taking decisions and leading internal processes. Indeed, the CSO Advisory Group members exert a great deal of influence because they interact directly with the CFS, putting them at the junction of the CFS–CSM interface. Given the reality of decision making, these Advisory Group members at times have to take important decisions without time for proper consultation. This may counter the operating principles of the CSM but responds to the reality of the way the CFS works. At the same time, the CSM has not lost sight of the reality of having to make quick and informed decisions.

Given the scope and diversity of the Coordination Committee, as well as challenges that span linguistics, connectivity, time zones and various levels of engagement, decision making in the CSM has proven challenging. Processes are under way within the CSM to re-evaluate how this is done. One approach which has proved rather successful is the creation of smaller working groups tasked with specific decisions, such as deciding which CSO proposals should be selected for the CFS side events.

Thematic policy working groups

To better coordinate civil society efforts in relation to the CFS's OEWGs and task teams, the CSM has established working groups—building where possible on established working groups—to organize civil society engagement and inputs. The role of the CSM working groups is to circulate relevant information on specific policy issues, provide a space for dialogue and the exchange of views among CSOs on the issues under consideration, provide a space for CSOs to develop strong and well-articulated civil society positions, and to provide inputs back to the CFS. The thematic policy working groups of the CSM mirror policy processes under way in the CFS and are open to all interested civil society participants. These working groups help to ensure "effective, diverse and expertise-driven civil society inputs into the policy discussions and negotiations" (CSM 2012:5). There is no predefined hierarchy or decision-making structure when it comes to the working groups, which could in part account for their success.

In 2013 there were 12 policy working groups responding to the CFS work agenda including, land tenure, agricultural investment, GSF, gender, nutrition, price volatility, protracted crisis and conflict, monitoring and mapping, social protection, climate change, biofuels, and the CFS program of work. In line with:

> the mandate of the CSM, working groups prioritize the participation of, and inputs from, small food producers and other people most affected by food insecurity and malnutrition, whilst ensuring civil society participation during meetings are representative of a regional, gender and constituency balance.
>
> (CSM 2012:5)

The Secretariat of the CSM tracked the number of active members in the working groups that operated in 2012. "Active" is qualified as follows:

> For most instances, "active" members of the working groups represent an entire network of CSOs, whereby they reach out and collate policy positions from a wider range of CSOs. Therefore, it is difficult to accurately account for and quantify the hundreds of civil society representatives who provide their expertise and inputs into the WGs [working groups] on a collective basis.
>
> (CSM 2012:5)

From 2010–2013, the numbers broke down as follows:

- Land Tenure: 75 active working group members
- Global Strategic Framework (GSF): 64 active working group members
- Responsible Agricultural Investment: 100 active working group members
- Climate Change: 40 active working group members
- Social Protection: 16 active working group members
- Protracted Crises: 94 active working group members
- Nutrition: 15 active working group members

What is included in the tally is the individual number of people who have requested to participate. This does not mean that they necessarily contributed or communicated back to their networks.

That the working groups are issue focused makes them appealing to a wide range of actors. One former member of the Coordination Committee explained:

> I think overall the Working Groups have worked quite well and there has been a lot of enthusiasm and engagement but occasionally some of the Working Groups are not as inclusive as they could be. The VGGT Working Group is always held up as a key example where diverse actors worked together and the voices of social movements were heard.
>
> (Interview, July 2014, Skype)

Building on this, the CSM working groups are structured to have a coordinator from a social movement and a resource person often from an NGO. In cases where a social movement actor is not found to act as coordinator, NGO actors would step in. The NGO participants tend to be very conscious of the political responsibility entrusted to them. One NGO actor coordinating a working group noted:

> as an NGO person, it shouldn't be my role and it's not what I wanted to do. But, also, I think that there was sufficient trust between each other and there was also kind of, I think a relatively good, how do you say that … reporting back and preparation and reporting back what the issues were … I also felt that there was sufficient backing in terms of the positions that we defended, so it wasn't really a difficulty. There was kind of a mandate by a broader group.
>
> (Interview, June 2012, Rome)

There remains ongoing concern and resistance on the part of social movements to ensure that NGO actors do not co-opt processes and that the CSM maintains its commitment to ensuring that the voices of those most affected by food insecurity are heard.

However, in the working groups, tensions between social movements and NGOs, often prevalent in Coordination Committee interactions have tended

to soften. One way that some working groups have made use of the NGO/
social movement divide has been to play on the strengths of each group. Not
exclusively, but broadly, NGOs provide strong technical support and facilitation capacity and social movements provide the political legitimacy and
grounded rationales when negotiations turn counter to the approaches favored
by CSOs. This strategy was most obvious and effective in negotiations on the
Voluntary Guidelines for the Responsible Governance of Tenure of Land,
Fisheries and Forests in the Context of National Food Security. That said,
the tensions between NGOs and social movements will not go away, and nor
should they necessarily.

Funding

Funding for the Civil Society Mechanism has been an issue since its inception and is likely to remain so.[5] Early on in the process one social movement
coordinator noted:

> Financing is always a difficult issue … Governments are usually surprised
> on how we participate with no resources. Oxfam has contributed human
> resources, how does it compare with the inputs of IPC? How far should
> we go in our contribution? Where does it end? … It is difficult to find
> finances for the Secretariat. Translation is another issue that has to be
> addressed. At this point the Secretariat is conceptual as they are not funded
> … It is our collective responsibility for funding. It is important for us to
> dialogue with governments that normally give us money.
>
> (Field notes, June 2011, Cordoba)

The difference in funding for social movements and NGO funding has been a
central tension. It is undeniable that Oxfam has more financial resources than
the IPC. This raises important issues with respect to representation and the
priorities of the CSM. These concerns were captured in the comments of one
civil society representative who asked: "If there isn't sufficient funding, what
do we do, send the NGO who can self-fund and give legitimacy to a process
that is being seriously derailed?" (field notes, June 2011, Cordoba).

NGO resources donated to the CSM in 2012 provided needed reserves
while the CSM waited for the release of funds through the multi-donor trust
fund administered by the FAO. After a great deal of lobbying, the CSM secured
funds through donations from member states. The Coordination Committee
members made a decision to partner with NGOs that had the capacity to manage funds. It was agreed that the holding of funds should be rotational and
that new NGOs should be brought in to help administer CSM funds. This
decision was a political one with many social movement actors fearing that an
international NGO held a disproportionate amount of power because it was
holding the funds. In 2013, the CSM transferred its funds to a smaller Italian
NGO. One limitation of the move was that the CSM was not able to rely on

this NGO to advance resources and cover funding gaps (CSM 2013), a security provided to them when the international NGO had held the funds. Such issues raise the question of whether the CSM should seek legal status so that it can manage its own funds independently.

The CSM uses its fund to ensure the active participation of CSOs in CFS processes. During the first quarter of 2012, the CSM spent €101,449 on four CFS Advisory Group meetings (including preparatory teleconferences and meetings in all three languages, as well as the translation of briefing notes); the CFS-rai meeting in January 2012, including a two days preparatory meeting; and other CFS OEWGs (i.e., monitoring, program of work and priorities, and finance). The money also goes towards paying for office costs and salaries of the Secretariat (three staff people).

One significant cost to the CSM is translation. In 2012 the CSM spent 21 percent of its resources on interpretation and translation. During the first quarter of 2013 the percentage of these expenses rose to 31 percent of total expenditures (CSM 2013). Interpretation and translation are vital for ensuring the full participation of all actors in the CSM and the CFS, especially social movements. However, there may be a need for the Coordination Committee to reflect on how money is spent as more money spent on translation means less funds available to support direct participation in CSM and CFS meetings (CSM 2013).

Internal challenges facing the CSM

The CSM is a novel mechanism for coordinating the effective participation of a diversity of actors in multilateral governance processes, but there have been growing pains. In what follows, key internal challenges faced by the CSM in its first three years of operation are presented along with a review of how participants sought to address them. The aim here is to illustrate how civil society actors are collectively managing their participation in the CFS.

The Coordination Committee: Growing pains

One of the key challenges within the organization of the CSM has been the operationalization of the Coordination Committee. The development of the Coordination Committee took much longer than expected, and by the end of the second year, 13 seats remained unfilled. Reasons for this included lack of contacts or networks in specific regions and constituencies as well as failure of interested parties to undertake an appropriate selection process and/or to submit these processes for approval. These challenges serve to highlight the difficulties of widening participation to include actors who previously stood outside of the process or whose current struggles and focus are localized. Indeed, key groups that have been marginalized by, or worked outside of and/or against, these processes are now faced with the task of determining ways of moving into these circles (Peine and McMichael 2005:32). Central to this transitional process from outsiders to insiders is the development of trust, networks, new skills and working through issues of representation and legitimacy. At the same time, in other fora, and especially in local contexts, these actors continue to push and resist dominant governance structures, adding another layer of complexity.

A major limitation in the design of the Coordination Committee is that there are few incentives for those who currently sit as focal points to review or develop accountability mechanisms or to find ways to improve decision making from a transparency and efficiency perspective. One EU-based food security analyst noted: "The Terms of Reference of the CC [Coordination Committee] talks about what the collective does but not the responsibilities of the individual CC members when they go back" (field notes, June 2011, Cordoba).

It was originally decided that the CSM's Terms of Reference would undergo formal review after one year, at which point changes and improvements could be made. The review never happened. This was in part due to a delayed start to the functioning of the Coordination Committee. Identifying constituency and sub-regional focal points through approved processes took more time than anticipated and by the end of the first year not enough had be accomplished within the operation of the CSM to warrant evaluation and review. Another reason was resources. A third and ongoing reason links to power: there is little incentive for those currently in power to review the Mechanism or to lose their power. As one expert noted:

> Anyone who understands power struggles in social movements sees the CSM as a platform for them to push their political platform. So the enthusiasm is less about the CSM perhaps and more about CSM becoming a platform for advancing political agendas.
>
> (Interview, June 2014, Skype)

Those constituencies and sub-regions that have undergone processes to appoint new focal points have predominantly been from wealthy countries and/or more internationally established organizations suggesting at least three things. First, there is arguably greater awareness in and across these regions and constituencies about the CFS and the CSM as well as opportunities for leadership through the Coordination Committee. Second, such processes require capital and capacity. Third, it illustrates the power and influence that such a position can bring to civil society actors, especially in the global South. Engagement in the CFS can expand the networks of CSOs and act as a gateway to other processes and fora. As one Coordination Committee member from a social movement explained:

> Through the constituency approach, through the CSM, now we are able to prioritize. [We] know our issues. Because we are quite actively involved in the CFS ... UNEP is now interested in inviting [us] to engage. Through the CFS access, we gain more opportunities across the UN system.
>
> (Interview, June 2014, Skype)

This exposure strengthens the networks of civil society actors participating in CFS activities through the CSM. It provides exposure, capacity building and greater opportunities to lobby for, educate about, and promote their issues. Such opportunities can also increase the social capital of actors back in their home communities as their frequent international travel is evidence of their influence and importance.

At the same time, there are risks. These individuals have been, at least in principle, selected on the basis of their communication and leadership skills. Bringing them into the UN system has the benefits noted above but it also risks removing community leaders from their communities. Furthermore, inability to properly engage across the constituency or region due to over-engagement in other fora could serve to delegitimize members of the Coordination Committee and the CFS more broadly.

A lack of consideration and processes around monitoring, accountability (i.e. how to ensure Focal Points are actually consulting and communicating with their regions or constituencies) and a lack of measures for recourse against those who do not fulfil their roles are all potentially significant challenges and limitations in the operation of the CSM. Time will tell if the Coordination Committee is able to develop, implement and then uphold such measures and if they find a way to rotate Coordination Committee members.

At the same time, the original Terms of Reference call for a complete change-over of the Coordination Committee every two years. This could be devastating to the functioning of the Mechanism. The CSM would have been well advised to develop a rotational mechanism when this problem was first anticipated. For example, at the 2010 CSO Consultation a proposal was made suggesting that each region and constituency create a committee that rotates members every two years. This would provide the benefit of support, training and knowledge transfer to members on the committee while working to ensure better diversity and sharing of power. The proposal was not taken on by any of the groups. At that same meeting, a key actor in the CSM noted that:

> there are still issues that need to be addressed: inclusivity, accountability mechanisms. Reviewing constituencies and making sure no one is falling through the gaps. Clarify the decision-making processes in the mechanism. Ensure gender is addressed through the mechanism. What are the criteria for membership? How will we ensure documents are translated? How do we make sure this is working at the national and regional levels … we need to build on this good start, keep moving forward so that in one year we are more organized and more inclusive and working together.
> (Field notes, October 2010, Rome)

These calls were set aside and discussion turned to issues related to process.

Some actors engaged in the CFS have identified the Coordination Committee's focus on internal process as limiting and have expressed this publicly in CSM meetings. As one participant from a prominent rural network lamented during the 2011 Civil Society Forum in advance of the 37th Session of the CFS: "I feel like this is a waste of time. I came here to talk about issues, about solutions, and they spent the whole meeting talking about how they will organize themselves. I don't have time for that" (interview, October 2011, Rome).

At the same meeting, the Coordination Committee began organizing meetings in camera to address more sensitive issues. While this does raise worrying questions about transparency and legitimacy, this is not necessarily negative. Instead, despite the growing pains, these actions can be seen as social movement actors coming to own the process and the Mechanism and working through the issues in a way they deem appropriate.

Recognizing that the CSM builds on a distinct history of engagement and operates within a particular governance space that allows it to function as it does, there are some lessons that can be identified and that can serve to both improve the organization of the CSM and inform the development of similar mechanisms.

The first lesson is that a 41-person executive, while admirable for its inclusive nature, is simply too large to be effective. The challenges are amplified when working across three languages and multiple time zones. One approach would be to reconsider the current weighting given to sub-regional focal points and constituency focal points. While regional distribution is important in has also served to create factions within the Coordination Committee. Another approach would be to implement rotational leadership across sub-regions and constituencies to streamline the Committee. A rotation system would also ensure that the Coordination Committee can take advantage of experience and expertise and mentor new members instead of starting from scratch every two years.

The CSM Coordination Committee also requires transparent and enforceable accountability mechanisms with recourse measures for non-compliance. Such mechanisms need to be flexible and to adapt to the capacities and realities of focal points and there must be support (both financial and in terms of capacity building) so that focal points can fulfil their responsibilities. This is admittedly easier said than done given limited financial resources and time.

The Coordination Committee needs to make a transition from a heavy focus on inward decision making and internal processes towards an outward focus on the broader work of the CSM. Understandably, the work of getting the CMS operationalized has meant that the Coordination Committee needed to reflect on process, but now that the CSM is operational there is a need for the leadership to engage more actively in the policy, outreach and communication work of the CSM, notably through the policy working groups. As a former member of the Coordination Committee explained:

> While the Working Groups can work well to an extent with an internally focused Coordination Committee, they are only able to be

effective in a limited sense. If the CSM cannot engage more CSOs and social movements in ongoing processes and build on moment, then the CSM will stand still or even move backwards. The way the CSM ensures that the voices of the social movements are heard is through the outreach of the CC members and regional consultations. This has impacts on how you spend the money. Do you support regional outreach through constituencies or do you enable the Working Groups to go out and conduct consultations?

(Interview, July 2014, Skype)

The working groups are increasingly the public face of the Mechanisms and are also the sites through which new actors get involved in the CSM. As such they are fundamental to maintaining the legitimacy of the CSM.

Participation versus representation

One of the main functions of the CSM is to facilitate the participation of people from sub-regions and constituencies in the CFS. Members of the CSM, especially members of the Coordination Committee, are not meant to represent the views of their organization. Rather, they are meant to play a communicative and networking function: they are meant to be facilitators. The final report of the Civil Society Consultation in advance of the 36th Session (Duncan and von Anrep 2010:8) explains:

> The Coordination Committee is the backbone of the CSM. One of the Coordination Committee's roles is to work hard to facilitate the participation of those in subregions and constituencies. In no way is the CC to be seen as a committee of people representing the views of their organization. Rather, they play a communicative and networking function.

This is easier said than done and as alluded to above, is in fact not being done very effectively. CSO participants are politically, intellectually and emotionally tied to their personal positions and those of their organization. To separate themselves from their values presents a challenge. However, the fact that this conversation has happened within the CSM points to an awareness of the roles and responsibilities of civil society as well as potential critics. Furthermore, the discussion highlights a deep awareness and understanding of the politics of representation and legitimacy held by the designers of the CSM.

Another important issue to consider is the implications of participation. In order to effectively participate in the CFS, civil society actors have had to undergo a process of internalizing not only the values of liberalism and neoliberalism but also the logic of bureaucratization (evident through their fluency in UN processes and language). This is not to suggest that CSOs have become pawns in the process. Indeed much of their engagement is strategic and well deliberated. Furthermore, resistance can emerge when actors question or redefine social norms and the identities ascribed to them by way of these norms (i.e., "peasant farmer," "poor African"). Resistance begins by challenging these socially prescribed identities and by transforming their subjectivity. An example of this can be seen in the way in which La Via Campesina has effectively challenged the discourse and social construction of the peasant or *campesino* (Desmarais 2007). For members of La Via Campesina, peasants are not poor, powerless, antiquated farmers; they are a coalition of savvy producers with a great deal of traditional and localized knowledge who are not on the fringes of industrial production but in fact in the majority.

Within the CFS, civil society and governments from the global South are increasingly aware of the power of influence and legitimacy that can be summoned up by drawing on lived experience of oppression, poverty and injustice. As global governance processes move towards increased participation and new definitions of expertise and knowledge, new experts can rise up and claim authority and legitimacy based on their lived experience. In line with theories of embedded neoliberalism (Chapter 2), they do so within a governance framework that seeks to maintain the influence of the dominant system that contributed to the oppression in the first place.

Time

Decisions taken by the Coordination Committee require translation, consultation, deliberation and decision making, both within the Coordination Committee and between the Focal Points and constituents. However, often the CFS does not give adequate time for this process and thus decisions are made without full consultation or even participation. There are also Coordination Committee members who despite having agreed to play a communication function do not respond to requests for decisions in a timely fashion, if at all. Similar challenges are faced by the working groups who are often expected to provide quick feedback on proposals. CSOs have found ways of addressing this problem by building trust among participants, trying to maintain open and transparent communication, translating all documents when possible and ensuring that clear deadlines are attached to requests for feedback. Of course, such deadlines are only useful if people are able to read their correspondence in a timely fashion and in a language they understand.

Consensus versus maintaining diversity

A central principle of the CSM is respecting diversity. CSO actors in the CSM works to find points of agreement on policy issues and to forward united positions and statements agreed upon by consensus by all participants. While there is recognition of the diversity of perspectives across CSOs working within the

CSM, there is also awareness of the political impact gained through united positions. Yet, CSOs participating in the CFS, especially in negotiations, face pressure to speak with a united voice. For example, at a plenary session of the 37th Session of the CFS (October 2011), the CFS chair encouraged civil society participants to speak with a unified voice, suggesting multiple CSO perspectives add confusion to an already complicated process. One government delegate noted that from his perspective, a united CSO endorsement of a specific recommendation carries more weight than that of some member states (interview, October 2011, Rome). Another negotiator noted:

> it would help to moderate and articulate and make more reasonable the positions and the views of civil society. Some in civil society would view this as co-option ... But is it a co-option or is it people getting together to understand the reasons behind some proposal and trying to find a way around it and so on and so on?
>
> (Interview, October 2011, Rome)

Arriving at a point of consensus often involves long discussions and processes of compromise on the part of all actors thereby moving them away from their original objectives. Chantal Mouffe (2000:17) warns that this process of consensus building "always entails some form of exclusion." Thus, while these processes of deliberation and consensus building form a fundamental part of the CSM, and the UN decision-making process more broadly, they also inevitably result in a form of social exclusion where the ideas of some actors are left out.

More specifically, within the CSM, coming to consensus has proved challenging not only for lack of shared approaches but also for lack of engagement. The membership of the CSM spans the world and actors possess varying levels of commitment and connectivity. Furthermore, working in three languages has proven, not surprisingly, challenging. Getting the working groups and Coordination Committee to come to consensus (note that in the structure of the CSM, silence is not taken as agreement) on issues in a timely fashion has meant frustration, delays and sometimes moving ahead without consensus, as often the CSM is only given a few days to react to documents or prepare for meetings. Here again, the commitment to transparency and the development of strong relations of trust are key to the successful operation of the CSM within the political space of the CFS.

Language

As noted above, one the largest expenses of the CSM is translation and interpretation. Across the CSM, within the Coordination Committee and among the CSO Advisory Group members, language is an issue. The linguistic challenges extend beyond spoken language to the ways in which different actors speak and who they are speaking for. There are also differences in how people speak that impact communication.

Consider that in one discussion, a peasant farmer from Argentina spoke about the wisdom of potatoes and the importance of listening and learning from potatoes (field notes, August 2011, Jokkmokk). For those not familiar with indigenous systems of knowledge, such a statement is immediately interpreted as quaint at best and is likely to be overlooked and widely dismissed. However, the meaning behind what was being said relates to specific technical knowledge about plant health and changing ecological conditions with important implications for food security. Because of the narrative way in which the issue is presented, the "policy impact" is overlook or missed entirely. This amounts to cross-cultural misunderstandings that extend beyond linguistics. It also illuminates the contrast between the processes undertaken by many social movements through their gatherings, and the often sterile and bureaucratic nature of the CSM which has to conform to the working processes of a UN committee.

"The voices of those most affected by food security"

The CSM remains committed to ensuring the participation of those most affected by food security in the CFS. This is reflected in the makeup of the CSM Coordination Committee and in the structure of the working groups as well as in the discourse of CSM participants. In the 2012 Annual Report (CSM 2012:4) this point is made explicit: "At the core of the CSM is the understanding that those most affected must be the agents of their own development and change." Towards this end, there is a widely held but contentious view within the CSM that participating NGOs have a key role to play in supporting social movements. As key actor in the CSM noted:

> Now we have the opportunity, through the CFS reform and the CSM, we have an opportunity to make change. We have a process and structure in place to engage people. It is important for NGOs to support the CFS process and broad engagement by civil society.
>
> (Field notes, October 2010, Rome)

Later, this actor clarified why their NGO supported the CSM:

> One, the organizing principles that are laid out and the structure of the mechanism: inclusiveness, transparency and openness. Two, because there is now a mechanism to ensure that it [participation] is broad, inclusive, etcetera. They [the drafting committee] took a look at these principles and tried to reflect these principles. This means some of the traditional leaders took a step back and let others move forward because this is fundamental if the mechanism is to succeed.
>
> (Field notes, October 2010, Rome)

This tension between NGOs and social movements permeates civil society engagement in food policy at all levels and raises a few key issues. First, NGOs do not need to engage with the CSM to participate in the CFS and could easily avoid engagement all together. This would effectively serve to challenge the legitimacy of the CSM as the facilitating mechanism for the CFS. The fact that they do engage is illustrative of their commitment to the values of the CSM. Second, NGOs have provided important technical support in the development of the mechanism and continue to provide support in the working groups and in the development of political strategies. Third, some financial support for the mechanism has been provided by supportive NGOs. For example, Canadian Foodgrains Bank, Oxfam, Action Aid and Welthungerhilfe have all supported the CSM financially. Finally, attempts to exclude a constituency of the Coordination Committee from positions of power are also cause for concern. Yet, they continues to highlight an ongoing lack of trust and fear on the part of social movement actors to previous formulations of power within the CSM and beyond, which relied (at times heavily) on technical and methodological support from Western NGOs. Social movement concerns also serve to continuously reinforce the CSM value of ensuring that those most affected by food security are not simply engaged but are leading the process.

Engaging with the CFS

Through the reform process and initial reform years of the CFS, the engagement of CSOs in the CFS was, on the whole, positively perceived. As one EU diplomat noted:

> [T]here was a sense of optimism from the [country] to say that the CFS actually is inclusive. We think that the management of the CFS needs to be improved, but the principles and the tenets of the CFS are sound. What we really valued in 2010 was the inclusion of the Civil Society Mechanism.
>
> (Interview, June 2012, Rome)

This sentiment was repeated in conversations and interviews other negotiators. When asked about the role of civil society in the CFS, one negotiator from a G20 country responded:

> I think it was fundamental because it was the momentum and the push, the voices, the voices were clearly articulated and powerful and also getting at the right points. That helped move the process along. I think they were vital and I think that lots of things would not have turned out the way they did if lots of factors weren't in place at that moment. So it was not taken for granted at all.
>
> (Interview, October 2011, Rome)

However, the engagement of CSO actors can also support weaker states. As a representative from a major international NGO based in Rome reflected:

This is the important role of civil society, because civil society is reducing, in a sense, power inequalities, because of the openness and transparency of the process. In a closed-door thing you can have just the big powerful countries that go and just shut out countries, and that's it. But in something like the CFS, you cannot do that, because everything is about agreement and the linkage with food security. You show that it is good for food security, and also you can kind of empower African states, because they are the most affected and so they are the ones that know more what they need. And this kind of changes power dynamics at the negotiations, and you can have even really small countries making a lot of impact.

(Interview, October 2012, Rome)

This view was shared and expanded on by the negotiator from a G20 country:

Sometimes the benefit is that we push things that perhaps wouldn't be pushed for if civil society wasn't there. The other benefit, once you give people an opportunity to really engage and be part of the decision-making process—some countries object to that—civil society is part of the decision-making process, just not of the decision-making itself. The decision making, yes, not the decision. But if people are part of the decision-making process, it's much more difficult to then just say no to everything and to come in with radical positions. You are extending a hand to them and inviting them to get in the process and as a result you benefit from much more reasonable positions from both sides.

(Interview, October 2012, Rome)

Recognizing the contributions they are making to the process, civil society actors do not take their participation for granted and recognize the looming potential for things to revert to how they were. For example, at the first meeting of the Coordination Committee, a key actor in the CSM stated: "There is a constant battle to ensure civil society participation. We cannot just sit back and relax" (field notes, June 2011, Cordoba). Reflecting on the first three years of engagement in the reformed CFS, an NGO actor from the North reflected on the frustration of the ongoing struggle to have their participatory status recognized: "Before consensus we should be equal participants in the discussion and contribute our own expertise. But this is a process that we go through with every single chair" (interview, Skype, June 2014).

Reflections on scaling out the CSM and CFS models

Since the initial success of the CSM, CSOs have been considering whether the experience of the reformed CFS and CSM should be duplicated for other multilateral processes (in particular for the UNFCCC). Two separate issues require reflection on these issues: institutional reform and civil society mobilization.

With respect to the first, the reform of the CFS came about due to a variety of factors that proved central to its success. First, there is the long history of civil society engagement in the FAO and the CFS. Furthermore, there is a history of CSOs working towards greater participation in the Committee specifically. This means that there was time for relationships to develop and for the institution to adapt. In line with this, direct challenges to dominant understandings of "expertise" within the Committee have been widely accepted as made evident not only through the engagement of CSOs on the Advisory Group, as well as on task teams and OEWGs, but also in the structure and principles of the CFS's HLPE. These factors created a more favorable environment for this sort of reform.

A key point to consider is the importance of individuals. The reform of the CFS was successful in part because people involved truly believed in the importance of CSO engagement. The chairs of the CFS have supported the engagement of CSO and now the Director-General of the FAO is championing civil society engagement. It remains to be seen who at the UNFCCC could be the champion of such a reform. The most obvious contender is the Climate Action Network.

While not the primary impetus for change, the reform of the CFS gained traction as a reaction to a major humanitarian crisis: 1 billion people hungry. The severity of the situation gave the reform political urgency. The acuteness of the crisis opened up space for institutional change. Another related point is that the CFS remains politically benign: especially as the G8, G20 and other "more influential actors" continue to focus on food security. Because the CFS cannot take binding decisions, there is little political risk of bringing CSOs to the table. However, this can also be seen as an opportunity: keeping the activities below ministerial level means that there is more flexibility, less politicking and more space for creativity. However, it also means that the outcomes carry less weight. What has been interesting to watch is the way in which CSOs have dealt with this by linking policy recommendations back to international commitments.

The stability of the Committee, which remains based in Rome, is also an important and distinguishing feature. Unlike the UNFCCC which hosts plenary meetings in different countries, despite having the Secretariat in Bonn, having the Committee in Rome and attended predominantly by Rome-based country representatives means that there are people in one spot, working on the issues, in contact with technical staff and each other. This is important for the lobbying work of CSOs, for consistency, for networking and for getting people to the table.

At the height of the food price crisis, the FAO was put on the defensive as they faced the threat of a loss of power and authority as new players (e.g., G8, G20, HLTF, World Economic Forum) began to seek out more prominent positions within the transnational policy space mediating global food security governance. This suggests that a widening of participation across the FAO and within the CFS was in part strategic: increasing participation allowed the

Committee to tap into calls for increased transparency and participation, notably by G77 countries and CSOs.

A final issue comes down to decision making, which remains the responsibility of member states. In the area of food security, there is relative cohesion and consensus around food security. This is not the case when it comes to climate change. This level of agreement in turn provides space for the voices of civil society. However, when it comes to climate change negotiations, the lack of agreement among member states makes it harder for them to come together and agree to give CSOs a voice, "knowing that it might contribute to shift power balances" (email correspondence with representative of a large international NGO active in the CSM since the beginning, November 2012).

The second level of analysis must consider the CSM itself. The CSM worked well initially because it had a core group of politically astute and relatively well-paid (or at least financially stable, for the most part) people with a history of engagement who could dedicate time on the ground to developing the proposal, conducting a consultation and presenting a document that could be endorsed by a broad range of civil society actors. What is more, they had legitimacy, authority and trust for the most part and this was really important at the beginning. The IPC was clearly central in this (along with Rome-based NGOs).

The work of the IPC and others included a broad (although not uniform) commitment to a political framework and a positive vision of change (food sovereignty). This created a political grounding and a starting point that has served to unify a lot of the actors. Of course not everyone subscribes to food sovereignty as an approach or as a label, but there is widespread acceptance of the principles (such as human rights, people's choice, ecological principles, gender equality). So while there is a diversity of opinions within the CSM, there are few who disagree fundamentally with a food sovereignty approach. This has been fundamental to ensuring that infighting among CSOs remains limited. A mechanism to address issues such as climate change or biodiversity would benefit from a similar overarching framework, grounded in the struggle and realities of those most affected by the issues. There is also the issue of who should be engaged in the mechanism. The CSM relied on categories defined by the FAO, but it is not clear how such categories could be defined in other fora.

Along these lines, a key strength of the CSM is its commitment to facilitating the inclusion of the voices of those most affected by food insecurity. This builds on the longer-term experience of CSOs working through the IPC. At the same time, the IPC has had to open up its own mechanism to other CSOs working on food security, including larger NGOs and nutrition groups. This can be seen in the way in which the IPC initially facilitated the CSM process but also in the development of IPC+, which brings together the farmers' organizations and social movements active in the IPC as well as NGOs. In summary, while the expansion of civil society engagement in multilateral policy fora should be welcomed and encouraged, the political and historic realities that bring about institutional change must be carefully considered.

Conclusion

The reform of the CFS and establishment of the CSM is illustrative of a participatory turn in global governance. Examining how this unfolds in practice not only uncovers new complexities and challenges but can also show how these are being addressed. These challenges are being navigated by networks that have been expanded to incorporate actors who have predominantly been committed to deconstructing and contesting the logic of embedded neoliberalism within food security policy, most notably through the advancement of a food sovereignty framework. The understanding of civil society actors of the impacts of embedded neoliberalism was made visible in a statement made by the leader of a farmers' movement in West Africa on an expert panel on food price volatility:

> Instead of responding to the causes of our poverty and of price volatility, we have seen whole catalogues of projects and programs financed in the name of the agricultural sector, billions of dollars are mobilized every year, but the truth is that more than half of the peasant families in the majority of our countries do not have access to money to buy a plough, a couple of oxen, a cart, or a donkey.
>
> (Coulibaly 2011)

The farmers' movement leader from West Africa further elaborated upon the process of neoliberalism and its impact:

> About thirty years ago I was in school and we were told that it was better to produce for external markets … We were then told that the state was inefficient and that more space had to be given to the private sector. At the same time, our states were forced to go even more into debt in order to re-establish macroeconomic equilibrium. We were told that any support to peasant agriculture—deemed to be non-performing—had to be cut … Then we were told to become competitive according to the criteria of international financial institutions, and that our states were not allowed to protect us any longer. All custom tariffs have been dismantled and our markets have been liberalized, food products produced elsewhere have started dumping into our markets at low prices, making us even more vulnerable to price volatility … However, none of these "solutions" that have been imposed on us moved us out of poverty. Worse, we became even more vulnerable. It is within this context that peasant agriculture is being asked to perform.
>
> (Coulibaly 2011)

The approach to food security programing and policy critiqued above exemplifies the deep entrenchment of neoliberalism within the institutional behavior, political processes and understandings of socioeconomic "realities"

(Cerny 2008:3). Food security programs and agriculture policies have been transformed by and within this process. Within the reformed CFS, farmers and peasants, pastoralists and fisherfolk are faced with the difficult task of balancing their approaches, their knowledge and their livelihood strategies not only with those of other civil society actors but also with nation-states, the private sector and international financial institutions, many of which serve to maintain and strengthen the logic of neoliberalism. Despite this, and some growing pains, the organization of the CSM has been successful. Its success has led to much interest in the Mechanism and raised questions about the potential to scale-out the model to other transnational spaces.

Just as the previous chapter made the case that the CFS should be seen as a benchmark, rather than a model, for participatory governance at the global level, so too must the CSM be understood as part of a unique trajectory. This was not lost on those involved in the broader CFS process. At the first meeting of the Mechanism's Coordination Committee, one FAO representative acknowledged that:

> This meeting is historic, the fruit of many years of hard preparatory work, from social organizations comprised of many social groups and social movements and other movements who have been advocating and affecting change for many decades. The engagement of CSOs as participants in the CFS process builds on the collective experience of this group. Contributions to the World Food Summit, World Food Summit +5, development of the IPC, inception and adoption for the guidelines for the realization of the right to food.
>
> (Field notes, June 2011, Cordoba)

The recognition of the process and actors involved has been fundamental to the ordering, structuring and functioning of the CSM over the first years of operation. At the same time, the CSM is an innovative mechanism that is adapting to the changing governance architecture of food security. As such, throughout the development and implementation of the CSM, there has been recognition that the process will not be perfect. What has been stressed is the need for transparency, to follow the established processes and to maximize communication.

While understanding how the CSM operates is interesting in and of itself, it tells us very little about efficacy in terms of influencing CFS processes. In the next three chapters the engagement of CSOs in CFS negotiations is reviewed to provide insight into how the CSM engages with the CFS and where the engagement leads to change.

Notes

1 For a review of this, see Bitzer et al. (2012) and Fuchs et al. (2009).
2 For a review of the use of these terms in the UN see McKeon (2009:11–16).

3 It is interesting to note that in many ways the CSM process mirrors the CFS process for consultation and drafting (see for example Chapter 7 on the Voluntary Guidelines).
4 In practice, policy working groups mostly do this but under the "guidance" of the Coordination Committee members.
5 Given the political and sensitive nature of finances, a decision has been made to provide only a broad summary based on publicly available information.

References

Bitzer, V., P. Glasbergen, and B. Arts. 2012. "Exploring the Potential of Intersectoral Partnerships to Improve the Position of Farmers in Global Agrifood Chains: Findings from the Coffee Sector in Peru." *Agriculture and Human Values* 30(1):5–20. Retrieved May 1, 2014 (http://link.springer.com/10.1007/s10460-012-9372-z).

Cerny, P. 2008. "Embedding Neoliberalism: The Evolution of a Hegemonic Paradigm." *The Journal of International Trade and Diplomacy* 2(1):1–46.

CFS. 1998. *Possible Modalities for NGO Participation in the Work of the Committee on World Food Security.* Rome: FAO. Retrieved (www.fao.org/docrep/meeting/W8327e.htm).

CFS. 1999. *Report of the 25th Session of the Committee on World Food Security.* Rome: FAO. Retrieved (www.fao.org/docrep/meeting/X2194e.htm#P190_21846).

CFS. 2008. *Proposals to Strengthen the Committee on World Food Security to Meet New Challenges (CFS:2008/6).* Rome: FAO. Retrieved (ftp://ftp.fao.org/docrep/fao/meeting/014/k3029e.pdf).

CFS. 2009. *Reform of the Committee on World Food Security Final Version.* Rome: FAO. Retrieved (www.fao.org/fileadmin/templates/cfs/Docs0910/ReformDoc/CFS_2009_2_Rev_2_E_K7197.pdf).

CFS. 2010. *Proposal for an International Food Security and Nutrition Civil Society Mechanism for Relations with CFS.* CFS:2010/9. Rome: FAO.

Coulibaly, I. 2011. *Presentation to Policy Roundtable on Food Price Volatility, 37th Session of the Committee on World Food Security (19 October).* Rome: FAO.

CSM. 2012. *Annual Report 2012.* Rome: FAO. Retrieved (www.csm4cfs.org/files/SottoPagine/86/csm_annual_report_2012.pdf).

CSM. 2013. *CSM Financial Report for the 1st Quarter of 2013.* Rome: FAO. Retrieved (www.csm4cfs.org/files/SottoPagine/87/1q_report_new_en.pdf).

Desmarais, A. A. 2007. *La Vía Campesina: Globalization and the Power of Peasants.* Halifax, Nova Scotia: Fernwood.

Duncan, J., and D. Barling. 2012. "Renewal through Participation in Global Food Security Governance: Implementing the International Food Security and Nutrition Civil Society Mechanism to the Committee on World Food Security." *International Journal of Sociology of Agriculture and Food* 19:143–61.

Duncan, J., and A. von Anrep. 2010. *Civil Society Consultation to the 36th Session of the Committee on World Food Security.* Rome: CFS.

FAO. 1997. *Resolution 8/97 Report of the Conference of FAO. Twenty-Ninth Session.* Rome: FAO. Retrieved (www.fao.org/docrep/W7475e/W7475e0a.htm).

FAO. 2002. *World Food Summit: Five Years Later.* Rome: FAO. Retrieved (www.fao.org/docrep/MEETING/005/Y7106e/Y7106E09.htm).

FAO. 2006. *Report of the Council of FAO: Hundred and Thirty-First Session.* Rome: FAO. Retrieved (ftp://ftp.fao.org/docrep/fao/meeting/011/j8664e.pdf).

Fuchs, D., A. Kalfagianni, and T. Havinga. 2009. "Actors in Private Food Governance: The Legitimacy of Retail Standards and Multistakeholder Initiatives with Civil Society

Participation." *Agriculture and Human Values* 28(3):353–67. Retrieved May 1, 2014 (http://link.springer.com/10.1007/s10460-009-9236-3).

Henkel, H., and R. Stirrat. 2001. "Participation as Spiritual Duty; Empowerment as Secular Subjection." pp. 168–84 in *Participation: The New Tyranny?*, edited by B Cooke and U Kothari. London: Zed Press.

Holt-Giménez, E., and M. A. Altieri. 2013. "Agroecology, Food Sovereignty and the New Green Revolution." *Journal of Sustainable Agriculture* 37(1):90–102. Retrieved (www.tandfonline.com/doi/abs/10.1080/10440046.2012.716388).

Hospes, O. 2013. "Food Sovereignty: The Debate, the Deadlock, and a Suggested Detour." *Agriculture and Human Values* 31(1): 119–130.

Joseph, J. 2012. *The Social in the Global*. Cambridge: Cambridge University Press. Retrieved May 2, 2014 (http://ebooks.cambridge.org/ref/id/CBO9781139149143).

McKeon, N. 2009. *The United Nations and Civil Society: Legitmating Global Governance – Whose Voice?* London: Zed Books.

Mouffe, C. 2000. *Deliberative Democracy or Agonistic Pluralism*. Political Science Series no. 72. Retrieved (www.ihs.ac.at/publications/pol/pw_72.pdf).

Pateman, C. 2012. "Participatory Democracy Revisited." *Perspective on Politics* 10(1):7–19.

Peine, E., and M. McMichael. 2005. "Globalization and Global Governance," pp. 19–33 in *Agriculture Governance: Globalization and the New Politics of Regulation*, edited by V. Higgins and G. Lawrence. New York: Routledge.

Saurugger, S. 2010. "The Social Construction of the Participatory Turn: The Emergence of a Norm in the European Union." *European Journal of Political Research* 49(4):471–95. Retrieved (http://doi.wiley.com/10.1111/j.1475-6765.2009.01905.x).

6   Multilateral power dynamics

Comparing outcomes of policy roundtables

Introduction

After the 2007–2008 food price crisis, there was swell of activity at that the global level to address a food system that pushed the number of hungry people in the world to over 1 billion. In a race for leadership over a changing architecture of global food security governance, the UN's CFS emerged as the foremost and inclusive intergovernmental platform for food security policy. In accordance with reform objectives, agreed to by the CFS's member countries, the role of the CFS is to: provide a platform for discussion and coordination to strengthen collaborative action; promote greater policy convergence and coordination; and, provide support and advice to countries and regions (CFS 2009: para 5). Furthermore, the CFS is committed to ensuring that the voices of all relevant stakeholders, particularly those most affected by food insecurity, are heard in the policy debate on food security (CFS 2009: para 7). Towards this end, the CFS undertakes consultations and includes a broad range of actors as participants in its sessional and inter-sessional work, including developing policy proposals on key issues relating to food security.

In line with theories of transnational neopluralism, powerful economic actors continue to maintain a great deal of influence and capacity when it comes to intergovernmental negotiations. Admittedly, democratic and participatory mechanisms can only go so far. Many actors continue to face limited capacity, linguistic limitations (although there is language interpretation, the texts under negotiation are in English) and inadequate resources to ensure enough trained staff can attend to the long and often overlapping negotiations. Yet, what is of interest with respect to the CFS is that due to reform structure, traditional power disparities are limited and new forms of legitimacy are shifting dynamics of intergovernmental negotiations.

This chapter explores how these changing dynamics play out through a review and comparison of two CFS policy roundtables: "How to Increase Food Security and Smallholder-Sensitive Investment in Agriculture," and "Food Price Volatility." In turn, the policy themes are presented, followed by an analysis of the negotiations. Particular attention is paid to the ways in which CSOs engaged in the roundtables, the impact they had on discussions and policy-making processes, as well as changes they were able to make. The chapter thus provides examples of how civil society participants are influencing intergovernmental food security policy processes while shedding light on the internal dynamics and power struggles in the newly reformed CFS. The review also contributes to debates on the role of participation in addressing a democratic deficit in global governance. The findings reinforce theories of transnational neopluralism (see Chapter 2) but importantly also illustrate opportunities and strategies for ensuring more meaningful participation in multilateral policy processes.

The two selected policy roundtables were deemed appropriate roundtables to compare for several reasons. First, they occurred during the same session and thus played out within the same context. Both issues were very topical and dealt with issues that are central to food security policy at the global level: investment and price volatility. Whereas civil society actors proved very influential on smallholder investment, securing many important changes to the decision box, they were less successful in negotiations on food price volatility.

CFS policy roundtables

One of the primary roles of the CFS is to:

> [p]romote greater policy convergence and coordination, including through the development of international strategies and Voluntary Guidelines on food security and nutrition on the basis of best practices, lessons learned from local experience, inputs received from the national and regional levels, and expert advice and opinions from different stakeholders.
>
> (CFS 2009: para 5.2)

Policy roundtables are meant to support these aims. More specifically, the objective of the policy roundtables "is to arrive at concrete recommendations for consideration by the Committee ... with a view to the formulation of actionable recommendations for approval" (CFS 2011e: para 6).

The organization of the roundtables proceeds as follows. The CFS identifies a theme for the policy roundtables and tasks the CFS's independent HLPE to produce a report with recommendations. In preparation for the roundtables, the CFS also forms task teams. These task teams draft discussion papers and compile "decision boxes" informed by the report of the HLPE. Decision boxes (sets of actionable policy recommendations) preface the discussion papers and form the starting point of the policy negotiations.

The roundtables employ an innovative participatory approach to negotiation. Each roundtable begins with a panel of experts, including experts identified by civil society actors. These experts are meant to provide context from multiple perspectives to help frame the negotiations. The negotiations are facilitated by a chair (a country delegate) and chronicled by a rapporteur (these are usually volunteers from country delegations or experts in the area) and a scribe. The rapporteur is responsible for identifying key outcomes, points of agreement and advancing recommendations. As noted above, the negotiations start from the text included in the decision boxes. Member states and participants identify themselves to the chair and then the chair calls on them to make interventions in the order they are seen. It is not uncommon to hear the chair say "Civil Society Mechanism please, to be followed by Canada and then the World Bank," illustrating not only a fundamental change in the way the CFS operates, but also in the ordering of intergovernmental negotiations.

The text under negotiation is projected onto a large screen. When changes to the text are suggested, the scribe inserts them in the working document using the Microsoft Word track changes function so that changes are visible to all participants. Text that is not agreed upon or finalized is placed in square brackets.

The chair works with the members and participants to come to consensus. As official participants under the reformed CFS, non-state actors, including civil society actors, have the right to intervene in debates and propose wording up the point where the members have reached consensus. At this point, only member states are allowed to intervene. When states reach consensus on the text, the roundtable concludes and the negotiated decisions are submitted to the Plenary for approval.

Following the procedure described above, at the 36th Session, the CFS identified key issues requiring further attention and requested the HLPE undertake studies to be presented at the 37th Session. The topics to be reviewed included an examination of the respective roles of large-scale plantations and of small-scale farming, including social, gender and environmental impacts; a review of the existing tools allowing the mapping of available land; and comparative analysis of tools to align large-scale investments with country food security strategies (CFS 2011b: para 26.iv).

From these requests, the HLPE produced two reports: *Price Volatility and Food Security* (HLPE 2011a) and *Land Tenure and International Investments in Agriculture* (HLPE 2011b). Building on these reports, the Bureau, with the support of the Advisory Group, identified the themes for the policy roundtables: investing how to increase food security and smallholder sensitive investment in agriculture; and food price volatility. They also organized a third roundtable on gender, food security and nutrition.

In preparation for the roundtables, the CFS Bureau established three task teams. Members of the advisory groups were invited to join and CSOs were allotted four seats on each of the task teams. These task teams, supported by the Secretariat, were asked to draft discussion papers and compile decision boxes. The discussion papers, complete with decision boxes, were submitted to the Bureau for consideration with the understanding that in the end, all documentation would be the responsibility of the CFS Secretariat.

Before attention turns to a review of the two policy roundtables, it is first important to note that institutional shifts such as those proposed by the CFS reform, take time. At the session under review in this chapter, the CFS was very much learning-while-doing. Furthermore, most of the actors were doing this for the first time. This was reinforced by a representative of a large international NGO who explained:

> I think it takes time, not only for people to understand ... when you didn't participate in the reform process itself, and you come after that there are many things that you don't know what the importance is, or the reasons why how it has been built.
>
> (Interview, June 2012, Rome)

Alongside the issue of time is a cultural challenge: many states are less open to the engagement of non-state actors in intergovernmental negotiations. During the 37th Session, the chair and the secretary of the CFS were asked by civil society actors to intervene on issues of protocol several times. With their intervention, most procedural problems were remedied. However, as will be shown in the case of the roundtable on food price volatility, the chair of the roundtable failed to adequately uphold the reform principles.

How to increase food security and smallholder sensitive investment

Over the last 30 years, investment in agriculture has steadily declined due in part to a growing perception that agriculture was unprofitable. In 1979 international aid to agriculture was 18 percent of total assistance (Kanayo et al. 2012). By 2006, it was just 2.9 percent. The food price spikes of 2007–2008 led to widespread calls for increased investment in agriculture alongside recognition that to ensure food security and reduce levels of poverty investments, investment had to target and support smallholder food producers. As food prices increased, the perception that investing in agriculture was unprofitable began to shift. This shift was made visible through increased speculation on agricultural commodities and investment in agricultural land through large-scale land acquisitions. Within this context the CFS recognized the need to establish best practices for increasing investment in smallholder sensitive agriculture.

The roundtable on increasing food security and smallholder sensitive investment in agriculture began by reviewing the text of the decision box contained in the background document. The decision box contained a chapeau comprised of four points that framed ten specific recommendations. The chapeau originally stated that the Committee "recognizes that the bulk of investment in agriculture is undertaken by a multiplicity of private actors, in particular farmers themselves, their cooperatives and other rural enterprises."

Leading up to the policy roundtable, the CSM Working Group on Agricultural Investment debated whether they should use the word "investment" at all, as it is a word that denotes and reinforces a capitalist logic which many opposed. They questioned whether it would be more useful to use language that better reflected what they meant by investment. It was argued that by (re)claiming the word, or changing to another word, "we can ensure that our language reflects and suits our purposes" (field notes, May 2012, Cordoba). Building on this, one civil society actor explained:

> when you talk about investment, you have to ask who needs investment and who is investing. The trickle-down theory of investment affects us adversely and is grabbing land from the poor … Investment is linked to the land and those who do not have title to land. Fisherfolk and pastoralists, for example, do not benefit from investment. They are completely left out of systems of investment.
>
> (Field notes, May 2012, Cordoba)

The CSM Working Group arrived at a general agreement around two understandings of investment. As another civil society actor emphasized: "when we talk about investment, we are talking about farmers investing in the land and this is not the same logic as multinational corporations investing in large plots of land" (field notes, May 2012, Cordoba). A social movement actor raised the issue that no one spoke about agrarian reform. Investment is needed to develop a conducive environment for small-scale food producers and developing a system of investment that incorporates the principles of food sovereignty: "this means farmer empowerment and the development of systems that allow for farmers to invest where they need to invest in order to control their livelihoods" (field notes, May 2012, Cordoba).

Civil society actors, facilitated by the CSM Working Group on Agricultural Investment, pushed to have farmers placed at the front of the statement, effectively shifting focus away from the investment of private actors towards the recognition that "the bulk of investment in agriculture is undertaken by farmers and smallholders themselves, their cooperatives and other rural enterprises with the rest being provided by a multiplicity of private actors as well as governments."

The change was significant and represented a major win for civil society actors who were supported by the rapporteur and Ethiopia[1] (for the Africa Group). This intervention was also highly strategic and reflected the long discussion and debate that had taken place among engaged CSOs.

Another key point of contention in the chapeau of the decision box was how to reference recognition and support for the HLPE report. A proposal was made for the CFS to "consider" the HLPE report, instead of "duly take note of its recommendations." The change was proposed by representatives from Canada and supported by representatives from Argentina, Australia, Brazil and the US. It was originally opposed by representatives from EU, Eritrea and civil society actors. The role of the HLPE is to provide independent, scientific and knowledge-based advice to underpin CFS policy formulations. The change is illustrative of a push on the part of some member states to weaken support for the report. Weakened support for the report illustrates a tension between the agreement of a collective of experts and the policy objectives of key states and showcases tensions at the science–policy interface. In the final text, the Committee opted for conviction with respect to uptake, "urging" member

Table 6.1 Changes to CFS decision on how to increase food security and smallholder sensitive investment in agriculture

Draft decision box	Final decision
The Committee:	*The Committee:*
• Underlines the paramount importance of increased and improved investment in agriculture for achieving food security and nutrition for all	24. Underlined the paramount importance of increased and improved investment in agriculture for achieving food security and nutrition for all
• Recognizes that the bulk of investment in agriculture is undertaken by a multiplicity of private actors, in particular farmers themselves, their cooperatives and other rural enterprises	25. Recognized that the bulk of investment in agriculture is undertaken by farmers and smallholders themselves, their cooperatives and other rural enterprises with the rest being provided by a multiplicity of private actors as well as governments
• Acknowledges that smallholder farmers, many of which are women, play a central role in producing most of the food consumed locally in many developing regions and are the primary investors in agriculture in many developing countries	26. Acknowledged that smallholder farmers, many of whom are women, play a central role in producing most of the food consumed locally in many developing regions and are the primary investors in agriculture in many developing countries
• Welcomes the report of the High Level panel of Experts (HLPE) on "Land Tenure and International Investments in Agriculture" and recommends its consideration by all stakeholders	27. Welcomed the report of the High Level Panel of Experts (HLPE) on "Land Tenure and International Investments in Agriculture," and duly takes note of its recommendations

governments, international partners and other stakeholders to "follow up" on the recommendations.

When agreement was reached on the chapeau, the member states and participants set to work on the recommendations. There were originally 13 recommendations but by the end of the roundtable the Committee had come to agreement on 11. For reasons of time and space, each proposal will not be considered. Instead, focus will be on key points.

In the draft text, the third proposal read: "Ensure that public policies and investments play a catalytic role in the formation of partnerships among agricultural investors, including private–public partnerships." On this issue, the CSM Working Group on Agricultural Investment argued that given the theme of the roundtable, the interests of smallholders needed to be prioritized. They proposed that after "private–public" the text be modified to include:

> farmer cooperative–private and private–private partnerships to ensure that the interests of smallholders are being served and preserved by these

partnerships, and recognize that, in many cases, the State has a crucial role to play in facilitating access of smallholders to credit, technical and extension services, insurance and markets.

(Field notes, October 2011, Rome)

The change was accepted. Importantly, this change served to qualify the types of investment that were needed, thereby contributing to international calls for greater investment. The eventually successful CSO proposal was supported by the representative from Zimbabwe (for the Africa Group) and opposed by representatives from Canada, Guatemala and the organization representing the private sector.

The fifth recommendation addressed participation in policy-making processes, a relevant and sensitive topic within the newly reformed Committee. Originally, the recommendation was to "actively involve organizations representing agricultural producers, notably smallholders and agricultural workers." CSOs successfully proposed to revise the text to "actively involve organizations representing smallholder agricultural workers." The rationale for the revision was to clarify who should participate and to create a direct link to the CFS's commitment to ensure that the voices of those most affected by food insecurity are heard (CFS 2009: para 7). Furthermore, the inclusion of agricultural workers is important as they are often neglected in discussions on investment.

Despite reservations about the *Land Tenure and International Investments in Agriculture* report (HLPE 2011b), the draft decision box included a recommendation for a new study to be undertaken by the HLPE on the constraints to smallholder investment in agriculture across different contexts. The decision noted that the study should take into consideration "the work done on this topic by IFAD, and by FAO in the context of COAG [FAO's Committee on Agriculture], and the work of other key partners." CSOs argued unsuccessfully that the HLPE, as an independent expert body, should not be told which references to consider. It is indeed not appropriate for the Committee to mandate what sources its independent expert panel consider. At the same time, the recommendation is a clear request for the HLPE to provide research to address a policy gap. In 2013 the HLPE followed up by releasing a report called *Investing in Smallholder Agriculture for Food Security*, that informed a policy roundtable by the same name at the 40th Session of the CFS.

At the 36th Session, the CFS had also agreed not to endorse PRAI. The suggested text in the proposed decision box was for the CFS to launch a CFS consultation on principles for responsible agricultural investment, taking into account existing frameworks, including PRAI. There was strong political opposition from some countries (most vocally negotiators from Canada) and the private sector. They argued that PRAI were strong interagency principles and called on the CFS to endorse PRAI. They further argued that such a decision would avoid a lengthy and costly consultation process. Civil society actors (supported by Argentina and Venezuela) resisted. For CSOs it was fundamental the Committee undertake consultations and negotiate principles for responsible investment. Furthermore, it was important that the discussions on the Voluntary Guidelines be completed before the Committee began considering such principles. The argument was that only once best practices for the governance of land tenure had been established did it make sense to move on to investment. In the end, the rapporteur proposed language which was approved by consensus and adopted in the ninth recommendation: "the consultation process will be initiated promptly after approval of the Voluntary Guidelines" (CFS 2011c: para 29.ix). This reinforcement of the previous decision was seen as an important victory for civil society actors and weaker countries who had gone up against powerful countries and won.

During the negotiations, the CSM Working Group on Agricultural Investment proposed a final recommendation requesting the "CFS Secretariat, in collaboration with the Advisory Group and based on the information made available by the relevant stakeholders, to prepare a general report on the state of implementation of the above recommendations to be presented to CFS" (CFS 2011c: para 29.xi). The aim was to ensure that the CFS followed-up on the topic of smallholder sensitive investments and that civil society was able to participate in the assessment as members of the advisory group. The strategy was successful. In their final decision, the Committee also encouraged governments and stakeholders to: enable national policies, governance and their evidence base; promote access to assets, public goods, social services, research and extension and technology; enable investment, access to markets, productive services and resources (CFS 2013).

Overall, the most significant change to come from civil society participation in the negotiations was a fundamental shift in the terms of debate on investment away from favoring corporate investment, public–private partnerships and global value chains, towards recognition of the role of sustainable smallholder food production as major investors in agriculture. This shift in perspective was championed by civil society actors not only in the policy roundtable but also on the CFS task team and advisory group. Their success however was not repeated in the roundtable on Food Price Volatility.

Food price volatility

Food price volatility threatens food security and deepens poverty. Extreme food price volatility is increasingly the norm and thus increasingly cause for concern. The price spikes in 2008 "pushed an additional 80 million people into hunger, increasing the number of hungry and malnourished to one billion" (CFS 2011d: para 2).

It is thus not surprising that food price volatility became a focus of international attention with groups like the G20 taking it on as a policy issue. At their November 2010 summit, G20 leaders requested that multilateral actors work with stakeholders "to develop options for G20 consideration on how to better mitigate and manage the risks associated with the price volatility of food and other agriculture commodities, without distorting market behaviour, ultimately to protect the most vulnerable" (G20 2010). This was followed up by a declaration for action on food price volatility by the G20 agricultural ministers (G20 2011). The FAO's (2011) annual *State of Food Insecurity* report also focused on food price volatility. The CFS, acknowledging a need for international policy coherence, organized a roundtable on the issue.

Given the politically sensitive nature of the roundtable it is perhaps not surprising that the CFS was unable to conclude negotiations in the single session allotted. A key challenge for the CFS came down to timing. The policy roundtable fell after the release of the G20 ministers of agriculture's Action Plan and before the G20 Summit where the plan was to be endorsed. This gave the policy roundtable heightened political importance which in turn served to undermine reform values of transparency, inclusivity and participation. When negotiations got under way it was clear that the world's 20 largest economies were going to push to have their priorities endorsed.

When the first round of negotiations ended, another round had to be scheduled. In the time between the first and second round, G20 countries worked to secure text that would support the G20 agricultural ministers' Action Plan at an impromptu drafting meeting. When civil society actors described the process, they explained that the rapporteur, who was also chair of the Drafting Committee, "didn't invite [CSOs] for the drafting committee he created in the second round ... and even if we were clearly opposing the text, we were kind of side-lined in the process" (interview, July 2012, Rome). CSOs were able to gain access to these meetings once they were informed of them. However, they were only informed by sympathetic country delegates suggesting a lack of protocol was in place within the CFS to ensure participation in all of its activities.

The CFS adheres to the democratic and inclusive principle of one vote per country, but works towards building consensus. It is also committed to considering the voices of those most affected by food insecurity. The G20 operates along a different set of principles. For the CFS to uphold its reform objectives it cannot simply rubber stamp policies and frameworks. This is not to say that such policies cannot be endorsed by the CFS but that there must be a transparent and participatory discussion and negotiation in order to do so. CSOs argued that policies recommended through the CFS should come from the membership and participants and should not be dictated by the world's 20 largest economies. While they had managed to convince the CFS not to endorse PRAI, this time, they were less successful at moving focus away from the G20's agenda.

With respect to the outcome of the negotiations, just as they had done in the roundtable on smallholder sensitive investment, the Committee downgraded their support for the HLPE's report from welcoming the report and recommending its consideration by all stakeholders, to "expressing its appreciation for the efforts by the High Level Panel of Experts for its work on price volatility and food security, and taking note of its report on Price Volatility and Food Security and recommendations contained therein" (CFS 2011a: para 46).

This change suggests a rejection by the CFS of its own expert panel's work. The rejection of the HLPE report becomes more obvious when contrasted with the following point wherein the Committee "welcomes the Action Plan on Food Price Volatility and Agriculture of the G20 as a positive effort to address a number of the main causes and implications of food price volatility" (CFS 2011a: para 47). Immediately, the influence and privileging of the G20's agenda becomes clear.

Moving from the chapeau to the recommendations, the first thing to note is that the Committee opted to develop "action points" rather than "recommendations," creating another link to the G20 Action Plan and breaking with the format used in other policy recommendations. On this point, the delegate from Norway,[2] with support from CSOs, argued that it was not suitable for the CFS to make decisions based on outside organizations' recommendations. However, negotiators from G20 countries stressed the political importance of the G20's Plan, noting it was a primary reference on food price volatility and the paragraph stayed in the final decision.

In total the Committee finalized 17 actions, organized into three sections: actions to increase food production and availability and enhance resilience to shocks; actions to reduce volatility; and actions to mitigate the negative impacts of volatility. The first section contained four recommendations targeted towards increasing food production and enhancing resilience to shocks. In this section CSOs working through the CSM Working Group on Food Price Volatility managed to secure some language in the final text. For example, in the first action point, they manage to include reference to strengthening smallholder production systems and fostering rural development, to an original decision that focused strictly on increasing "stable and sustainable public and private investment to boost agricultural productivity." CSOs had argued that the reformed CFS had a mandate to promote and protect smallholders and that the proposal CSOs put forth would enhance cohesion with the recommendations negotiated in the roundtable on increasing smallholder sensitive investment. During the negotiations, CSOs also tried to remove the reference to "boost agricultural productivity" but they were not successful.

For the rest of the action points, few changes were made. There was the inclusion of language to support the inclusion of "all key partners" in the development of comprehensive country-led food security strategies. The same paragraph placed emphasis on "evidenced based" processes. CSOs understood this to be an exclusion strategy. Referencing the chair of the CFS Task Team, one CSO actor noted "also, what they insist a lot upon is evidence-based and things like that, so, arguments like that were also being used [to discredit CSO proposals]" (interview, July 2012, Rome). This stands in contradiction to efforts of the CFS to open itself up to "alternative" forms of knowledge as illustrated through the structure and operating principles of the HLPE and through the inclusion of CSOs as participants.

Within the policy roundtable, member states agreed that there was a need to review biofuels policy. CSOs challenged the EU (often one of their allies) on this point. CSOs claimed that the EU was using the HLPE study as a delay tactic so as to avoid the need to take policy decisions until the research was complete. The US and Brazil supported the EU and effectively shifted the discussion from one of mandates, subsidies and tariffs to one about what kind of research is needed. The action point again invoked a positivist discourse, noting that the review be "according to balanced science-based assessments." The Committee mandated the HLPE to conduct "a science-based comparative literature analysis, taking into account the work produced by the FAO and the Global Bioenergy Partnership (GBEP), of the positive and negative effects of biofuels on food security" (CFS 2011a: para 50i). Two main issues can be raised with this action point. First, as was seen in the roundtable on investing in smallholder sensitive agriculture, the CFS member states were again attempting to dictate the content to be review by the independent HLPE. And again, while it is in their right to request studies, it is outside their jurisdiction to mandate sources. Second, that two references to "science-based" work are made the same action point is telling and reinforces a discourse that serves to rationalize neoliberal policy processes while simultaneously delegitimizing other forms of knowledge and expertise.

The CFS added a new action point during the roundtable, asking "relevant international organizations, in consultation with all relevant stakeholders, to further assess the constraints and effectiveness of local, national and regional food reserves" (CFS 2011a: para 50j). This says very little but does present an opportunity to develop a study to assess the role of food reserves and stocks. Of prime importance will be which international organization leads the process moving forward.

During the roundtables CSOs managed to make small gains on issues of food reserves and speculation and a reference about the to include the Economic Community of West African States (ECOWAS) and West African countries in the development of targeted emergency humanitarian food reserves in the region. Overall, and when compared to the roundtable on smallholder sensitive investment, CSOs were unsuccessful in the negotiations on food price volatility. While not happy with the reification of the G20's Action Plan through the CFS, this was in fact not the major concern. CSOs recognized that they were participants. They had a role to play in pushing negotiations and challenging decisions but they were not decision makers. Decisions are the responsibility of the states. While they did not support the decision, they were prepared to accept it under the operating principles of the reformed CFS.

The main issue for CSOs was the way in which negotiations had proceeded. They were consistently ignored and their proposals were not incorporated into the working document. They were also not informed about important meetings that they were entitled to attend. The Russian chair of the roundtable had to be reminded of CFS procedures and still failed to uphold them. The failure of the chair was widely recognized. This led him to withdraw himself from the candidates for CFS chair selection which was scheduled to take place at the end of the 37th Session.

Frustrated by the systematic marginalization of their participation and the direction of the negotiations, including the promotion of the G20 agenda and a failure on the part of the Committee to recognize key drivers of food price volatility, CSOs decided to walked out of the discussions in protest at 22:45. When the CSOs left the room, their departure was not recognized officially in the Plenary or in the interventions or final report. Discussions continued at a relatively quick pace and negotiations were closed before midnight. The walk out was a risky move given that this was only the second session of the reformed CFS, and thus the relationships between member states and participants were new and fragile. However, in the end, the walk out had little impact. Overall, the policy roundtable negotiations on food price volatility served to reinforce the G20 action plan on food price volatility. Participation from non-G20 countries was limited and civil society contributions were largely ignored.

Conclusion

A review of the policy roundtables on food price volatility and smallholder sensitive investment provides insight into the functioning and implications for increased participation and policy outputs within the CFS. When it came to negotiating on smallholder sensitive investment, CSOs secured important textual changes through the negotiations. In this policy roundtable, CSOs had the advantage of a positive framing: few would be willing to withdraw support from policies to support smallholders or to explicitly promote policies that were not sensitive to smallholders. Importantly, the issue of smallholder investment has remained on the CFS agenda in more meaningful ways than food price volatility (e.g., the HLPE report and a roundtable on investing in smallholder agriculture for food security at the 40th Session of the CFS).

On the more technical issue of food price volatility, and when pitted against the interests of the G20, CSOs had less influence and legitimacy and non-G20 countries played a less active role in negotiations. The outcomes of the policy roundtable suggest that on issues of international trade and markets, the CFS was less willing or able to move away from a business-as-usual approach. This supports the theory of embedded neoliberalism. It is also important to note that in supporting the G20's Action Plan, the CFS was fulfilling its role of enhancing cohesion around food security policy. The problem this raises for proponents of the CFS is that it is precisely the role of the CFS to lead and coordinate these discussions in an inclusive manner that prioritizes food security. When they endorsed the reforms, G20 countries agreed that the CFS was the foremost platform for actors to work together in a coordinated manner to work towards the elimination of hunger. To develop action plans outside of the CFS can potentially undermine the CFS and its processes.

Given these conclusions, CSOs would be advised to continue to push the CFS to focus on issues that build on its explicit areas of expertise and its strengths. However, for CFS policies to have an impact in so far of advancing the goal of eradicating hunger, the CFS cannot shy away from contentious issues such

Table 6.2 Summary of CSO wins and losses in two policy roundtables at the 37th Session

CFS	Output	CFS wins	CSO losses
37 (2011)	How to increase food security and smallholder sensitive investment in agriculture (policy roundtable)	• Decision box was changed to be smallholder focused (references to smallholders or farmers frame the actions). • Recognition of smallholder investment. • Awareness of the need to strengthen smallholder production systems, reflecting a shift in focus from external investments to investments made by and for small-scale food producers. • Removal of generic references to agriculture, highlighting diversity in modes of food production. • Food security was presented as a parameter for investment. • Secured an assessment of impact of partnerships on smallholders.	• Value and political weight of the HLPE reports (weak language); predetermining inputs into HLPE reports. • Mapping described as Framework. For CSOs the Global Strategic Framework is the overarching framework of the CFS.
	Food price volatility (policy roundtable)	• The decision box recognized food reserves as an instrument for mitigating food price volatility but also as key in emergency contexts. • Discussion on contentious issues. • Mandate for an HLPE report on biofuels. • Recognized the role of speculation in volatility. • Although vague, the CFS recognized the need to "improve transparency, regulation and supervision of agricultural derivative markets." • The initiative to improve markets transparency was supported.	• Value and political weight of the HLPE reports (weak language). • Promotion of the G20's agenda. • Unable to shift away for the productionist paradigm (desire to "boost agricultural production"). • Failure of the CFS to acknowledge key drivers of food price volatility. • Limited engagement from non-G20 countries. • Marginalization of CSOs throughout the process (for food price volatility roundtable).

as trade. Indeed, the CFS needs to continue to address these issues from a food security perspective. This is how it can best fulfil its reform objectives.

While the engagement of civil society clearly served to broaden debate, there were other important outcomes. This being only the second session of the reformed CFS, the negotiations provided important learning and capacity building for civil society actors as well as other participants and member states. CSOs became further politicized to intergovernmental negotiations and gained valuable insight on effective and non-effective techniques. These were translated into future strategies.

The policy roundtables reviewed in this chapter show that while enhanced CSO participation does not necessarily overcome existing power relations nor fully address the democratic deficit that marks global governance processes, it can be concluded that given proper mechanism, financial support and goodwill, the meaningful participation of civil society actors can expand the scope of debate and can have an impact on policy positions.

However, the CFS also faces challenges, including the influence of power politics. In theory, the CFS has implemented mechanisms to balance out relations of power. In practice, this will require greater resources for permanent representatives from poorer countries, as well as an examination of how the CFS conducts negotiations. Operating parallel sessions, night sessions without interpretation and negotiating texts in English are key barriers to ensuring meaningful participation.

What this review illustrates is that in a few short years the CFS has implemented and operationalized an innovative approach to participatory policy making at the global level. This is of itself noteworthy and valuable. Furthermore, it can be concluded that while the CFS remains weak on issues of economics and trade, overall the expansion of participation in the CFS has resulted in changes to policies that ensure stronger support for smallholders and prioritize food security.

Notes

1 The CFS Sessions are understood to be "public." For this reason, and to better understand the geopolitical realities and tensions under way in the CFS, countries have been identified with their interventions. To reflect the fact that there may be a disconnect between the position presented at the CFS and an official country position, and/or in recognition of the fact that policy cohesion and approached at the national level on issues related to food security is often lacking, reference is made to delegates, negotiator or representatives. These terms are used interchangeably and refer to the individual or individuals making interventions in the name of a member country. This should also serve to remind readers that personalities play an important role in multi-stakeholder and intergovernmental negotiations.
2 Norway is a vocal critic of the G20, with Foreign Minister Jonas Gahr Støre publicly calling the G20 "one of the greatest setbacks since World War II." Støre further argued the G20 is a self-appointed group composed by the world's major powers (Ertel 2010). Norway is not an EU member state and is thus not represented at the G20.

References

CFS. 2009. *Reform of the Committee on World Food Security Final Version.* Rome: FAO. Retrieved (www.fao.org/fileadmin/templates/cfs/Docs0910/ReformDoc/CFS_2009_2_Rev_2_E_K7197.pdf).

CFS. 2010. *Final Report Thirty-Sixth Session Committee on World Food Security.* Rome: FAO.

CFS. 2011a. *37th Session of the Committee on World Food Security: Final Report.* Rome: FAO.

CFS. 2011b. *Final Report Thirty-Seventh Session Committee on World Food Security.* Rome: FAO. Retrieved (www.fao.org/fileadmin/templates/cfs/Docs1011/CFS37/documents/CFS_37_Final_Report_FINAL.pdf).

CFS. 2011c. *Policy Roundtable: How to Increase Food Security and Smallholder-Sensitive Investment in Agriculture.* Rome: FAO.

CFS. 2011d. *Policy Rountable: Food Price Volatility.* Rome: FAO.

CFS. 2011e. *Provisional Annotated Agenda.* Rome: FAO.

CFS. 2013. *Report of the Fortieth Session of the Committee on World Food Security (CFS).* Rome: FAO. Retrieved (www.fao.org/docrep/meeting/029/mi744e.pdf).

Ertel, M. 2010. "Norway Takes Aim at G-20." *Spiegel Online International.* Retrieved (www.spiegel.de/international/europe/norway-takes-aim-at-g-20-one-of-the-greatest-setbacks-since-world-war-ii-a-702104.html).

FAO. 2011. *The State of Food Insecurity in the World 2011: How Does International Price Volatility Affect Domestic Economies and Food Security?* Rome: FAO. Retrieved (www.fao.org/docrep/014/i2330e/i2330e.pdf).

G20. 2010. *Multi-Year Action Plan on Development (Annex II).* Seoul: G20.

G20. 2011. *Ministerial Declaration: Action Plan on Food Price Volatility and Agriculture.* Paris: G20.

HLPE. 2011a. *Price Volatility and Food Security.* Rome: FAO. Retrieved (www.fao.org/fileadmin/user_upload/hlpe/hlpe_documents/HLPE-price-volatility-and-foodsecurity-report-July-2011.pdf).

HLPE. 2011b. *Land Tenure and International Investments in Agriculture.* Rome: FAO. Retrieved (www.fao.org/fileadmin/user_upload/hlpe/hlpe_documents/HLPE-Landtenure-and-international-investments-in-agriculture-2011.pdf).

HLPE. 2013. *Investing in Smallholder Agriculture for Food Security.* Rome: FAO. Retrieved (www.fao.org/3/a-i2953e.pdf).

Kanayo, O., O. U. Maurice, and O. O. Emmanuel. 2012. "Food Security, Policies and Institutions in Africa: Prospects for a Revolution." *Journal of Economic Cooperation and Development*, 33(4): 87–115.

7 Best practice

The Voluntary Guidelines on the Responsible Governance of Tenure

Introduction

Since its reform in 2009, the CFS has placed considerable emphasis on issues related to land, with particular focus on tenure and investment. At their 36th Session (October 2010), the CFS organized a policy roundtable on land tenure and international investment in agriculture. They also requested the HLPE to produce a report, which was later titled *Land Tenure and International Investment in Agriculture* (see HLPE 2011). At that same session, the Committee gave its support to the development of what was then called the Voluntary Guidelines on the Responsible Governance of Tenure of Land and Other Natural Resources, and decided to establish an OEWG of the CFS to review the first draft of the Guidelines with a view to submitting them for consideration to the 37th Session of CFS (October 2011) (CFS 2010: para 26.i).

The Guidelines were not submitted to the 37th Session for reasons that will become clear below. However in May 2012, the CFS did endorse the Voluntary Guidelines on the Responsible Governance of Tenure of Land, Fisheries and Forests in the Context of National Food Security (VGGT), marking a key moment in the evolution of the reformed CFS. Since the endorsement, their implementation has been encouraged by the G20, Rio+20 and the Francophone Assembly of Parliamentarians, among others.

On December 21, 2012, the UN General Assembly adopted a resolution on Agriculture Development and Food Security which:

> [e]ncourages countries to give due consideration to implementing the Voluntary Guidelines on the Responsible Governance of Tenure of Land, Fisheries and Forests in the Context of National Food Security, as endorsed by the Committee on World Food Security on 11 May 2012.
>
> (UN General Assembly 2012)

It also requested "relevant entities of the United Nations system, in accordance with their respective mandates and in the most cost-effective manner, to ensure the speedy dissemination and promotion of the Guidelines" (UN General Assembly 2012).

On January 19, 2013, at the Fifth Berlin Agriculture Ministers' Summit, ministers from 80 countries issued a communiqué on responsible investment in food and agriculture that called on parties to confirm their intention to implement the VGGT in accordance with national priorities, and further called on business enterprises to comply with them domestically and abroad. The VGGT have also become a priority for the FAO. By February 2013, the FAO had supported 10 awareness raising workshops, 17 country-level workshops had been requested and 53 briefings in 33 countries had been completed (Hilton 2013). A range of additional documents (e.g., supplementary guidelines that provide technical details on specific aspects when necessary, training and advocacy materials, and strategies for implementation) are developed by the FAO to support uptake and application of the Guidelines (FAO 2012a). In May 2014, the CFS hosted an event—VGGT Two Years On: Where We Are and Where We Are Going—to reflect on progress made.

To say that the VGGT represent a landmark in the evolution of the reformed CFS would not be hyperbole. According to the FAO, they represent "an unprecedented international agreement on tenure governance" (Hilton 2013). This case study focuses on the development and negotiation of the VGGT and analyses the outcomes and possible implications. Given the objectives of this book, there is an added focus on, and insight into, the role and impact of civil society actors.

It is important to reiterate that civil society actors do not necessarily speak with one voice. However, the CSM's Working Group on Land Tenure, aided by a strong facilitator, did manage to develop an engagement strategy and joint positions while making most effective use of the legitimacy and political skills of social movements and the technical expertise and capacity of NGOs. Their participation throughout the process strengthened the rationale for their inclusion as official participants in the reformed CFS.

This case study is organized as follows. First the issue of land tenure is introduced. From there, the process of negotiating Voluntary Guidelines on the governance of land tenure is presented along with the methodology for undertaking consultation on prepared drafts. This is followed by a review of the negotiation process that led from the First Draft to the final text. The analysis highlights the fragmented nature of negotiations while illustrating how in the case of the VGGT alliances were formed around issues and not necessarily along regional or historic lines. Tensions raised by language and culture are highlighted, as are challenges resulting from a disconnect between negotiators and technical staff in the national capitals. What is perhaps most apparent in this review is the active role that civil society actors played in these negotiations and the way in which their contributions are taken on par with those of states and other CFS participants such as the World Bank, highlighting a shift in the operation of intergovernmental negotiations. The case study concludes with consideration of next steps.

Land tenure and food security

Land is a fundamental resource that secures the livelihoods of many, especially the rural poor, who often rely on access to and control over natural
resources. Land provides food and shelter and is a key factor in economic
growth (Behrman et al. 2012; Deere and Leon 1997; Deininger et al. 2007;
Sietchiping 2010). While the notion of land is generally associated with surface
and underground resources, land is also a physical object, an asset and the site
of emotional, cultural, historic and spiritual practices. Ensuring sustainable land
use and eradicating food insecurity is dependent upon how people and communities gain, maintain and control access to land. However, access to land is
increasingly scarce as a result of a growing world population, environmental
degradation, breakdown of customary authority and climate change, and is in
turn becoming subject to intensified competition (Harvey and Pilgrim 2011).
This competition has been made visible through the rapid rise in land grabbing and large-scale land acquisitions (Borras et al. 2011; De Schutter 2011;
GRAIN 2008; Hall 2011).

Access to land and other natural resources is defined and regulated in societies through complex systems of tenure. Tenure defines who can use which
resources, the duration and the conditions of use. Tenure constitutes a web of
intersecting interests and forms an important part of social, political and economic structures at the household, community and national level (FAO 2002).
In a report on land tenure and rural development, the FAO (2002) defined
land tenure in the following way:

> 3.1 Land tenure is the relationship, whether legally or customarily defined,
> among people, as individuals or groups, with respect to land. (For conven-
> ience, "land" is used here to include other natural resources such as water
> and trees.) Land tenure is an institution, i.e., rules invented by societies
> to regulate behaviour. Rules of tenure define how property rights to land
> are to be allocated within societies. They define how access is granted to
> rights to use, control, and transfer land, as well as associated responsibilities
> and restraints. In simple terms, land tenure systems determine who can use
> what resources for how long, and under what conditions.

> 3.2 Land tenure is an important part of social, political and economic
> structures. It is multi-dimensional, bringing into play social, technical,
> economic, institutional, legal and political aspects that are often ignored
> but must be taken into account. Land tenure relationships may be well-
> defined and enforceable in a formal court of law or through customary
> structures in a community. Alternatively, they may be relatively poorly
> defined with ambiguities open to exploitation.

This definition highlights the political, social and cultural significance of tenure while alluding to the diversity of ways in which these social norms are
regulated. Tenure systems include informal and unwritten customary rights

of access to and use of land and natural resources as well as more "formal" arrangements (e.g., individual tiling, freehold and leasehold) mediated by written contracts, policies and laws. There are also secondary rights that include access to migratory routes and grazing lands. Formal and customary tenure systems often co-exist but customary systems are under threat as land scarcity increases. Insecure tenure rights enhance vulnerability, conflict, food insecurity and poverty and can lead to increased environmental degradation and conflict when competing users fight for control over the resources (FAO 2012b; Sietchiping 2010). The governance of tenure is a crucial factor in determining rights and associated duties to use and control land, fisheries and forests. Many tenure problems arise as a result of weak governance which in turn adversely affects social stability, sustainable resource use and the economy.

Establishing guidelines for tenure of natural resources

Cognizant of the centrality of tenure to food security, and in response to specific requests from member states for guidance on the governance of tenure, the FAO began a process of developing Voluntary Guidelines on the governance of land tenure in 2006. Voluntary guidelines set out principles and internationally accepted standards for responsible practices by providing a framework that states can use when developing their own strategies, policies, legislation and programs. Furthermore, they can be used by all actors to judge whether proposed actions (e.g., policies, investments) constitute acceptable practice. The VGGT follow the format of other FAO voluntary instruments such as the Code of Conduct for Responsible Fisheries; International Code of Conduct on the Distribution and Use of Pesticides; Responsible Management of Planted Forests: Voluntary Guidelines; and Fire Management Voluntary Guidelines: Principles and Strategic Actions.

Notably, the VGGT build on and support the Voluntary Guidelines to Support the Progressive Realization of the Right to Adequate Food in the Context of National Food Security, enforced by the 30th Session of the CFS and then adopted by the FAO Council at the 127th Session (November 2004). The VGGT are grounded in a rights-based approach and list the realization of the right to adequate food as a primary goal (FAO 2012c: para 1.1), but the links between the two sets of guidelines go deeper.

The Voluntary Guidelines on the Right to Food make specific reference to access to resources and assets. They encourage states to facilitate stable and non-discriminatory access and utilization of resources and to protect the rights of individuals with respect to resources. They also encourage states to undertake land reforms consistent with their human rights obligations. Guideline 8B, which is specifically on the issue of land, states:

> States should take measures to promote and protect the security of land tenure, especially with respect to women, and poor and disadvantaged segments of society, through legislation that protects the full and equal right to

own land and other property, including the right to inherit. As appropriate, States should consider establishing legal and other policy mechanisms, consistent with their international human rights obligations and in accordance with the rule of law, that advance land reform to enhance access for the poor and women. Such mechanisms should also promote conservation and sustainable use of land. Special consideration should be given to the situation of indigenous communities.

(FAO 2005: para 8.10)

The VGGT also build on the discussions and outcomes of the International Conference on Agrarian Reform and Rural Development (ICARRD) held in March 2006. ICARRD had established several commissions to tackle key issues around agrarian reform and rural development. Commission 1 was established to address Agrarian Reform and Access to Land: Challenges and Opportunities. The Commission's report highlighted the need to approach agrarian reform with a broad focus that includes participatory approaches to respond to diverse national contexts (ICARRD 2006: para 32). The Commission recognized the challenge of achieving balance between agro-business, foreign investment and the interest of small-scale famers but reiterated that family agriculture should be a competitive enterprise.[1]

Building on the findings of the Commission's Report, the final declaration of ICAARD, adopted by 92 states, focused on the importance of secure and sustainable access to land, water and other natural resources. Specifically, it called for an increase in the participation of stakeholders in agrarian reform processes to develop efficient institutions to apply policies, and to respect the role of customary practices where they play a positive role in land management, especially common property management. The value of titling and registries as instruments for transparency and certainty of property were emphasized, as was the importance of internal and external markets and market mechanisms. They also agreed that issues of land are related to conflict and must be addressed with prudence in the context of stakeholder participation. Interestingly, no reference was made to the Voluntary Guidelines on the Right to Food, although the final report "emphasized that policy-makers should give high importance to issues of food sovereignty and a rights-based approach to agrarian reform and rural development" (ICARRD 2006: para 59). These are not the only guidelines developed to address issues of investment and land tenure. A list of principles and guidelines related to investment in agriculture appears in Table 7.1.

In 2009, the FAO's Land Tenure and Management Unit issued a Discussion Paper titled *Towards Voluntary Guidelines on Responsible Governance of Tenure of Land and Other Natural Resources* with the aim of seeking views and comments (FAO 2009). The paper provided examples of what could be included as guidelines, noting that the Voluntary Guidelines would be prepared through a participatory process involving international organizations, governments and civil society.

Table 7.1 Principles and guidelines related to investment in agriculture

Name	When	Who
• Basic Principles on the Purchase and Leasing of Large Areas of Land in Developing Countries	2009	• German government (BMZ)
• Elements for a code of conduct for foreign land acquisition	2009	• International Food Policy Research Institute
• Equator Principles (III)	2012	• 76 adopting financial institutions
• Extractive Industry Transparency Initiative Principles	2003	• Extractive Industry Transparency Initiative
• Large-Scale Land Acquisition and Responsible Agricultural Investment: For an Approach Respecting Human Rights, Food Security and Sustainable Development	2010	• Government of France
• Minimum Human Rights Principles Applicable to Large-Scale Land Acquisitions or Lease	2009	• Special Rapporteur on the Right to Food
• Principles for Responsible Agricultural Investment that Respect Rights, Livelihoods and Resources (PRAI)	2010	• Inter-Agency Working Group: FAO, IFAD, UNCTAD and the World Bank
• Promoting responsible international investment in agriculture	2009	• Japanese government (Ministry of Foreign Affairs)
• Santiago Principles (Generally Accepted Principles and Practices)	2008	• International Working Group of Sovereign Wealth Funds
• Voluntary Guidelines to Support the Progressive Realisation of the Right to Adequate Food in the Context of National Food Security	2004	• FAO
• Voluntary Guidelines for Responsible Governance of Tenure of Land, Fisheries and Forests in the Context of National Food Security	2012	• CFS
• Principles for Responsible Agricultural Investments in Agriculture and Food Systems	2014	• CFS

When the idea for Voluntary Guidelines on land tenure was conceived, it was assumed they would be a technical document aimed at policy makers and fieldworkers and that they would receive, at most, two hours of review in the CFS, be approved and then become a resource applied by the FAO (interview, March 2012, London). However, a year after the release of the FAO's discussion paper, at their 36th Session, the CFS:

> encouraged the continuation of the inclusive process for the development of the Voluntary Guidelines (Voluntary Guidelines on the Responsible Governance of Tenure of Land and Other Natural Resources—VGGT)

building on existing regional processes with a view to submitting the guidelines for the consideration of the 37th Session of CFS and decided to establish an open-ended working group of the CFS to review the first draft of the Voluntary Guidelines.

(CFS 2010: para 26.i)

By bringing them into the CFS, the nature of the guidelines shifted from a technical to a political nature and their influence and interest increased. A major rationale, especially for CSOs, for the negotiation of the guidelines within the CFS was to add an additional level of influence and standing. Many hoped that intergovernmentally negotiated guidelines would provide a counterbalance to emerging guidelines and principles on responsible investment, most notably PRAI. When questioned about the shift from a technical process to a political one, an FAO technical staff member suggested that the move was viewed positively in so far as it gave the VGGT far more political weight. It was noted that "we were lucky to have a CFS that was looking for something to do" (field notes, June 2013, Berlin).

Bringing the Voluntary Guidelines into the CFS

As mentioned above, at the 36th Session of the CFS there was agreement to establish an OEWP of the CFS to review the first draft of the Voluntary Guidelines. This particular decision was the result of a debate principally led by civil society actors who believed that beyond a clear need for guidelines on land tenure governance, the CFS needed to undertake a process to counter PRAI. CSOs worked hard to block an endorsement of the then RAI, now referred to as PRAI, which were developed by the World Bank, UNCTAD, FAO and IFAD in 2009. The reasoning was that PRAI was developed without proper consultation. The principles were not grounded in a rights-based approach and did not give primacy to goal of improving food security. Furthermore, PRAI lacked institutional legitimacy insofar as they were never submitted for approval by their respective governing bodies.

Civil society actors could agree that principles to address large-scale land acquisition and foreign investment in agriculture were needed, despite concerns that they could be seen as rationalizing land grab and the problematic assumption that investments are not responsible: all investments should be responsible. However, civil society actors argued that before such principles could be identified, guidelines for the responsible governance of tenure were needed.

At the 36th Session, the CFS held a discussion on land tenure with a view to endorsing the VGGT and PRAI. As is the procedure in the reformed CFS, there was a discussion between member states and participants to arrive at a decision. Table 7.2 provides a comparison of the draft decisions presented to the CFS policy roundtable by the Secretariat and the final decisions taken by the CFS in the form of recommendations.

Comparing the draft decision box (the text presented for negotiation to the Committee) to the final recommendations of the CFS, some key changes can

Table 7.2 Outcomes of the Policy Roundtable on Land Tenure and International Investment in Agriculture (CFS 36)

Draft decision box (August 2010)	*Final recommendations of the 36th Session of the CFS (October 2010)*
Endorsing the ongoing inclusive process of development of the Voluntary Guidelines on Responsible Governance of Tenure of Land and Other Natural Resources and requesting FAO to submit the Voluntary Guidelines for review and approval by CFS and FAO governing bodies.	Encouraged the continuation of the inclusive process for the development of the Voluntary Guidelines (Voluntary Guidelines on the Responsible Governance of Tenure of Land and Other Natural Resources—VGGT) building on existing regional processes with a view to submitting the guidelines for the consideration of the 37th Session of CFS and decided to establish an OEWG of the CFS to review the first draft of the Voluntary Guidelines.
Endorsing the ongoing elaboration of Principles for Responsible Agricultural Investment that Respect Rights, Livelihoods and Resources initiated by the World Bank, FAO, IFAD and UNCTAD and recommending that the consultation process be pursued and include all relevant stakeholders.	Taking note of the on-going process of developing Principles for Responsible Agricultural Investments that Respect Rights, Livelihoods and Resources (RAI), and, in line with its role, decided to start an inclusive process of consideration of the principles within the CFS.
Urging FAO and the other international organizations involved to continue ensuring the consistency and complementarity between the two processes and to keep focus on their food security and poverty reduction objectives.	Urged governments and other stakeholders involved in the drafting process of both the VGGT and the RAI to ensure consistency and complementarity between the two processes.
	Requested the HLPE to undertake studies, to be presented at the 37th Session of the CFS, on the following important issues, in accordance with the CFS reform document agreed in 2009, and the Rules and Procedures for the work of the HLPE: the respective roles of large-scale plantations and of small-scale farming, including economic, social, gender and environmental impacts; review of the existing tools allowing the mapping of available land; comparative analysis of tools to align large-scale investments with country food security strategies.
	Encouraged member state support for capacity building toward effectively addressing land governance.

be identified. These include a deadline for the submission of the Guidelines to the CFS and the removal of FAO governing bodies from the approval process. This was a risk, as the reformed CFS had not yet proven itself. The move could be seen as a way to weaken the political impact of the outputs by having the documents endorsed by a historically weak Committee. However, the overwhelming sentiment was that the CFS, with its enhanced participation, was the most appropriate forum for endorsement as it was positioned to be the foremost intergovernmental platform for addressing food security policy.

For the RAI process, the draft language calling for "endorsement" of their elaboration was weakened to "taking note," after a long negotiation between member states but notably between representatives of the World Bank and La Via Campesina that went on past 2 a.m. without language interpretation. As an aside, this round of negotiations was a turning point for many: it was evidence of the willingness of member states to accept the implications of participation. States had every right to reach consensus and stop the back and forth between the participants, and end the negotiations much earlier. Instead they made a concerted effort to work through the differences and to move towards consensus. Some might suggest that this is further evidence of vertical shifts evident across global governance where states pass responsibility onto other actors, but those in the room, who engaged until the end, agree that this was much more. This was evidence of a concerted effort on part of all actors to enact the reform vision of the CFS.

The outcome of the negotiations was perceived as a victory by civil society actors who had made a statement calling on the CFS to:

> not endorse the Principles for Responsible Agricultural Investment that Respects Rights, Livelihoods and Resources (RAI): the RAI is not an adequate instrument to regulate private investment; moreover, RAI principles have been formulated through an exclusive process without the participation of communities and constituencies most affected by agricultural investments, especially private investments. What is needed instead are nationally and internationally enforceable laws and public regulations on all investments pertaining to land, including provisions on extra-territorial obligations of states to regulate and make private companies accountable for their operations abroad.
>
> (Field notes, October 2010, Rome)

However, CSOs did lose on a few key issues. Specific reference food security and poverty reduction objectives were lost but emphasis on consistency and complementary was retained, in line with the overall mandate of the CFS. The negotiations resulted in two additional points. The first point was a request to the HLPE to undertake a study into land tenure and investment. The final point encouraged member state support for capacity building toward effectively addressing land governance. The major impact of the policy roundtable was that the CFS would proceed with a review of the VGGT.

Methodology

The FAO and the CFS committed to ensuring that the VGGT were developed in a consultative and participatory way. Participatory policy making is necessarily a time-consuming process. That said, the VGGT managed to undertake widespread, meaningful consultation in a reasonable amount of time. The methodology used in the drafting of the Guidelines was applauded by all stakeholders for their participatory and consultative effectiveness. In total, ten regional, one private sector and four civil society consultation meetings were organized between September 2009 and November 2010. The FAO coordinated regional consultations in Brazil, Burkina Faso, Ethiopia, Jordan, Namibia, Panama, Romania, the Russian Federation, Samoa and Viet Nam. These meetings brought together almost 1,000 representatives from government institutions, civil society, private sector, academia and UN agencies from across 130 countries. Each consultation meeting included an assessment to identify issues and actions to be included in the Guidelines in the context of governance of tenure. Building on the consultations, FAO technical staff developed a Zero Draft of the Guidelines. On April 15, 2011, there was a public reading in FAO of the Zero Draft. From April 18 to May 1, 2011, an electronic consultation on the Zero Draft was organized. Then, from July 12 to 15, 2011 the CFS hosted intergovernmental negotiations. It is important to remember that under the reform of the CFS, these negotiations were open to the participation of civil society and private sector actors, among others.

Following the electronic consultation on the Zero Draft, a First Draft was developed by FAO technical staff. It was written so as to be consistent with international and regional instruments that address human rights and tenure rights. It was also informed by the broad and inclusive process of consultation that took place from 2009–2010. In terms of including the outcomes of the consultation into the First Draft, it was noted that:

> Some proposals were not included in this revised draft because they provided a greater level of detail than that which can be accommodated in an instrument of this nature, and they may be more suited for supporting material that will become available later. In other cases, several different views were put forward in ways that did not allow them to be reconciled into a single proposed change. The reconciliation of such different views will be addressed along with other matters during the CFS-led negotiations and open-ended working group meetings which are intended to lead to a final text of the Voluntary Guidelines in July 2011.
>
> (FAO 2012a:4)

The First Draft was submitted to the OEWG on June 1, 2011 and comments were compiled by the CFS Secretariat. From June 15–17 the OEWG tried to focus the discussion and prepare for the negotiations.

The process of negotiation unrolled as follows. Working in English with the proposed text projected onto a large screen, participants would identify themselves to the chair and then the chair would call on them to make suggestions. Scribes noted the suggestions in the working document using the Microsoft Word track changes function. This visibly tracked all of the inclusions and deletions. All members of the Committee, including civil society, governments and the private sector, had the right to make suggestions and all suggestions had to be taken into account. Negotiations continued until member states reached consensus on the text.

Proposed text was inserted into the working text and if it was contentious it was put into square brackets. Proposed text that had been rejected was crossed out. In the cases where it became apparent that the Plenary was unlikely to find consensus, the problematic paragraphs were sent to a "Friends of the Chair" (FOC) group. For this, the chair identified an agreeably neutral "friend" (most often a government representative from a member state with little stake in the issue) to facilitate negotiations between interested (disagreeing) parties. These groups were in theory open to all interested CFS participants. However, often these groups met while the plenary negotiations continued. This restricted participation as many delegations did not have enough people or resources to cover both meetings. Consequently, wealthier countries were better represented in these groups. Less well-staffed delegations tended to develop regional alliances and divide the work among themselves. Once the FOC reached consensus, the facilitator reported back to the chair, and often Plenary, with a text that had the agreement group and consensus was sought from Plenary to approve the language. When consensus was reached among member states, the changes were accepted and the text was "cleaned" (meaning that the track changes were accepted) and the paragraph was then closed. Some of the most contentious paragraphs within the negotiations related to: state-owned land; responsible investment; provisions for investment; climate change and emergencies; and implementation. This sheds light on the various tensions that exist within the CFS.

Here it is important to note that the negotiations of the VGGT were technically not negotiations but discussions and consultations by the OEWG. Even after the Guidelines had been finalized in the Working Group, member states had the right to reopen the text and launch negotiations in the CFS Plenary. While the Working Group was only "consulting" on the text so that it could presented it to the CFS plenary for endorsement, in practice and especially by the March 2012 session, the Working Group functioned very much like a session of the Plenary. Members and participants adopted the language of "negotiation" and worked in a manner that was indistinguishable from the negotiations that take place during the CFS sessions. Furthermore, in promoting the VGGT, actors including the CFS and the FAO speak about them as being the result of intergovernmental negotiations. Because of this, the language used herein relates to negotiations as it is a more adequate reflection of the process and to distinguish the efforts of the CFS OEWG from the consultations that took place around the Zero and First Draft.

From July 12–15, the OEWG met in Rome to negotiate the text but they were unable to come to consensus on all paragraphs and thus did not complete the process.[2] A second round of negotiations took place the week before the 37th Session. Still the negotiations did not conclude and a final session was added for March 2012. Instead of endorsing the VGGT, at their 37th Session, the CFS "recognized that additional time will be required to complete the process and endorsed its continuation and finalization" while also acknowledging that "substantial progress [had been] gained so far and recommended building on the solid base which has been achieved, while concentrating on remaining paragraphs and respecting and maintaining the spirit of understanding reached during the July and October negotiations" (CFS 2011: paras 11–12). Despite the extended work plan, there was widespread and growing agreement of the value of the process and the potential of the outcome.

The phrase "concentrating on remaining paragraphs and respecting and maintaining the spirit of understanding reached" was key. The OEWG had deliberated and facilitated intergovernmental negotiations that had led to consensus on the majority of the text and there was a great deal of concern that reopening negotiations on specific paragraphs would at best slow down, and at worst derail, the process. That said, as the Canadian negotiators frequently reminded the Committee, nothing decided in the working groups was final. Final decisions could only be taken by the Plenary and every government has the right to raise concerns in Plenary, thereby blocking consensus. After an extended negotiation in March 2012, the OEWG reached consensus and an extraordinary meeting of the CFS was called in May 2012 for the CFS to endorse the VGGT. The VGGT were endorsed unanimously by 96 member countries.

Review of the First Draft

It is here argued that the transition from Zero Draft to the final version of the Voluntary Guidelines is evidence of the value of meaningful and diverse consultation and participatory negotiations. As will be shown below, the First Draft failed to adequately recognize structural problems linked to land tenure and assumed weak tenure to be weak management. Furthermore, it failed to give sufficient weight to issues related to discrimination (e.g., race, class, ethnicity, wealth and age) and related restrictions to access to land, and recognition of tenure or rights to land.

The First Draft contained several weaknesses. First, it started from the assumption that states own land and that they have the authority to distribute tenure rights, so long as the actions conform to a set of guidelines. Viewed this way, the Guidelines are no longer a tool for responsible governance but instead a tool for states and/or elite groups to rationalize or legitimize control over natural resources. Framing land tenure this way opens the Guidelines to challenges arising from the multiple uses and roles of land across contexts. The First Draft failed to live up to claims of being aligned with existing human rights instruments insofar as it did not uphold or reinforce existing rights, such as those included in the

UN Declaration on Indigenous Peoples (UNDIP). CSOs raised concerns that failure to include such existing rights into the Guidelines could lead the VGGT to be used to dilute rights. CSOs reminded the CFS that rights are not negotiable and nor should people have to negotiate for their land. Talk of negotiation contradicts the UNDIP commitment to free, prior and informed consent.

Related to this point, between the Zero and First Drafts, wording had changed from stating countries should act in ways that are "consistent with international and regional human rights obligations" to "consistent with their obligations and voluntary commitments to applicable international and regional human rights norms and standards." While the inclusion of voluntary commitments is good, the revised sentence is arguably weaker overall. Given the voluntary and thus non-binding nature of the Guidelines, it is not likely that they could easily (if at all) undermine a UN Declaration on Rights. However, the fact that states were unwilling to ensure coherence between the pre-existing rights defined in UNDIP and the Guidelines, and that they failed to use the Guidelines to strengthen the rights of vulnerable people, including indigenous peoples, is problematic.

The controversial issues of markets and investment remained highly problematic across both drafts. On this matter, CSOs consistently argued for the need to recognize that there are other types of land-based investment beyond agriculture that impact on small-scale food producers (e.g. mining, development, military). CSOs also raised concern that the discourse of development could be used to rationalize changes in land tenure systems. They cited examples of the development of beach resorts for tourism, noting that such processes often disregard food producers and customary uses of, and rights to, these lands and resources. Land rights are also restricted by projects undertaken in the name of conservation, where communities are pushed off their land or their access to natural resources is restricted so as to protect a specific species of animal or biodiversity.

Some of these concerns were addressed between the First Draft and the final version of the VGGT. Most notably, the final version of the VGGT ground the VGGT in a rights-based approach:

> 4.2 States should ensure that all actions regarding tenure and its governance are consistent with their existing obligations under national and international law, and with due regard to voluntary commitments under the applicable regional and international instruments.
>
> (FAO 2012c)

A rights-based approach strengthens the VGGT. Insofar as while they remain voluntary, the guidelines build on and take form existing international obligations and commitments. Grounding the VGGT in a rights-based approach was a direct outcome of strong interventions and negotiation by civil society actors and the Special Rapporteur on the Right to Food, who developed a strong strategy and rationale for grounding the document in a rights-based approach.

Such an approach further strengthens the links between the VGGT and the CFS which is meant to "strive for a world free from hunger where countries implement the Voluntary Guidelines for the progressive realization of the right to adequate food in the context of national food security" (CFS 2009: para 4).

Negotiating the Voluntary Guidelines: Insight into process and participation

Securing buy-in and convincing member states about the relevance and potential of these Guidelines took time. This is perhaps not surprising given the politically sensitive nature of land tenure and related issues. When the FAO launched the process, it was mainly European countries that financially supported the process. There was hesitation on the part of many African countries due to the fact that in 2009 the African Union had adopted a Land Policy Framework and there were concerns over how the two documents would correlate. That said, the Africa Group ended up playing a critical role in the negotiations, often forging political alliances with the EU and rejecting claims by other governments that such guidelines were not needed, giving concrete examples of why they were needed. Indeed, the insistence of African governments on the potential value of guidelines for the governance of land, fisheries and forests provided motivation and legitimacy throughout the negotiation process.

Asian countries were largely absent from the negotiations, though the delegate from Afghanistan was an exception. The Chinese delegation also followed the negotiation closely and contributed to discussions on tenure in the context of state-owned land and markets. That the negotiations were based on an English language text can be given as part of the reason. India was completely absent from the discussions, which was surprising in part given that India had been active in processes linked to the Voluntary Guidelines on the Progressive Realization on the Right to Food, but perhaps less surprisingly when one considers that India is involved in 65 land investment deals whereof 39 are transnational and 26 domestic (International Land Coalition 2013). The conflict related to Kashmir could have also limited a desire to enter into international discussions on land tenure.

Analysis of the Voluntary Guidelines

The purpose of the VGGT is to:

> serve as a reference and provide guidance to improve the governance of tenure of land fisheries and forests with the overarching goal of achieving food security for all and to support the progressive realization of the right to adequate food in the context of national food security.
>
> (FAO 2012c:iv)

Towards this end, the VGGT cover seven key areas related to the responsible tenure of land, fisheries and forests: legal recognition and allocation of tenure rights and duties, including safeguards, public resources, indigenous peoples and informal tenure; transfer and other changes to tenure rights and duties, specifically as they relate to markets, investments and land consolidation; restitution; redistributive reform; the administration of tenure including records of tenure rights, valuation, taxation, resolution of disputes and transboundary matters; responses to climate change and emergencies; and the promotion, implementation, monitoring and evaluation.

These areas are all framed by a set of guiding principles of responsible tenure governance as well as principles for implementation. The former declare that states should recognize and respect all legitimate tenure right holders, safeguard legitimate tenure rights and provide access to justice to deal with infringement of legitimate tenure rights. Furthermore, non-state actors including businesses have a responsibility to respect human rights and legitimate tenure rights. With respect to implementation, there are ten principles:

1   Human dignity.
2   Non-discrimination.
3   Equity and justice.
4   Gender equity.
5   Holistic and sustainable approach.
6   Consultation and participation.
7   Rule of law.
8   Transparency.
9   Accountability.
10 Continuous improvement.

In the First Draft there were only nine principles, with "Gender and social equity, and gender and social justice" constituting a single principle recognizing that "equality between individuals may require acknowledging differences between individuals, and taking positive action, including empowerment, to ensure equitable treatment and outcomes for all, women and men, and vulnerable and marginalized people" (FAO 2012a). In the final document, the social focus was lost when the principle was split into "Gender equality" and "Equity and justice." The principle of equity and justice recognizes:

> that equality between individuals may require acknowledging differences between individuals, and taking positive action, including empowerment, in order to promote equitable tenure rights and access to land, fisheries and forests, for all, women and men, youth and vulnerable and traditionally marginalized people, within the national context.
>
> (FAO 2012c)

Section 1.2 outline the objectives of the Guidelines, specifically:

> 1.2.4 strengthen the capacities and operations of implementing agencies; judicial authorities; local governments; organizations of farmers and small-scale producers, of fishers, and of forest users; pastoralists; indigenous peoples and other communities; civil society; private sector; academia; and all persons concerned with tenure governance as well as to promote the cooperation between the actors mentioned.
>
> (FAO 2012c)

This paragraph represented a key battle for CSOs that fought for a definition of small-scale producers to be included. It is noteworthy that the term "small-scale producers" is used over smallholders as it shifts the focus to the production. Another change was that in the First Draft, civil society came after the private sector in the listing and judicial authorities replaced reference to courts thereby increasing relevance across multiple contexts and respecting systems of traditional authority. This was changed in the final version.

To improve on the implementing principle of transparency, a proposal was made by the Office of the High Commissioner for Human Rights, represented by the Special Rapporteur on the Right to Food, who sits on the Advisory Group to the CFS. The proposal was to explicitly state the need to make information available in formats accessible to all "including women, communities in remote areas and persons with disabilities." The proposal was rejected. The final principle reads: "3B.8 Transparency: clearly defining and widely publicizing policies, laws and procedures in applicable languages, and widely publicizing decisions in applicable languages and in formats accessible to all."

Some delegations argued that rather than have a "bucket list," it was more appropriate to ensure accessibility for all. The limitation of this being that a focus on everyone depoliticizes or shifts focus away from the groups of people who are most often ignored. However, in the spirit of language harmonization, and to avoid inevitably leaving groups off the list, throughout the document the application of the implementing principles and relevant guidelines applies broadly "to all," with the notable exception of Section 9, which relates specifically to indigenous peoples and other communities with customary tenure systems.

Tensions related to issues of state sovereignty and definitions were inevitable and correspondingly took a prominent position in the negotiations. These tensions are raised immediately in paragraph 1.1, where, referring to the objectives of the Guidelines, it notes that the "Voluntary Guidelines seek to improve governance of tenure of land,* fisheries and forests." The asterisk refers to a footnote that states "there is no international definition of land within the context of tenure. The meaning of the word may be defined within the national context" (FAO 2012c). This is problematic given that the guidelines are meant to provide guidance on the tenure of land and that becomes challenging if land remains undefined. Throughout the negotiations countries were adamant about maintaining their right to define land within a national context. While this does remain the right of countries, a definition of what "land" is would certainly have strengthened the Guidelines. Broad definitions of land do exist. The FAO discussion paper on the development of guidelines did provide a definition that could have been used:

> Terminology is problematic in any material of this nature. In order to simplify the text, the term "land" is used to include any human–made improvements to the land, including housing and other buildings, and infrastructure such as irrigation systems. In addition to land, the discussion paper addresses other natural resources (such as trees and forests, pastures and other vegetation, water and fisheries) that cover the land or are otherwise related to it.
>
> (FAO 2009:1–2)

Building on the theme of state sovereignty, the final version of the Guidelines includes a new paragraph (2.5) which states that the "Guidelines should be interpreted and applied in accordance with national legal systems and their institutions." This directive is reiterated in paragraph 3.1.2 with reference to the principles that should be upheld by states. In reference to safeguards, language was added to clarify that states should protect tenure rights holders against the arbitrary loss of their tenure rights, including forced evictions "that are inconsistent with their existing obligations under national and international law." In that same section, language related to the prevention of corruption was weakened for the final document. The First Draft mentioned that states "should prevent opportunities for corruption in all forms, at all levels, and in all settings" but this was changed to "should *endeavour to* prevent corruption." The shift is subtle but important and reflects awareness on the part of governments that they could be held to these Guidelines.

The selective review of the negotiations highlights the complexity of the process but also the high level of engagement and interaction across participants. What inarguably sets the CFS negotiations apart from other intergovernmental negotiations is not simply the inclusion of participants in such a meaningful way, but also the level of debate and dialogue among member state delegates. Within these negotiations there are prepared positions but no prepared statements orated by ministers forwarding grandiose visions but failing to address concrete issue or advance the process. The move away from prepared statements makes room for negotiation, compromise and eventually consensus.

That the VGGT respect and protect human rights in the context of tenure is key not only for ensuring coherence with CFS policies and the Voluntary Guidelines on the Right to Food, but also insofar as this links the VGGT to existing international commitments and therefore strengthens them from a legal and enforcement perspective. The emphasis on women, peasant farmers, fishing communities, pastoralists and indigenous peoples is valuable, as are the principles of implementation. CSOs were pleased to have secured the use of the term "small-scale producers" over the term "smallholder farmer," noting that focus needs to be on those who produce food, a category that extends well beyond what is commonly understood to be farming. Finally, the importance of the VGGT extends beyond having an intergovernmentally negotiated and endorsed set of best practices for responsible governance of tenure to evidence of the capacity of the CFS to live up to its reform mandate and deliver relevant and useful outcomes.

That said, there are limitations within the document. First and foremost, there is no definition of land, fisheries or forests. While initially a glossary had been proposed, this was later rejected because it was evident that member states would be unlikely to reach consensus and that they preferred to define the terms within their national context. CSOs wanted a glossary but were aware of the potential for the glossary to contain weak definitions.

The failure of the VGGT to address water is perhaps the greatest weakness. Changes in land tenure can result in changes to access of fishers to waterways and fishing grounds. Moreover, irrigation, water for animals and transport, and rights and access to water (beyond fisheries) stand to be challenged with shifts in land tenure. CSOs pushed for this to be recognized in the Guidelines but were not successful. Migratory routes were also not given adequate consideration and the assumption that large-scale investments in industrial agriculture, fisheries and forests are essential for development remains unchallenged within the VGGT.

Throughout the negotiations participants were keenly aware of the increasing number of large-scale land acquisitions taking place, particularly in food inse-cure countries. For some, this contributed to a sense of urgency to complete the Guidelines. While these Guidelines were not specifically meant to address land grabbing (Seufert 2013:183), the links between the responsible governance of tenure and increasing large-scale acquisitions of land could not be avoided. CSOs pushed for an international ban on land grabbing while governments from several developing country governments argued in favor of the large-scale acqui-sition of tenure rights as central to fostering national and regional economic development (Seufert 2013). In the end, the VGGT address safeguards to enact with respect to the large-scale acquisition of tenure rights and resulting impacts.

Another limitation of the VGGT is that they do not prioritize support for small-scale food producer groups. Furthermore, they do not consolidate the recognized rights of indigenous peoples as articulated in UNDIP and other international instruments.

As CSOs noted in their analysis, the longer-term implications of tenure on youth and future generations are also not adequately addressed. Nor is there enough clarification on different modes of production. CSOs also noted that not enough emphasis had been placed on enforcement and that the document lacked adequate propositions for mechanism of enforcement.

Implications and next steps

As their name suggests, the Voluntary Guidelines are voluntary. In practice they are an instrument of international soft law and do not replace existing national or international laws, treaties or agreements. Not enforceable, the Guidelines represent intergovernmental consensus on accepted principles and standards for responsible land tenure governance practices. Importantly, "they explicitly refer to existing binding international human rights obligations related to land and natural resources and provide interpretation and guidance on how to implement these obligations" (Seufert 2013:182).

The question of why bother if the end result is a set of non-enforceable, Voluntary Guidelines needs to be addressed. First and foremost, the VGGT respond to a need expressed by several states: applicable guidance for good governance of tenure. Second, the VGGT are an entry point to begin to talk about land govern- ance and to foster public engagement. Third, the VGGT can be effectively used at the national level to evaluate existing land tenure and easily identify gaps in policy. Fourth, the rights-based approach is important as it shifts focus of land tenure to the most vulnerable populations. Fifth, the VGGT are a useful tool for assessing and monitoring the actions of governments and non-governmental investors.

The final document represents what one leading UN expert on food security declared to be a "contribution to those struggling to address power relations" (field notes, June 2013, Berlin). While an initial reading of this com- ment suggests that this is a rather positive statement, it is important to note the focus is not on the responsibility of states but rather it is placed on CSOs. This is a trend that must be monitored. To frame the VGGT as a success for those struggling against stronger powers is not incorrect, but the VGGT are not to be seen as limited to CSOs. For the VGGT to be most effective and to fulfil their purpose, they must be taken up at the national level, in national laws and policies. The move towards strong national or regional policies around the governance of land fisheries and forests is not something that will come about overnight. Furthermore, it is a process that must be undertaken carefully and with sensitivity. At the same time, there is urgency, not least due to the links between tenure of natural resources and food security. While moving forward cautiously, there are several issues that remain to be addressed, notably com- munication, implementation and monitoring.

In terms of next steps, a lot of focus has been placed on communication and awareness building. This is of course of important but there are potential implications which must be taken into consideration. For example, the issue of language must be addressed. The VGGT are not available in some lan- guages and, furthermore, the language used therein is quite technical. There are efforts under way to translate the document into other languages and to make the content more accessible. However, as the review of the negotiations highlights, the language within the VGGT is highly negotiated and must be interpreted with upmost caution.

Beyond efforts to disperse the VGGT and build awareness, there is a need for capacity building, for example in cases where states do not have surveyors or records of tenure or documentation. Also, governments must be prepared to develop complaints mechanisms and clear processes to address grievances in line with the Guidelines. This is something that to date has been inadequately considered.

Implementation of the VGGT is not simply a technical issue; it is also a highly political issue that will require a great deal of political will. Since their endorsement there has been an assumption about the goodwill to implement, but in actuality, implementing guidelines on such a contentious issue will likely be avoided by most governments. In order to address this challenge, focus could be scaled-up to the regional level and regional groupings of countries could work towards implementation of relevant aspects, employing regional pressure and resources. The point on relevance is important. The VGGT are not to be seen as a one-size-fits-all solution that should be wholly incorporated into national law and policy. Instead, the VGGT seek to provide best practices on a range of tenure-related issues allowing governments and policy makers to pick and choose what is needed given their specific context.

Another way of supporting implementation would be to build on the links to existing human rights obligations. Here it could be advantageous for the FAO to work closely with interested countries and with countries that have a strong human rights record to begin to implement sections of the VGGT into the national context and to then use their experiences to help motivate or guide other countries.

Across civil society organizations there are tensions around leadership and authority with respect to monitoring and implementation with the IPC and IPC+ (which includes select NGOs) forging ahead to develop CSO guidelines, but excluding actors keen to participate. The IPC, which liaises with FAO, has also made it clear that the CFS has no capacity to implement and therefore by extension the CSM does not have a mandate to work on implementation. The CSM is only a facilitation mechanism but its members are able to work on whatever projects they deem appropriate. The rising tensions between the IPC and CSM are politically sensitive and illustrate the factions and turf wars that emerge within these international fora.

With respect to implementation, accountability needs to be at the fore, which in turn requires monitoring. Monitoring is as technical as it is political. The purpose of the VGGT is to provide guidance to improve the governance of tenure of land, fisheries and forests with the goal of achieving food security for all. CSOs have proposed two possibilities for monitoring. First is the establishment of an independent body to review progress made towards improved governance of tenure, using the VGGT as a baseline. Alternatively, a process could be identified whereby states report on their progress in implementing the Voluntary Guidelines. This process could be peer reviewed by other states, CSOs and other CFS participants (Seufert 2013). While innovative and forward looking, these proposals are unlikely to see any traction. With respect to the first suggestion, the questions of who and how need to be addressed. Also it remains to be seen how such a body would be funded and how it would select the countries to be monitored. With respect to the second proposal, member states have been explicitly clear in their rejection of mandatory reporting or paperwork in the reformed CFS.

Despite the limitations of the CSO proposals, the fact remains that monitoring is key to achieving the objectives of the VGGT. The FAO has a role to play in supporting countries and building capacity but their role in monitoring is less clear. While there is agreement that the CFS is not an implementing body, there is arguably a role for the CFS in monitoring. The Global Strategic Framework (GSF) of the CFS (2012: para 101) notes that:

> In line with the CFS mandate, some way should be found to monitor the state of implementation of the Committee's own decisions and recommendations, so as to allow for the reinforcement of the coordination and policy convergence roles of the CFS. To this end, the Secretariat was tasked with reporting, in collaboration with the Advisory Group, on the state of implementation of numerous CFS decisions and recommendations, including the VGGT.

The CFS has also launched an OEWG on monitoring:

> The open-ended working group on monitoring, established by the CFS Bureau, has decided to focus its first efforts on this component, and will further debate possible options, modalities and required resources for the follow-up of the state of implementation of CFS recommendations by the Secretariat, according to the role of CFS to promote accountability as defined in the Reform Document. The GSF, by providing a consolidated body of CFS outputs, will, in conjunction with the VGGT and future similar instruments, contribute to the task of knowing what recommendations to monitor.
>
> (CFS 2012: para 102)

Moving forward, the OEWG has decided to focus on the monitoring of the VGGT. In line with the reformed roles of the CFS, the monitoring group has expressed interest in sharing best practices. Case studies usefully provide a review of the context and provide a sense of where things stand. However, careful attention must be paid to the method used to select case studies. The method should ensure that case studies are collected from a variety of actors (e.g., government, private sector, social movements, NGOs, research institutes) to ensure that multiple perspectives are reflected.

While case studies provide a useful starting point, indicators are needed to begin to assess impact and implication. For the VGGT, both qualitative and quantitative indicators would be advisable. The CFS's GSF (see Chapter 7) contains suggestions for developing indicators in a gender-sensitive approach and within a human-rights based framework. Given the complexity of land governance and the importance of location and context, indicators will need to be considered and designed to suit specific cases.

Multi-stakeholder platforms will also be central to effective monitoring, while supporting the principles of the VGGT and the CFS. These need to meaningfully involve all actors, be multi-sectoral and respect differentiations of power. Correspondingly, a clear methodology is needed for establishing the multi-sectoral platforms and ensuring transparency. It is also important to note that with respect to monitoring and indicators, the question of attribution must be addressed: how can change be attributed to the VGGT or related actions? This is something that has received inadequate attention and requires further research.

Conclusion

The successful negotiation of the VGGT is evidence of the value of the reformed CFS as well as participatory policy making at the global level. This case study began by reviewing land tenure and highlighting the importance of good governance of land tenure to the eradication of hunger. The methodology employed in the development of the VGGT was presented and followed by a review of the negotiations. The interactive and participatory nature of the CFS was illustrated through a review of the negotiations, wherein social dynamics were also elucidated. While there are limitations with the VGGT there is also growing interest and awareness and discussions about next steps. Strategies for implementation and monitoring at the national and regional levels are being considered along with extraterritorial obligations, suggesting that the VGGT could have an important impact on policy.

The analysis of the negotiations illustrates the important role that consultation and participation of a wider range of stakeholders can have on policy outcomes. The process of negotiating the VGGT also provides insight into key tensions in participatory policy making that can inform wider scholarship and practice. It is important to note that finalizing the VGGT was an important step in the evolution of the CFS but the process was in part successful because the CFS was able to avoid discussion on some highly contentious issues, notably related to trade and investment, by tabling them to be addressed in the CFS negotiations on CFS-rai. The CFS had agreed to postpone the development of the CFS-rai until after they had endorsed the VGGT. This facilitated progress on the VGGT but set up a very difficult CFS-rai process.

Further lessons can be learnt from this case study. For example, the value of consultation was made evident through the analysis but what was perhaps not as well captured was the role of resources: not only financial resources (which were significant), but also less tangible resources such as time, expertise, trust and patience. This process demanded a high quantity of these resources. The case study also raises important questions to be addressed through future research including reflecting on implications for policy when a technical process becomes co-opted by a political process, albeit a consultative and participatory political process. Impacts of expertise and the implications of consensus building require more consideration. Finally, the VGGT map out an important relationship between the FAO and the CFS in so far as the FAO initiated the process in response to requests by member states, the CFS took over the process, expanded consultations and secured intergovernmental agreement on the document, and now the FAO is taking the lead on developing tools to effectively operationalize the Guidelines. The reinforcing nature of the CFS process and FAO work is another area that requires further investigation, wherein questions are asked about who is being included, who is being left out and who is making use of the resources developed by the FAO.

Notes

1 Reflecting on the process of developing the VGGT, one participant in the negotiation process noted "at a later stage in the process, Brazil made it clear that the Voluntary Guidelines had to be understood as part of ICARRD follow-up, which was not the case at the beginning of the consultation process" (Seufert 2013:183).
2 Sections where consensus had been reached include: Preface; Section 1 (Objectives); Section 2 (Nature and scope); Section 3 (Guiding principles) up to and including 3B.6.; Paragraph 9.8 of Section 9 (Indigenous peoples and other communities with customary tenure systems); Paragraph 12.5 of Section 12 (Investments and concessions); Section 13 (Land consolidation and other readjustment approaches); Section 14 (Restitution); Section 15 (Redistributive reforms); Section 16 (Expropriation and compensation).

References

Behrman, J., R. Meinzen-Dick, and A. Quisumbing. 2012. "The Gender Implications of Large-Scale Land Deals." *Journal of Peasant Studies* 39(1):49–79.

Borras, S. M., R. Hall, I. Scoones, B. White, and W. Wolford. 2011. "Towards a Better Understanding of Global Land Grabbing: An Editorial Introduction." *Journal of Peasant Studies* 38(2):209–16. Retrieved (www.tandfonline.com/doi/pdf/10.1080/03066150.2011.559005).

CFS. 2009. *Reform of the Committee on World Food Security Final Version.* Rome: FAO. Retrieved (www.fao.org/fileadmin/templates/cfs/Docs0910/ReformDoc/CFS_2009_2_Rev_2_E_K7197.pdf).

CFS. 2010. *Final Report Thirty-Sixth Session Committee on World Food Security.* Rome: FAO.

CFS. 2011. *Report of the 37th Session of the Committe on World Food Security.* Rome: FAO.

CFS. 2012. *Global Strategic Framework for Food Security and Nutrition (First Version).* Rome: FAO. Retrieved (www.fao.org/docrep/meeting/026/ME498E.pdf).

Deere, C. D., and M. Leon. 1997. *Women and Land Rights in the Latin American Neo-Liberal Counter-Reforms.* Retrieved (http://gencen.isp.msu.edu/documents/Working_Papers/WP264.pdf).

Deininger, K., Jin, S., & Nagaranjan, H. K. 2007. "Land Reforms, Poverty Reduction, and Economic Growth: Evidence from India." *Journal of Development Studies* 45(4):496–521.

De Schutter, O. 2011. "How Not to Think of Land-Grabbing: Three Critiques of Large-Scale Investments in Farmland." *Journal of Peasant Studies* 38(2):249–79. Retrieved (www.tandfonline.com/doi/abs/10.1080/03066150.2011.559008).

FAO. 2002. *Land Tenure and Rural Development.* Rome: FAO.

FAO. 2005. *Voluntary Guidelines to Support the Progressive Realization Of The Right to Adequate Food in the Context of National Food Security.* Rome: FAO. Retrieved (ftp://ftp.fao.org/docrep/fao/meeting/009/y9825e/y9825e.pdf).

FAO. 2009. *Towards Voluntary Guideleines on Responsible Governance of Tenure of Land and Other Natural Resources: Discussion Paper.* Rome: FAO.

FAO. 2012a. *First Draft: Voluntary Guidelines on the Responsible Governance of Tenure of Land, Fisheries and Forests*. Rome: FAO.

FAO. 2012b. *Governance of Tenure: Finding Common Ground*. Rome: FAO.

FAO. 2012c. *Voluntary Guidelines on the Responsible Governance of Tenure of Land, Fisheries and Forests in the Context of National Food Security*. Rome: FAO.

GRAIN. 2008. *Seized! The 2008 Land Grab for Food and Financial Security*. Barcelona: GRAIN.

Hall, D. 2011. "Land Grabs, Land Control, and Southeast Asian Crop Booms." *Journal of Peasant Studies* 38(4):837–57. Retrieved (www.tandfonline.com/doi/abs/10.1080/0306 6150.2011.607706).

Harvey, M., and S. Pilgrim. 2011. "The New Competition for Land: Food, Energy, and Climate Change." *Food Policy* 36:S40–S51. Retrieved (http://linkinghub.elsevier.com/retrieve/pii/S0306919210001235).

Hilton, A. 2013. *Update on the Support Programme for the Implementation of the Voluntary Guidelines on the Responsible Governance of Tenure of Land, Fisheries and Forests in the Context of National Food Security*. Rome: FAO.

HLPE. 2011. *Land Tenure and International Investments in Agriculture*. Rome: FAO. Retrieved (www.fao.org/fileadmin/user_upload/hlpe/hlpe_documents/HLPE-Land-tenure-and-international-investments-in-agriculture-2011.pdf).

ICARRD. 2006. *Report of the International Conference on Agrarian Reform and Rural Development*. Porto Alegre: ICARRD. Retrieved (www.agter.asso.fr/IMG/pdf/ICARRD_final_report_En.pdf).

International Land Coalition. 2013. "Land Matrix." Retrieved (http://landmatrix.org/get-the-idea/global-map-investments/#).

Seufert, P. 2013. "The FAO Voluntary Guidelines on the Responsible Governance of Tenure of Land, Fisheries and Forests." *Globalizations* 10(1):181–186.

Sietchiping, R. 2010. "Political Economy of Land Access and Control Over Natural and Land-Based Resources: A Means for Conflicts Prevention and Management?" pp. 1–12 in *CAPRi Workshop on Collective Action, Property Rights, and Conflict in Natural Resource Management*. Siem Reap, Cambodia.

UN General Assembly. 2012. *Agriculture Development and Food Security: Report of the Second Committee*. Sixty-Seventh Session (Agenda Item 26). New York: UN.

8 Policy coordination at the global level

The Global Strategic Framework

Introduction

Following the food price spikes of 2007–2008, the international community called for coordinated responses to avoid future crises (FAO et al. 2011; G8 2009; HLPE 2011). Toward this end, in 2009 the CFS reformed with three key roles: coordination at the global level; policy convergence; and support and advice to countries and regions (CFS 2009: para 5).

To begin to fulfil these roles, the CFS agreed to develop the Global Strategic Framework for Food Security and Nutrition (GSF) so as to "improve coordination and guide synchronized action by a wide range of stakeholders" (CFS 2009: para 6.iii). The GSF is meant to provide an overarching framework and act as a single reference document with practical guidance on core recommendations for food security and nutrition strategies, policies and actions validated by the wide ownership, participation and consultation afforded by the CFS (2012b: para 7). The idea is that it provides a "one-stop-shop" for policy makers and thus reinforces the CFS's role in global policy convergence.

Food security is a complex issue that is impacted and influenced by multiple policy areas including agriculture, environment, health, trade, development, climate change and finance, to name but a few. While there is broad agreement on what food security means in terms of an end goal, there is little agreement on why the world faces such extreme food insecurity and what solutions are needed to remedy the situation. As such, policy convergence and coordination are extremely difficult and vitally important. Furthermore, coherence is needed to ensure targeted and coordinated actions do not serve to undermine development. Policy coherence is also key for monitoring and agreement on objectives and pathways are key to ensuring impact at the country level. In this respect, the GSF has the potential to play an important role in global food security governance.

In this chapter, concepts of policy convergence, coordination and coherence are introduced. This is followed by a review of the process of developing and negotiating the GSF within the reformed CFS. An assessment of the GSF is then provided. The chapter concludes by arguing that the GSF is the most comprehensive and fit-for-purpose framework for coordinating food security policy at the global level.

Policy convergence

The reformed CFS works to develop policy recommendations on key issues related to food security so as to support countries achieve food security. Given the diverse realities and challenges when it comes to securing food for its citizens, questions about the value and/or implications of policy coherence should be raised. Surprisingly, within the CFS, such questions have not been asked. In fact, there is a widely held view that policy convergence, coherence and coordination are fundamental to ensuring food security.

Convergence is undertaken to support coherence in regulatory regimes, which then allows for enhanced coordination. Policy convergence can be defined as "the tendency of policies to grow more alike, in the form of increasing similarity in structures, processes, and performances" (Drezner 2014:53; Kerr 1983:3). Drezner (2014:78) notes that a state's ability to cooperate and agree on norms of governance determines the extent of policy convergence. However, while cooperation and agreement are fundamental to establishing the baseline, the uptake of intergovernmentally negotiated policies and the application of them is arguably a stronger indication of actual convergence.

Academic assessments of policy convergence in an era of globalization differ. Indeed, the literature on convergence is fragmented: divided on the driving forces of both globalization and convergence, and unclear on the role of the state. Within the CFS, there is a stated political commitment to convergence and there is clear agreement on the roles and responsibilities of states: food security is a national responsibility. With respect to convergence at the global level, some argue it promotes a race to the bottom where ecological, social, health and labor rights come second to economic growth (Bonior 1999; Davies and Vadlamannati 2013; McKenzie and Lee 1991; Polanyi 2001; Rodrik 1997). Others are more optimistic, arguing that the architecture of transnational governance allows for negotiated convergence on regulations and has the potential to address a democratic deficit (Cerny 1999; Drezner 2014; Vogel 1995; Wheeler 2001).

The trajectory of policy convergence, be it to the bottom or the top, depends on the sector and the actors involved. It also mediated by the level of political influence the policy bodies have in the hierarchy of global governance. Evidence from the CFS suggests that within the Committee there is not a push for the lowest common denominator. Instead, in most instances, the Committee has aimed for the highest possible level of agreement. The outcomes of these agreements are recorded in the GSF.

Policy coherence remains a concept that is "easily understood but difficult to measure" (May et al. 2006:382). Indeed, there is general agreement that greater coherence of policies is desirable, but the concept still remains under-theorized and supported by little empirical data. Analyses of the food price crisis noted that the food system had been subject to disjointed agriculture policies at the national and international levels, resulting in distortions in trade and limited policy coherence at the national and international level

(Ahmad 2011:1). With respect to food security policy, there was international a demand for improved policy coherence. Towards this end, the CFS was tasked with promoting policy coherence. However, it is difficult to argue that there is not a level of coherence across agriculture, food and nutrition policy insofar as the implications of embedded neoliberablism suggest a move towards policy coherence.

Neoliberal hegemony provides a cohesive link across sectors from the national through to the international. Challenging this hegemony is possible and is undertaken by state and non-state actors alike, but given the nature to which it is embedded not only as common sense but also presented as the most logical and rational ideology to inform policy, contestation proves challenging. This is made visible in discussions below, for example on the inclusion of contentious issues into the GSF.

Alongside convergence and cohesion, there is the need to coordinate. Policy coordination is vital insofar as "[p]olicy outcomes in all but the simplest policy systems emerge from a complex of ecology of games featuring multiple actors, policy institutions, and issues, and not just single policies operating in isolation" (Lubell et al. 2011). Food security was originally conceived as a state responsibility, with states having the role to ensure that there was sufficient food to "sustain a steady expansion of food consumption and to offset fluctuations in production and prices" (United Nations 1975). The 156 states that have ratified the International Covenant on Economic, Social and Cultural Rights (Article 11), adopted in 1966, are legally bound to ensure the right to adequate food. Yet the increasingly interconnected nature of systems of food provisioning, coupled with increasing interdependence of food, financial and energy markets, illustrates the need for good policy and effective, coordinated governance at the global level. Coordinated action is necessary, and international responses and national strategies must take place not in isolation but must be part of a larger global sustainability, health and development framework.

Food security policy at the national and international levels is ripe with inconsistencies and contradictions. The unique context of each country with respect to their food security situation serves to further complicate matters. Peters (2005) argues that within a governance context, coherence requires enhanced coordination, but recognizes that coordination has always been a challenge for the public sector. In a policy context, coordination can refer to negative coordination (avoidance of producing negative impacts through interaction) or positive coordination (mutual recognition and agreement to cooperate) (Peters 2005). The CFS aims for the latter but in its first few years of reform often failed to secure recognition from other key actors in the architecture of global food security governance. The intention of the GSF was to create a single, living document that could support coherence by promoting convergence, while also promoting coordination through the leadership and legitimacy of the CFS.

Developing a global strategic framework

Leadership of the development of the GSF was tasked by the Bureau to an OEWG, led by representatives from Brazil, with the aim of developing a GSF by October 2012. At the 36th Session (October 2010), a concept note for a GSF for Food Security and Nutrition, developed by the CFS Secretariat, was presented to the Committee. In the presentation it was argued that the reformed CFS brings together a wide range of actors and countries at different stages of development, all working towards a common shared goal in the context of a complex environment. As such there is a need for a framework to harmonize, facilitate and organize the CFS in its newly identified roles.

The concept note highlighted six key objectives:

1   Improving coordination and synergy among all stakeholders.
2   Strengthening coherence and convergence among policies and programs.
3   Bringing together knowledge (HLPE) and field experience (Joint Secretariat).
4   Catalyzing country-level capacity building.
5   Improving communication and information exchange.
6   Creating an atmosphere of trust and shared responsibility.

Furthermore, the concept note argued that a GSF could be expected to add value to the CFS by promoting prioritization, partnership, accountability and ownership.

The CFS agreed that the Bureau, with the assistance of the Secretariat and in close collaboration with the Advisory Group, would launch a consultative and inclusive process to be conducted to develop the first version of the GSF. The consultation was to be inclusive and to establish agreement on purposes, basic principles and structure of the GSF while taking into account existing frameworks.

Following the consultation, the OEWG came to agreement on the nature, purpose and principles of the GSF. It was decided that the structure and content of the GSF should be consistent with the vision, roles and guiding principles of the CFS and that the content should be taken from CFS outcomes, country-level experience, existing best practices, stakeholder dialogues and evidence-based knowledge. The broad issues to be addressed by the GSF were also outlined and included: identifying challenges and opportunities for food security and nutrition; identifying priorities for action; promoting convergence; recommending and describing options for governance mechanisms; and consolidating macro-level warnings about challenges related to food security and nutrition. It was also agreed to describe and recommend strategies that could be adopted by stakeholders at different levels so as to encourage the adoption of national strategies following a twin-track approach, and to identify areas across policy and practice that could benefit from future consensus building and convergence.

An annotated outline was developed and two versions were presented (April and June 2011). Government buy-in and engagement in the GSF negotiations was proving to be quite low in comparison to the negotiations on the VGGT. For example, in discussions on Section V: Uniting and Organizing to Fight Hunger, only a small number of members and participants were present. Observations at the time noted that those present included Switzerland, France, Finland, Denmark, US, Mexico, Argentina, South Africa, Zimbabwe, Angola and China, along with FIAN International, La Via Campesina, Indigenous Caucus, International Union of Food Workers, World Alliance of Fisherfolk and an NGO working on protracted crisis and food security. When questioned about the low attendance, many felt that this was due in part to CFS overload brought about by an engaged and lengthy negotiation on the VGGT. Others felt that active participation on a document that aimed to bring together issues upon which there was already international consensus was not the best use of time and resources. However, the chair of the OEWG was committed to completing the process. This led one EU-based food security analyst to declare that "[i]t is clear that the strategy of Brazil, who have been carrying this process, is to take people by surprise to ensure it is not clear what the significant of [the GSF] is until it is too late to shut it down" (field notes, May 2011, Rome).

This strategy seemingly employed by the Brazilian chair was one echoed by CSOs: notably, to take advantage of limited national buy-in and engagement to advance more progressive solutions. Indeed one network of NGOs working in Europe deliberated at length as to whether or not they should lobby their national government on issues related to the CFS. The concern was that too much engagement and awareness on the part of civil servants and politicians could backfire insofar as they could potentially get increasingly engaged and then restrict the trajectory of more progressive policy-making processes and policy recommendations. In the end, this network opted not to lobby at the national level, recognizing that the government participated in the negotiations as part of the EU, which was generally considered to arrive at favorable positions and was seen as an ally by many of the civil society actors working through the CSM.

At the 37th Session of the CFS the Committee acknowledged the CFS Bureau-led consultative and inclusive process that resulted in the purposes, basic principles, structure and process of the GSF, as well the electronic consultation on the Annotated Outline. The Committee also underlined the critical role of planned consultations on the GSF and the role of the GSF as a dynamic instrument which reflects and consolidates the ongoing policy convergence work of CFS.

Following the 37th Session, a first draft of the GSF was developed and included in the official agenda of each FAO Regional Conference in 2012. It was also placed on the agendas of the CSO regional consultations. Based on the regional consultations and electronic inputs, a second draft of the GSF was developed and released. It served as the basis for negotiations during an OEWG meeting that took place in Rome at the FAO between June 27 and 29, 2012.

During the June meeting, as with other CFS negotiations, contentious sections that blocked consensus were sent to the Friends of the Chair (FOC). In this case, the FOC was an open group, coordinated (voluntarily) by a representative from the Swiss government. Originally, the chair recommended that the FOC run parallel to the Plenary, but this was rejected on the basis that it would restrict the participation of smaller delegations. One issue sent to the FOC was the discussion on paragraph 30, the chapeau of section IV Policy, Programme and Other Recommendations. The proposed text read:

> Based on the foundation of the right to adequate food, and in the context of the overarching frameworks described above, there is broad international consensus on the appropriate policy response to the underlying causes of hunger and malnutrition in a number of areas.

Delegates from Canada and the US wanted to delete reference to the right to adequate food and negotiations ensued. The final text now reads:

> Taking into account the progressive realization of the right to adequate food in the context of national food security and in the context of the overarching frameworks described in Chapter III, there is broad international consensus on appropriate policy responses to the underlying causes of hunger and malnutrition in a number of areas.

While the inclusion of the correct language around the right to food was seen positively, the shift from "being based on the foundation of the right to food," to "taking into account the progressive realization of the right to food" was a clear set-back for actors promoting a rights-based approach. Given that the CFS reform document gives primacy to achieving the right to food, the outcome of this negotiation can also be seen as a set-back for the CFS. Some also felt that the introduction of language about "national context" reflected a push for national sovereignty and an effort to limit the scope and influence of the document.

CSOs had better success in the negotiation on text related to gender. In Chapter IV, Section D: Addressing Gender Issues in Food Security and Nutrition, CSOs managed to secure language that recognized that women "are often subjected to structural violence." They also managed to include language related to role women play in securing nutrition: "Women make vital contributions to the food security and nutrition of developing countries, but they consistently enjoy less access than men to the resources and opportunities for being more productive farmers" (CFS 2012b).

At this June meeting, the CFS intergovernmental working group reached agreement on the first five chapters of the first version of the GSF on Food Security and Nutrition. A further meeting was scheduled for July 19, 2012 to finalize Chapter VI, the so-called "gap" section: Major Existing Gaps on Policy and Coordination Issues. The rationale for this section was to address the need for policy decisions in several areas, with a view to achieving convergence across and between sectors at the national and global levels. As such, the was section to list key issues upon which there was not yet international consensus but which the CFS should address.

In the Second Draft text (June 2012), areas where gaps in policy or coordination could be filled by way of promoting convergence or developing guidance in an underdeveloped topic were listed. The list was subdivided between policy-related gaps (as a complement to Chapter IV: Policy, Programmes and Other Recommendations) and gaps related to coordination and organization (as a complement to Chapter V: Uniting and Organizing to Fight Hunger). The draft document noted that the listing of an issue within the "gaps section" did not necessarily mean that it should become a priority or immediate focus of CFS policy debate or the CFS's HLPE. The list would however support the CFS in the elaboration of a Multi-Year Programme of Work, insofar as the CFS Bureau would be able to select and prioritize topics from this listing.

Several policy-related gaps were identified, including: conflict between the demands of agricultural production for food and for energy; matching the natural resource base to the demands of development; the international trading systems and the need for trade agreements to better incorporate food security concerns; deeper understanding of the effects of food quality standards on food security and nutrition and the integration of smallholder producers to markets; seeking consensus on the case for adopting and on definitions of the concepts of "food sovereignty" and the "green economy," and the implications for stakeholders; resolving the potential conflict between the demand of water for agricultural production and for other sectors; better guidance and improved consensus on the advantages, disadvantages, potential and limits of agro-ecological approaches; improving consensus and policy convergence on biotechnology, particularly genetically modified organisms (GMOs); and regulating large-scale acquisitions of land in developing countries in such a way as to protect the interests of local populations.

The main gaps proposed related to coordination, organization and accountability and included: strengthening food security and nutrition governance mechanisms; establishing principles for monitoring and accountability of governments and other stakeholders engaged in delivering food security and nutrition; and finding ways to improve the effectiveness of regional organizations and enhancing cross-border cooperation in areas such as infrastructure, ecosystem/resource use, markets and programing by donors.

The gaps section was clearly ambitious in its effort to identify contentious issues and related policy gaps that threaten advancement on food security. Yet, when it came to agreeing on the issues for which there was no international consensus, the CFS rather ironically failed to come to consensus and the section was reworked in favor of completing the negotiations. The CFS renamed the section "Issues that May Require Further Attention," noting that because "there is a diversity of views, some issues may require further attention by the international community where they are relevant to the international debate on food security and nutrition" (CFS 2013:50). That the CFS could not even agree that there were issues that did require further attention, elucidated the political nature of the negotiations. That certain governments (notably, the Canadian government) were so unwilling to commit to a list of policy gaps was frustrating for many participants but also serves to illustrate the potential political importance of the reformed CFS.

In the revised section, the matching of policy gaps to specific sections was dropped and replaced with nine issues, introduced with a statement declaring that the listing of issues was "not exhaustive and does not necessarily mean that they should be addressed by the CFS" (CFS 2013:50). The issues that made the cut were far from ambitious, with references to agro-ecology, food sovereignty, GMOs and large-scale land acquisitions all removed:

1 Ways to improve the integration into and access to markets of small-scale producers, especially women;
2 Ways to boost rural development to strengthen food security and nutrition in the context of rural–urban migration;
3 The demand for water for agricultural production and for other uses and ways of improving water management;
4 The need for the international trade system and trade policies to better recognize food security concerns;
5 The management of the food chain and its impact on food security and nutrition, including ways to promote fair and competitive practices, and to reduce post-harvest food losses and waste;
6 The effects of food standards, including private standards, on production, consumption and trade patterns, especially regarding food security and nutrition;
7 The use and transfer of appropriate technologies in agriculture, fisheries and forestry, including consideration of the impact of intellectual property regimes on agriculture, food security and nutrition;
8 Nutrition-sensitive approaches that are integral to the planning and programing for food security and sustainable agriculture;
9 Enhancing policy dialogue and promoting science-based decisions on biotechnology, in a manner that promotes sustainable agriculture and improves food security and nutrition.

(CFS 2013:50)

After the year-long process of developing and negotiating the GSF within the intergovernmental OEWG, the first version was finalized. The negotiated document was submitted for editorial review and the inclusion of case studies and a final version was sent for translation into all FAO official languages and then presented to the 39th Session of the CFS in October 2012 for endorsement. At this point the Committee also agreed that the GSF would be updated "regularly to reflect the outcomes and recommendations of CFS in a manner consistent with multilateral principles, agreements and mandates" (CFS 2012a).

The GSF is a living document to be updated annually with outcomes from the policy roundtables. At the 40th Session of the CFS, it was agreed that the statistical figures included in Section 1 of the GSF would be updated annually to reflect the conclusions of the annual *State of Food Insecurity* reports. It is foreseen that the GSF will be revised every three to four years to ensure it remains relevant. The first review and renegotiation are planned for 2016.

The second version of the GSF (2013), and therefore the first update, was reformatted so as to be more user friendly. The document moved away from the traditional FAO CFS report style, adding an image and title in the header of the document and reorganizing the table of contents by page and not by paragraphs. The second version also listed the case studies in the table of contents, making them easier to find. The outcomes of the policy roundtables of the CFS39 on "Social Protection for Food Security and Nutrition" and "Food Security and Climate Change" were also added to the second version.

To increase usability of the document, the CFS would be advised to work with its members, participants and international organizations to find innovative ways of translating the GSF into useful tools for policy makers and CSOs to hold governments to account. The process of implementing the VGGT could provide instructive practices in this regard, understanding that the GSF has limited funding and extends well beyond a single governance issue. Another example is the manual on how to use the GSF, developed and published by CSOs: *Using the Global Strategic Framework for Food Security and Nutrition to Promote and Defend the People's Right to Adequate Food* (Boincean et al. 2013).

Civil society engagement

While the engagement of CSOs in the negotiation of the GSF was discussed above, it is instructive to look deeper into their role and positioning, especially in the initial phases. In preparation for contributing to the development of the GSF, civil society actors developed a series of key messages that were shared during the 36th Session. Their key issues responded to the concept note and raised concern about the absence of reference to fundamental rights, including an absence of reference to the universal right of all human beings to adequate, affordable food. They also highlighted lack of engagement with broader rights-based frameworks such as the ILO conventions. The CSOs provided a list of references to be included into the GSF, including the resolution of the International Labour Conference's (2008) Committee on Rural Employment for Poverty Reduction; the Memorandum of Understanding between the ILO and FAO signed in September 2004; and the reform of the Food Aid Convention. CSOs reinforced the sovereign rights and responsibilities of states but highlighted the importance of elaborating the GSF through a broad and participatory process.

When the annotated outline was released in April and June 2011, there was very little time to organize comments. CSOs, facilitated through the CSM, attempted to come to a consolidated position but this proved impossible and they thus submitted one document with three sets of comments developed by different coalitions of actors. This is not to be seen as a failure of the Mechanism, but rather, it reinforced the principle of diversity that lies at the core of the CSM. While CSOs acknowledged that there was strength in submitting a unified proposal, the importance of diversity over-rode the desire for a strong political statement. This sheds light on when and where and how CSO actors negotiate their positions among themselves and when they are willing to compromise and perhaps more interestingly, when they are not. It further illustrates the challenge of arriving at compromise when issues are highly political and response time is limited. This limited timeframe also impacted the responses received by member states. As one leading human rights campaigner reflected: "Only 19 countries manifested comments on the annotated outline and most of them were negative, which caused countries like Canada and the US to claim that the process isn't working, no one is buying in" (field notes, May 2011, Rome).

The civil society members of the CFS Advisory Group raised concerns that the role of the CSM was not explicitly recognized in the online GSF consultation process and it was argued that by failing to coordinate CSO consultation through the CSM, the CSM was effectively being undermined. It is important to remember that the CSM has principles and processes in place to ensure that the voices of those most affected by food insecurity are prioritized and there was concern that an open consultation could be usurped by large NGOs. CSOs also raised concerns about the limitations of an electronic consultation, noting that those most affected by hunger and malnutrition would be unable to participate meaningfully and that therefore the consultation was inadequate. As one leader of a European farming social movement explained:

> Electronic space should not constitute a participatory space. We need money to find more innovative ways to bring stories forward. How can we use existing CFS structures to elaborate and deepen discussions but how this feeds into the GSF is key. We need to get out of the tight box of electronic consultation.
>
> (Field notes, September 2011, Rome)

In the spirit of action and engagement, CSOs decided that the CSM, led by the Working Group on the GSF, needed to coordinate an autonomous consultation to feed into the CFS consultation process. The outcome of this process fed into two CSO working documents (September 2011 and December 2011).

Within these documents, CSOs articulated their vision for the GSF. They expressed the view that the GSF should set criteria for policy makers, for civil society, for financial institutions, for UN agencies and all other actors. It was fundamental that the GSF be built around the aim of improving food and nutrition security and work towards the realization of the right to food and food sovereignty. Therefore, the GSF must create and enable an environment for states to take up their responsibilities for the realization of the right to food. There was also emphasis on focus on engaging states. Speaking of the GSF as a political battle, a central strategy for CSOs was to:

> politicize the debate towards the national level and towards governments. [We need to] explain to national parliaments what is happening at the CFS around the global governance of CFS. Don't leave it to the bureaucrats. This a way to politicize the debate through the issues and through the process.
>
> (Field notes, May 2011, Rome)

These sentiments were echoed by one EU-based food security analyst:

> We need to start lobbying and invest in engaging national governments on why the GSF is a useful tool. Because there is no money for consultation, we have to start planning now to take full advantage of the FAO regional conferences that will take place next year. The regional consultations are a stepping stone to the CFS process, they are meant to be part of the CFS.
>
> (Field notes, May 2011, Rome)

CSOs were aware of the importance of making explicit the link between the GSF and national-level policy processes. They recognized that the GSF would have no significance if it remained at the global level and noted that the process of "nationalizing" the GSF is crucial. They argued that the ultimate goal of the GSF is for it to achieve national ownership (understood as democratic ownership).

CSOs proposed that the CFS could articulate a strategy on how to operationalize the GSF at the national level. It should clarify the kinds of policies that must be adopted to strengthen small-scale food producers and their respective areas of concern, including cooperation with the private sector. On a related point, CSOs argued that the GSF should provide strategies for revitalizing the role of the public sector and of the state in addressing the causes of hunger and malnutrition. To be most meaningful, the GSF must contain policy recommendations that challenge assumptions of current models of consumption and production, as well as public–private for-profit partnerships and their inconsistencies, and denounce unequal trade relations as a factor contributing to malnutrition. As CSOs continued to work on their position, under the leadership of representatives from FIAN and La Via Campesina, their positions became increasingly sophisticated, especially with respect to the integration of a rights-based approach. The ideas developed in the working document informed many of the CSO interventions in the consultation as well as CSO interventions in the negotiations.

When the GSF was endorsed by the CFS, CSOs noted:

> The GSF constitutes a step forward in promoting a new model of governance on food, agriculture, and nutrition. This document built upon the

human rights approach, women's rights and the recognition of the central role of smallholder farmers, agriculture and food workers, artisanal fisherfolks, pastoralists, indigenous peoples, landless people, women and youth, to food and nutrition security … We expect countries and all actors to fully support the implementation of the GSF on all levels. We will contribute to make use of this important tool for our initiatives and struggles at local, national and international levels.

(Field notes, October 2012, Rome)

Assessing the global strategic framework

The GSF is a single living document with an aim to improve coordination and guide synchronized action by a wide range of stakeholders. This "living" nature is one aspect that sets the GSF apart from the other policy frameworks: it seeks to build on best practices and has developed mechanisms to ensure continuity. This is certainly the best way of ensuring policy coherence over the medium to long term. Furthermore, insofar as the GSF is a living document, it is flexible so that it can be adjusted as priorities change.

As a document, the GSF has the potential to improve coordination and guide synchronized action by a wide range of stakeholders. The first two versions of the Framework have chapters dedicated to the root causes of hunger, existing frameworks, policy and program recommendations (the outcomes of the CFS policy roundtables), uniting and organizing to fight hunger, and issues that may require further attention. However, the potential of the GSF is not in the document itself, but in how it is used, if at all.

Given the mandate and authority of the CFS, the GSF is not a legally binding instrument. Like all CFS documents, guidelines and recommendations are meant to be interpreted and applied in accordance with national policies, legal systems and institutions. This focus on the national level not only reinforces the theme of country-led plans, but it also suggests recognition that food security is a national responsibility. It also alludes to broader themes of state sovereignty and the role of the state in global governance. What the GSF does offer are:

> guidelines and recommendations for catalyzing coherent action at the global, regional and country levels by the full range of stakeholders, while emphasizing the primary responsibility of governments and the central role of country ownership of programmes to combat food insecurity and malnutrition.
>
> (CFS 2012b: para 8)

The GSF places emphasis on policy coherence designed to target decision and policy makers responsible for policy areas with a direct or indirect impact on food security and nutrition. This is another factor that separates the GSF from the other policy framework insofar as it moves beyond high-level rhetoric and focuses on the practice of policy making at the national level.

The breadth and technical capacity of the negotiators and related technical staff is also important. The negotiators representing countries are, for the most part, permanent representatives to the FAO or the Rome-based food agencies, and thus, if not experts, they are at least well versed and certainly immersed in issues related to food, agriculture and nutrition. This comes through not only in the negotiations but also in the breadth of recommendations. Comparing for example the way in which the CFS addresses the importance of a gender-sensitive approach, with recognition of the key role of women as food and nutrition providers and producers as well as the structural barriers they face, to the way in which the other policy documents at best recognize that gender is an issue to be addressed in food security, it becomes clear that CFS recommendations take a systems approach and are more useful in terms of informing and supporting positive policy change to work towards the eradication of hunger. The mechanisms for participation and inclusivity were key to the development of a useful and applicable one-stop policy document like the GSF and the CSF is showing that it has processes in place to make this happen.

It is informative to compare key policy documents selected for further examination with the overarching frameworks on food security and nutrition identified by the CFS. The intended "value added" of the GSF is that it provides "an overarching framework and a single reference document with practical guidance on core recommendations for food security and nutrition strategies, policies and actions validated by the wide ownership, participation and consultation afforded by the CFS" (CFS 2012b: para 7). The GSF identifies six primary frameworks that are important due to their particular connection to food security and nutrition.

It is interesting that the MDGs are listed first. The goals provide a political and operational framework for development and provide measurements of human development that are based on more than income. The MDGs have a target of reducing hunger, but fail to address agriculture or food security. They do not include a focus on participation and fail to emphasize sustainability. Some of the goals lack measurements, meaning assessment and monitoring is limited at best. Furthermore, while each of the goals has specifically stated targets and dates for achieving those targets, there are no clear guidelines on how they can or should be achieved. They are not used as a policy tool as much as an aspirational framework. When they are referenced in a post-2008 context, it is predominantly in the context that they are unlikely to be met, or in the context of post-MDG sustainable development goals.

The Voluntary Guidelines to support the progressive realization of the right to adequate food in the context of national food security are a useful addition to the GSF as they provide an overall framework for achieving food security and nutrition objectives. They call for the right to adequate food to be the main objective of food security policies, programs, strategies and legislation; that human rights principles (participation, accountability, non-discrimination, transparency, human dignity, empowerment and rule of law) should guide activities designed to improve food security; and that policies, programs,

Table 8.1 Overarching frameworks identified in the Global Strategic Framework for Food Security and Nutrition

1. The MDGs

2. The Voluntary Guidelines to support the progressive realization of the right to adequate food in the context of national food security

3. The Five Rome Principles for Sustainable Global Food Security

4. The VGGT

5. High-level fora on Aid Effectiveness

6. United Nations Updated Comprehensive Framework for Action (UCFA)

7. Other frameworks and documents:

   The 1989 Convention on the Rights of the Child (CRC)

   The 1981 International Code of Marketing of Breast-milk Substitutes

   The 1979 Convention on the Elimination of All Forms of Discrimination Against Women (CEDAW)

   The 1993 Declaration on the Elimination of Violence Against Women (DEVAW)

   The 1995 Beijing Platform for Action ensure women's rights

   ILO conventions 87, 98 and 169

   The International Assessment of Agricultural Knowledge, Science and Technology for Development (IAASTD)

   The final Declaration of the International Conference on Agrarian Reform and Rural Development (ICARRD)

   The UN Declaration on Rights of Indigenous People (UNDRIP)

   The Scaling-Up Nutrition (SUN) Framework and Roadmap

Source: CFS (2012b)

strategies and legislation need to enhance the empowerment of rights-holders and the accountability of duty-bearers, thus reinforcing the notions of rights and obligations as opposed to charity and benevolence.

A right to food approach has been central to the reform of the CFS, arguably for a few key reasons. The first is based on the broad recognition of the work of the Special Rapporteur on the Right to Food, Olivier De Schutter, who has consistently presented strong, legally grounded arguments promoting the value of a right to food approach to achieving food security in a sustainable and appropriate way. Efforts of the Special Rapporteur have ensured that more actors are aware of the importance of a right to food approach. An obvious example of this was the public exchange between Pascal Lamy, director of the WTO, and Olivier De Schutter (WTO 2011) relating to the impact of the WTO on the progressive realization of the right to food. Second, civil society actors involved in the CFS have consistently pushed for, and negotiated the inclusion of, language linked to a rights-based approach. For them, a rights-based approach is very much aligned with a food sovereignty approach and moreover provides a framework for holding states accountable. Also, the reform document of the CFS clearly expresses that the "CFS will strive for a world free from hunger where countries implement the Voluntary Guidelines for the progressive realization of the right to adequate food in the context of national food security" (CFS 2009: para 4). While a rights-based approach has been widely accepted by the CFS, a right to adequate food normative and analytical framework has yet to permeate policy fora outside the FAO, and even within the FAO and the UN there is ample work to be done (De Schutter 2013).

Finally, when reviewing GSF, one thing that stands out, especially in comparison to the other policy frameworks reviewed above, are the endnotes (a total of 100) referencing statements to existing documents. There are important implications and insights to be gained from this. First, the CFS has made a deliberate effort to ground the recommendations and policies in the GSF in existing commitments and best practices as negotiated or promoted by other multilateral fora. Second, and this came out clearly in the negotiations, the OEWG was pressured into defending and rationalizing what was included in the GSF to appease less-friendly governments. Third, the references strengthen the potential application and uptake of the policies therein insofar as policy makers will have not only the negotiated GSF text but can also easily access the origins of the recommendations, which can arguably strengthen the rationale for their implementation.

Conclusion

When compared to the other key policy documents that have been developed multilaterally to address food security in the wake of the food price spikes of 2007–2008 (e.g., the UN HLTF's Updated Comprehensive Framework for Action; World Bank's Agriculture Action Plan: FY2010–1; the G8's L'Aquila Joint Statement on Food Security; the Global Agriculture and Food Security Program Framework; the Declaration of the World Summit on Food Security; and the G20's Multi-Year Action Plan on Development), it becomes clear that while the GSF has perhaps the lowest level of recognition, it is by far the most comprehensive, useful and fit-for-purpose. Proponents of the GSF further argue its merits on the basis that it is a policy guidance document that has been developed through consultation and participation of a wide range of actors and has been inter-governmentally endorsed by members of the CFS.

The CFS is proving to be fastidious when it comes to detail and policy coherence because of the internal and external pressure that it faces. It is also motivated by the energy of the participants, notably those from civil society, who remain active in their engagement and commitment. Yet the legitimacy and authority of the CFS are consistently being undermined by other multilateral actors who continue to advance food security initiatives that are not coherent with the policies included in the GSF.

This raises questions about usefulness versus influence. Given that competing policy frameworks (e.g., CFA, L'Aquila) have been developed and endorsed at the level of country leaders, and given how little influence and notoriety the CFS has, influence and uptake remain a challenge. To begin to assess the impact and usefulness of the GSF, future research must consider the ways in which the GSF is being used by policy makers in the development of food security policies, as well as by CSOs looking to hold governments to account. Towards this end, the document has been used by CSOs to defend and reinforce their positions in CFS negotiations, particularly during policy roundtables at the 40th Session of the CFS and during negotiations on CFS-rai. Beyond the CSM, initial evidence suggests that few are making use of the GSF.

Finally, a future challenge for the GSF will be how to incorporate ongoing international efforts to address food security outside of the CSF, for example the Sustainable Development Goals or UNFCCC. The CFS must continue to prioritize food security and nutrition and be willing to address issues that are central to food security even if they are addressed elsewhere in different contexts. While this could appear to contradict efforts to move towards enhanced policy coherence, the value of the CFS is that it can tackle difficult issues and identify best practices from a food security perspective.

References

Ahmad, M. 2011. *Improving the International Governance of Food Security and Trade.* Geneva: ICTSD. Retrieved (http://ictsd.org/i/publications/114288/).

Boincean, S. et al. 2013. *Using the Global Strategic Framework for Food Security and Nutrition to Promote and Defence the People's Right to Adequate Food: A Manual for Social Movements and Civil Society Organizations.* Brussels: La Via Campesina. Retrieved (http://viacampesina.org/downloads/pdf/en/GSF-Manual_en.pdf).

Bonior, D. 1999. "Defending Democracy in the New Global Economy," in *Statement to an AFL-CIO Conference on Workers' Rights, Trade Development, and the World Trade Organization.* Seattle, WA.

Cerny, P. 1999. "Globalization and the Erosion of Democracy." *European Journal of Political Research* 36(1):1–26.

CFS. 2009. *Reform of the Committee on World Food Security Final Version.* Rome: FAO. Retrieved (www.fao.org/fileadmin/templates/cfs/Docs0910/ReformDoc/CFS_2009_2_Rev_2_E_K7197.pdf).

CFS. 2012a. *Final Report of the Thirty-Ninth Session of the Committee on World Food Security.* Rome: FAO. Retrieved (www.fao.org/fileadmin/user_upload/bodies/CFS_sessions/39th_Session/39emerg/MF027_CFS_39_FINAL_REPORT_compiled_E.pdf).

CFS. 2012b. *Global Strategic Framework for Food Security and Nutrition (First Version).* Rome: FAO. Retrieved (www.fao.org/docrep/meeting/026/ME498E.pdf).

CFS. 2013. *Global Strategic Framework for Food Security and Nutrition: Second Version.* Rome: FAO. Retrieved (www.fao.org/fileadmin/templates/cfs/Docs1213/gsf/GSF_Version_2_EN.pdf).

Davies, R.B., and K.C. Vadlamannati. 2013. "A Race to the Bottom in Labor Standards? An Empirical Investigation." *Journal of Development Economics* 103:1–14. Retrieved (http://linkinghub.elsevier.com/retrieve/pii/S0304387813000060).

De Schutter, O. 2013. *Mission to the Food and Agriculture Organization of the United Nations.* New York: UN.

Drezner, D.W. 2014. "Policy Convergence." *International Studies Review* 3(1):53–78.

FAO, IFAD, IMF,OECD, UNCTAD, WFP, World Bank, WTO, IFPRI and UN HLTF. 2011. *Price Volatility in Food and Agricultural Markets: Policy Responses.* Rome: UNCTAD. Retrieved (http://unctad.org/en/docs/2011_G20_FoodPriceVolatility_en.pdf).

G8. 2009. *"L'Aquila" Joint Statement on Global Food Security.* L'Aquila: G8. Retrieved (www.g8italia2009.it/static/G8_Allegato/LAquila_Joint_Statement_on_Global_Food_Security[1],0.pdf).

HLPE. 2011. *Price Volatility and Food Security.* Rome: FAO. Retrieved (www.fao.org/fileadmin/user_upload/hlpe/hlpe_documents/HLPE-price-volatility-and-food-security-report-July-2011.pdf).

Kerr, C. 1983. *The Future of Industrial Societies: Convergence or Continuing Diversity?* Cambridge, MA: Harvard University Press.

Lubell, M.N., G. Robins, and P. Wang. 2011. "Policy Coordination in an Ecology of Water Management Games," in *Political Networks Conference.* Ann Arbor: OpenSIUC. Retrieved (http://opensiuc.lib.siu.edu/pnconfs_2011/22).

May, P.J., J. Sapotichne, and S. Workman. 2006. "Policy Coherence and Policy Domains." *Policy Studies Journal* 34(3):381–403. Retrieved (http://doi.wiley.com/10.1111/j.1541-0072.2006.00178.x).

McKenzie, R., and D. Lee. 1991. *Quicksilver Capital: How the Rapid Movement of Wealth Has Changed the World.* New York: Free Press.

Peters, B.G. 2005. *The Search for Coordination and Coherence in Public Policy: Return to the Center?* Unpublished paper. Pittsburgh: Department of Political Science, University of Pittsburgh.

Polanyi, K. 2001. *The Great Transformation: The Political and Economic Origins of Our Time.* Boston: Beacon Press.

Rodrik, D. 1997. *Has Globalization Gone Too Far?* Washington DC: Institute for International Economics.

United Nations. 1975. *Report of the World Food Conference, Rome, November 5–16, 1974.* New York: United Nations.

Vogel, D. 1995. *Trading Up: Consumer and Environmental Regulation in a Global Economy.* Cambridge, MA: Harvard University Press.

Wheeler, D. 2001. "Racing to the Bottom? Foreign Investment and Air Pollution in Developing Countries." *The Journal of Environment* 10(3):225–45.

WTO. 2011. "Lamy Rebuts UN Food Rapporteur's Claim That WTO Talks Hold Food Rights 'hostage'." *News Items.* Retrieved (www.wto.org/english/news_e/news11_e/agcom_14dec11_e.htm).

9 Conclusion

Reflections on civil society
engagement in global food
security governance

Introduction

When the CFS reformed, it was responding to international calls for better coordination, cooperation, convergence and coherence around global food security policy. Through its reform, the CFS set out on an ambitious trajectory. By way of inclusive, participatory and consultative processes, the CFS effectively reinvented itself, transitioning from an inefficient and insignificant reporting and monitoring committee to a primary actor in global food security governance.

This book has provided a window onto this moment of transition. It is important to recognize that the CFS's transition carries on as the Committee continues defend its place in a changing architecture of global food security governance. Correspondingly, this book has not sought to offer an evaluation or complete assessment of the CFS. Instead, it has provided insight into the mechanisms and processes that have come to shape a UN committee that has emerged as a best practice in global governance.

The review of the participation of CSOs in the reformed Committee serves to elucidate some of the key boundary issues: issues that challenge and can transform the status quo. The participation of CSOs has served to expand debate, introduce new perspectives and therefore shift the direction of global food security policy. This is nothing new; NGOs and CSOs have been influencing the direction of global governance for decades. What is new is that they are now doing it as equal participants in the debate. Understanding how the CFS has implemented its participatory reforms provides useful insight into participatory governance processes.

In this final chapter, the impacts of CSO engagement are summarized. These impacts include: enthusiasm and awareness; improving and expanding debate; and supporting weaker states. From there, successful engagement strategies employed by CSOs are reviewed before attention turns to reflections on the implications of the CFS's experiences for global food security governance and global governance more broadly. The chapter concludes with a discussion of opportunities for future research.

Reflecting on the reformed CFS

Food security and nutrition are global goods, as well as national and local goods. Food is also a human right. Yet some nation-states and communities are unable to ensure food security. This suggests a need for global food security governance, but also raises a series of questions: Governance on behalf of whom? Governance by whom? What form of governance?

With respect to governance on behalf of whom, the CFS's vision is clear: governance on behalf of those most affected by food insecurity and for the achievement of "a world free from hunger where countries implement the Voluntary Guidelines for the progressive realization of the right to adequate food in the context of national food security" (CFS 2009: para 4). In practice, this is of course a more complicated question. States have clear agendas and objectives as well as restrictions: states govern on behalf of their own interests. However, the engagement of civil society actors allows discussions to move beyond redlines. As one organizing member of the CSM noted, referencing discussions on biofuels:

> The CFS was the only place where biofuel mandates subsidies and targets are discussed. In the G20 they talked about it for two seconds. One country says it is a red line and the conversation moves on. In the CFS it stayed on the agenda until the very end. At least there is a discussion. If the countries cannot agree, then that's life and we will go out to the media and shout, but at least you have a space where you cannot be eliminated.
>
> (Interview, June 2014, Skype)

Thus while the gap between vision and political reality will always shape the answer to "Governance on behalf of whom?" and powerful actors can be expected to maintain disproportionate influence, the organization of the CSF makes space for weaker states and non-state actors to force discussion on key issues and promote governance on behalf of those most affected by food security and nutrition.

The CFS's response to the question of "Governance by whom?" is central to its success. The CFS is the most inclusive, consultative, participatory and transparent intergovernmental committee addressing food security. The CFS recognizes that the governance of food security, in all its complexity, requires input and engagement of a broad range of actors. As such, it allows stakeholders to participate in and across the work of the Committee. However, there is also acknowledgement that states are accountable for ensuring food security and as such, states take final decisions for which they can be held accountable. How to hold them to account is, of course, another issue. The CFS has no mandate or capacity to implement policies that reflect decisions made at the CFS. This leads to the final question: "What form of governance?"

The CFS is a platform for a broad range of actors to work together in a coordinated manner. Its contribution to global food security governance is through coordination, wherein it seeks to strengthen collaborative action, promote policy convergence and provide support and advice. While it is mandated to support collaborative action and promote policy convergence, the CFS is restricted to doing this through knowledge sharing and the production of negotiated policy recommendations, principles and Voluntary Guidelines. As such, the CFS should not be evaluated on the basis of actions outside its role and scope of influence.

A challenge is that while the CFS has achieved normative legitimacy when it comes to its role and function, in reality, alternative governance processes, which can be seen as less legitimate or certainly less inclusive, continue to play key roles in the architecture of global food security and continue to hold a great deal of power and influence. Furthermore, in working outside of the CFS, their actions can serve to undermine the inter-governmentally approved roles of the CFS.

For the actions and outputs of the CFS to have an impact, actors, including states, the private sector, practitioners and civil society, need to use and implement them. Mapping the uptake and application of CFS outputs will require a great deal of work and resources. Evaluating the impact of CFS actions on the eradication of hunger is near impossible. This is in no way to suggest that the CFS has no value. Indeed, throughout this book, multiple examples of the potential and actual impact of the reformed CFS have been presented. This optimism was similarly expressed by representative of an international NGO:

> I see the CFS creating the building blocks, as well as consolidating political processes, with the CSM, with intensive consultation processes, with an independent HLPE, that eventually will help to deliver politically. It is still a bit early to see how this will translate into national changes and international engagements.
>
> (Personal correspondence, November 2012)

Impact of participation

Attention now turns to summarizing impact that CSOs have had in their role as participants. While the case studies have illustrated the changes CSOs have been able to successfully make to policy recommendations and other CFS outputs, it is useful to also consider less measurable impacts. These include: enhanced enthusiasm and awareness; quality of debate; and support for states.

Enthusiasm and awareness

The meaningful and active engagement of CSOs in the reformed CFS fostered increased interest in the activities of the CFS. Given their status as participants, international NGOs and social movement actors had a vested interest in stirring up interest in the Committee and its activities and the CFS inarguably gained increased notoriety and influence as a result.

Table 9.1 Key wins for CSOs in CFS negotiations

CFS	Output	CSO wins
36 (2010)	Addressing food insecurity in protracted crises: Issues and challenges (policy roundtable)	• Approval of an inclusive and consultative process for the elaboration of an Agenda for Action for Addressing Food Insecurity in Protracted Crisis.
	Land tenure and international investment in agriculture (policy roundtable)	• CFS blocked the endorsement of the PRAI.
		• Brought the voluntary guideline process into the CFS: established an OEWG to review the Voluntary Guidelines and to develop them for the consideration of the CFS.
		• Inclusion of focus on women, small-scale producers and vulnerable groups in decision box.
		• Legal accountability, remedies and measures for reparation and compensation.
37 (2011)	How to increase food security and smallholder sensitive investment in agriculture (policy roundtable)	• Decision box was changed to be smallholder focused (references to smallholders or farmers frame the actions).
		• Recognition of smallholder investment.
		• Awareness of the need to strengthen smallholder production systems, reflecting a shift in focus from external investments to investments made by and for small-scale food producers.
		• Removal of generic references to agriculture, highlighting diversity in modes of food production.
		• Food security was presented as a parameter for investment.
		• Secured an assessment of impact of partnerships on smallholders.
		• Inclusion of human rights language in the decision box.
	Gender, Food Security and Nutrition (policy roundtable)	• CFS recognized the crucial role of women in ensuring food and nutrition security.
		• The Committee affirmed that female smallholders should be given equal treatment in agricultural programming, both as a matter of human rights and to promote economic development.
		• Governments were asked to audit national legislation to amend discriminatory laws, and to enact and enforce laws against all kinds of violence.
	Food Price Volatility (policy roundtable)	• The decision box recognized food reserves as an instrument for mitigating food price volatility but also as key in emergency contexts.
		• Discussion on contentious issues.
		• Mandate for an HLPE report on biofuels.
		• Recognized the role of speculation in volatility. Although vague, the CFS recognized the need to "improve transparency, regulation and supervision of agricultural derivative markets."
		• The initiative to improve markets transparency was supported.

38 (2012)	Voluntary Guidelines on the Responsible Governance of Tenure of Land, Fisheries and Forests in the Context of National Food Security	• Consultative and inclusive process for developing the Guidelines. • CSOs participated at all stages including the negotiations, to draw attention to the real-life issues facing them and to make concrete proposals. • VGGT respect and protect human rights in the context of tenure. • Emphasis on women, peasant farmers, fishing communities, pastoralists and indigenous peoples. • Strong principles of implementation. • Evidence of the capacity of the CFS.
39 (2012)	Global Strategic Framework	• Grounded in a human rights approach. • Recognition of role of small-scale food providers, women's rights and living wages for agricultural workers. • Mentions potential of agro-ecology. • Framework for human rights-based approach to monitoring and accountability.
	Food Security and Climate Change	• Impact of climate change on small-scale producers for whom it is acknowledged that adaptation is a top priority. • Governments recognized their responsibility to ensure that all policies and actions are consistent with the right to food.
	Social Protection for Food Security and Nutrition	• Secured a strong human rights perspective. • Focus on meaningful participation of stakeholders. • Stronger gender perspective was achieved. • Inclusion of decent work, small-scale food producers in providing social protection, policies to support breastfeeding.
40 (2013)	Biofuels and Food Security	• Although unable to ensure political advances, CSOs ensured that the recommendations did not weaken existing global frameworks and agreements by ensuring references to the GSF, right to food and the VGGT. • In the end, the CFS welcomed the HLPE report and globally reaffirmed that biofuels should not compromise food security.

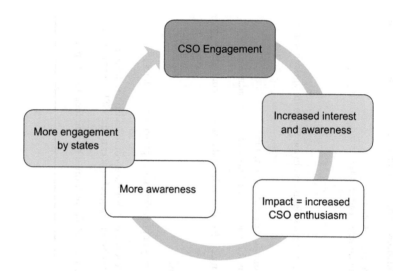

Figure 9.1 Enthusiasm and awareness cycle of CSO engagement in the CFS

CSO engagement can be seen as part of a cycle of enthusiasm and awareness. Through their participation, CSOs, with their vast networks and media
connections, created increased interest in the CFS. When they recognized
that their participation had an impact on outcomes, their enthusiasm for the
CFS increased, which in turn created more awareness. That CSOs were now
attending meetings and pushing the debates meant that other actors in the CFS,
notably states, needed to increase their level of preparedness and engagement.
In turn, many Rome-based delegations increased communication with experts
back in their capitals. This in turn increased awareness of the CFS outside of
Rome, in the capitals.

Greater engagement by states suggests greater influence and relevance for
the CFS, which in turn prompts greater CSO engagement. To date, this has
been the cycle of enthusiasm and awareness. However, the cycle could easily
shift if, for example, greater engagement by states created a less participatory
and inclusive space for non-state actors to engage. CSO enthusiasm would
decline, as would perceived legitimacy.

This relates to the need to find a balance between formalization and success,
ensuring adequate influence to warrant the ongoing work of the Committee,
and retaining a lower level of political engagement so as to allow for informal
modes of operation to continue.

The balance of the CFS is already changing. One NGO actor from the
North explained that: "States are sending new people to the CFS. For example,
Argentina sent people from the capital to participate in the biofuel debate [CFS
40]" (NGO actor from the North, June 2014, Skype). The implication is that

biofuels were an important thematic area for Argentina and they in turn sent an expert from their capital to help negotiate and ensure a favorable outcome. While this can be seen as evidence of the growing influence of the CSM—if the government of Argentina believed the CFS had no value, it is unlikely that they would have sent an expert—there are also potential limitations that could arise from increased influence. As one expert remarked: "People have recognized the power of the CFS and the strength of the CSM within it. It makes them nervous because there is a potential for them [countries] to lose control" (interview with expert on the CSM, June 2014, Skype).

Improving the quality of debate

Civil society actors have dynamically contributed to the operation of the reformed CFS. In the inter-sessional periods, CSOs contributed (with varying degrees of success) to the design of agendas and to the identification of expert panelists. As noted above, the participation of CSOs has also meant that delegations have needed to be more prepared so as to be able to address issues raised.

A key and measurable impact of CSO engagement in the CFS are changes to policy proposals. These were reviewed in detail in preceding chapters. While changes to text are central to the work of the CSM and fundamental to assessing and evaluating the impact of CSO participation in the Committee, many participants argue that their most important function is to open up discussion, including through the introduction of controversial ideas and statements. For example, "Our presence is important because we manage to bring in the real serious issues that big countries do not what to bring up and this changes the dynamics" (interview with member of the CSM, June 2014, Skype).

While CSOs can table issues and call for greater discussion:

> When it comes down to the real important issues for CSOs, like agro-ecology, genetic diversity and food sovereignty, these are taboo subjects at the CFS but these are fundamental issues for the CSM. But there have been small gains in relation to issues such as agro-ecology and genetic resources as a result of civil society lobbying with governments who are "pro" agro-ecology and food sovereignty. Because of these relations with some member governments, they [CSOs] have been able to at least keep these contentious words on paper.
>
> (Interview with expert on the CSM, June 2014, Skype)

In many instances, through their engagement, CSOs have ensured that the reformed CFS avoids race-to-the-bottom negotiations. One working group facilitator noted:

> civil society actors can go beyond the defense of national interests where governments are stuck. It is difficult to go beyond the lowest common denominator. Everyone is trying to compromise but with their own red

lines. There is a small area where the red lines can move, where we can shift them a bit, like in the VGs [Voluntary Guidelines]. So that we are better positioned and have the legitimacy to defend the consistencies on issues like food security, on the right to food, and we can go further, hearing the voice of those affected by food insecurity. And if not, we are in a position where we can challenge. Holding governments accountable is a bit optimistic but we can challenge them.

(Interview with working group facilitator, June 2014, Skype)

The autonomous participation of CSOs as full participants in the CFS has resulted in stronger debates and, in turn, stronger policy outcomes that prioritize food security.

Supporting states

One of the arguments put forward by supporters of the reformed CFS in the post-food price crisis battle for leadership was the commitment to the principle of "one country, one vote." In practice, the CFS works towards consensus. All participants have the right to intervene in negotiations up to the point where the chair believes consensus is being reached by member states. Proponents argue this serves to even out power imbalances, which would only be reinforced through a G8- or G20-led initiative. Indeed, within the reformed CFS, weaker states can play an important role and have had influence, not only in terms of their numbers, but also in terms of perceived legitimacy. When a developing country claims that a policy on land tenure is needed, it becomes hard for a developed country to call for the policy recommendations to be abolished. One of the implications of CSO engagement in the CFS is that they are able to create alliances or support governments with similar objectives. As such: "Some smaller countries feel that they can support issues with the backing of civil society" (interview with member of the CSM, June 2014, Skype).

Powerful states have also used this reformulated construction of legitimacy to their advantage in negotiations, drafting joint positions with developing countries and having them table the position to give it more political weight within the Committee. In other international fora, one would expect the more powerful state to make the intervention.

At the same time, the technical capacity of some civil society actors allows them to support or actively engage with traditionally strong states, as illustrated by this anecdote:

I don't know much about how are these things work in other parts of the world, but perhaps, I may be wrong, but I don't know of any other forum like this, intergovernmental forum, and so on, where civil society representatives can be there. [A CSO actor] … was there, going where the US delegation was seated and negotiating with them, and they were all taking notes of her words. And then saying "no, what if we did it this way, or that way."

(Interview, October 2011, Rome)

In an interview, one diplomat from a G20 country and active in the CFS explained that in his opinion, CSO statements or CSO support for positions advanced by governments now hold more weight in negotiations than those of some member countries, even though civil society does not vote (interview, March 2012, Rome). CSOs thus play a key role not only challenging states but also supporting them. Furthermore, within the CFS, definitions of legitimacy have are often based on experience and not on wealth. As such, CSOs and poorer states have the potential for a strengthened negotiating position. How they make use of this depends on the strategies they advance.

Successful strategies for CSO engagement in the CFS

The impact of CSOs in the reformed CFS has been significant. Yet their ability to have an impact has involved a great deal of learning, preparation and training. Key strategies can be identified as supporting the successful engagement of CSOs in the CFS and include:

- making use of experiential knowledge;
- balancing technical capacity with political legitimacy;
- taking advantage of network governance models;
- making use of frameworks to promote coherence;
- developing strong alliances with other actors;
- ensuring enough time for meaningful consultation and development;
- maintaining communication between CSOs, between the various levels of the mechanism (e.g., Coordination Committee, Advisory Group members, wider participants, Secretariat);
- reducing language barriers and potential cultural barriers;
- maintaining interest of existing participants;
- attracting new participants and ensuring that the mechanism continues to open up;
- balancing participation and representation;
- working towards consensus while respecting diversity;
- establishing clear, transparent decision making and accountability mechanisms;
- building trust among the different constituencies represented;
- ensuring the sustained meaningful engagement of those most affected by food insecurity in all processes.

Some of these are now explored in greater detail, notably network governance, making use of expertise, balancing technical capacity with political legitimacy, and making use of coherent frameworks to guide policy positions and build alliances.

The development of the CSM, with its unique blend of formal and informal governance structures, is an important example of how global networks can address challenges related to language, time, representation and legitimacy. As a network, the CSM represents an effective organizing model for food social movements engaging in global governance processes; it is a politicizing, engaging and connecting mechanism. It actively seeks out and supports the engagement of those "most affected by food security" and provides opportunities to hear alternative voices perhaps more connected to the realities on the ground. Its structure can also be replicated at various levels to support regional, national, local engagement and across sectors.

CSOs, notably larger NGOs, often have staff with technical expertise on issues being negotiated at the CFS (e.g., investment, land tenure, biofuels, climate change, protracted crisis). By contrast, member states are often represented by diplomats skilled in negotiation and politics but less knowledgeable on technical issues and therefore heavily reliant on technical civil servants, often working in the capitals. CSOs have earned the trust and respect of many of the state delegations because of their knowledgeable contributions and expertise.

Related to this, civil society actors have made a point of arriving at meetings well prepared, often sharing recommendations and thoughts in advance of the meetings. The policy working groups of the CSM work diligently to familiarize themselves with the texts. They develop priority areas to introduce and to defend. They identify their redlines. The large amount of work that goes into their preparations is illustrative of a high level of buy-in CSOs have for CFS process, but it also produces relevant and informed interventions which governments, on the whole, acknowledge. As noted above, this level of advanced preparation results not only in more strategic engagement in the roundtables, but also increased preparedness on the part of governments throughout the year.

While the range of expertise across the CSM is a strength, a former member of the CSM's Coordination Committee noted that there is still room for improvement in terms of making better use of what exists:

> I think CSOs have influence and power because they prepare. They research and analyze draft documents and generally have a responsible approach to negotiations. They know what the red lines are and what they are prepared to negotiate on. So because of these things, the CSM has influence in the negotiations. But that does not mean that CSOs cannot do a lot better and be even more influential.
>
> One of the ways of doing that is to substantiate the issues and arguments by providing examples from the local level. As happens in the CFS, the debates and discussions take on a bit of an ideological nature and sometimes civil society does not make sufficient use of who is in the room and who they are and the fact that they are farmers, or workers or fisherfolk, for example. I think they don't always bring in enough of the

personal and organizational experience and lessons learned to substantiate their arguments. This could dramatically influence the impact civil society has.

(Interview, July 2014, Skype)

To effectively make use of their unique position and perspective, CSOs require political fluency. Through ongoing engagement, civil society actors are becoming increasingly politically savvy about the processes and procedures of the Committee and are, as a result, becoming more influential and effective in negotiations. They are increasingly fluent in reading and analyzing UN texts and following the Committee's procedures. They are also more confident about what their rights are with respect to engaging in work and negotiations of the CFS. The challenge with the reformed CFS comes back to personalities. While indeed the initial post-reform members of the Committee had participated in the reform and were favorable to CSO engagement, this is subject to change. New actors are arriving in Rome with little or no awareness of how the CFS operates. CSOs must continuously push to have their rights recognized. Furthermore, as the CFS gains more influence, negotiations come to be seen as more important and technical experts can be added to delegations. This changes the dynamics and requires CSOs to revise their political strategies.

One successful way CSOs have made use of their experience and diversity is by dividing interventions into technical and political categories: the former normally led by an NGO actor and the latter, a social movement actor. CSOs assess the negotiations and determine what type of intervention is needed. For example, when a proposal is made that touches on one of the established redlines, a political statement articulating why the proposal is not acceptable can serve to shift the tone or terms of the debate.

There remain taboo issues within the CFS that CSOs find challenging to get traction on. Tactics that have worked well to overcome these issues include referencing existing CFS decisions, recalling the HLPE reports and quoting existing international precedence. Continuing to raise the issues in discussions also serves to create greater awareness and understanding. In turn this can help to create an environment wherein negotiators aim for the highest level outcome. The debates give delegations opportunities to more fully understand contentious issues allowing for agreement on more strongly worded statements.

While the CSM upholds principles of diversity, central to the success of the CSO interventions has been a united position. The development of these positions, through the policy working groups, has been guided by two increasingly inter-related frameworks: food sovereignty and the right to food (Claeys 2013). Food sovereignty is the vehicle of a global social movement: it is a unifying element of a growing network of peasants defending their right to food through the right to define and control their food systems. However, food sovereignty is also a political framework, developed to politicize food security, grounded by the right to food and flexible enough to allow for the incorporation and framing of multiple issues. It effectively revalues food, the way it is grown and the communities of people that grow, raise, catch or gather it, process it and bring it to table. It also places small-scale food producers as key decision makers for food systems.

As a political framework, food sovereignty undertakes a rigorous political analysis of agricultural policies and programs with a focus on relations of power and control of resources. It proposes solutions based on experiences of food producers and rooted in an approach that gives primacy to producer's rights, community rights, healthy food systems—through the promotion of agro-ecological production—and gender equality through a defense of the rights of women. Food sovereignty seeks out the maximization of local food systems but is not opposed to trade or exchange that is fair and respects agro-ecological principles and human rights. This framework guides the majority of CSO interventions and provides coherence, while grounding interventions.

While use of the term "food sovereignty" has been rejected by CFS, some of the principles have been included in outputs as a result of successful CSO lobbying. And while there is no consensus on food sovereignty, even among actors in the CSM, key principles are overwhelmingly shared and provide an overarching objective and framework under which a diversity of actors can come together to develop joint strategies and positions.

Similarly, CSOs have benefitted from the uptake of a rights-based framework and in turn from the experience and expertise of the Office of the Special Rapporteur on the Right to Food. The legal perspective offered by a rights-based approach has proven valuable to the construction and defense of CSO arguments. Furthermore, that the CFS's reform vision expresses an explicit commitment to strive for a world free from hunger where countries implement the Voluntary Guidelines for the progressive realization of the right to adequate food, gives weight to all calls a rights-based approach. Despite international obligations and the vision of the CFS, defenders of the right to food have had to consistently lobby and push the Committee to respect the rights-based approach. However, securing the approach and having it as a basis across CFS outputs has been perceived as a key success by many CSO actors.

Despite limitations to human rights frameworks (Charvet and Kaczynska-Nay 2008), the uptake of a rights-based framing by social movement actors and their allies supports the development of an alternative conception of rights, emphasizing the collective claims at multiple levels, the need to challenge neoliberalism in agriculture and food production, and the need to defend the autonomy and equality-reinforcing food systems: the right of peoples to food sovereignty (Claeys 2013:2).

Another key benefit of the food sovereignty approach is that it is inherently a positive framework. It is a pathway to achieving change. Being positive can be a strategic political tactic: Barack Obama did not win the 2010 US presidential election campaign by declaring "no we can't." CSOs, through an application of the food sovereignty framework, present positive proposals that include practical and actionable solutions. As the leader of a European farming social movement explained early on in the process:

> This reform only takes on the meaning if we come up with genuine contributions and solutions. The reformed CFS is not a space to forward demands but a space to put our recommendations on the table and to forward and negotiate our needs and move them forward with governments. It is not a list of what is not working. This has been done before. We need to push to have solutions we know will work forward. We need to forward solutions and makes sure that they are implemented and that governments follow through.
>
> (Field notes, October 2010, Rome)

Despite the limitations and challenges that come from using the term food security, CSOs were effective in shifting the terms of debate by linking their recommendations to the CFS's focus on food security and smallholders. This often helped keep negotiations focused on food security and limited drift towards private investment frames or market solutions. It also helped to ensure that the needs of smallholders were more visible in policy recommendations. Moreover, despite the Committee's attempt to limit the impact of the HLPE reports and recommendations, CSOs found it useful to reply to the reports to support their arguments. As noted above, CSOs also pursued a similar strategy to secure rights-based approaches.

CSOs have been developing strong alliances with national representatives who increasingly acknowledge the technical knowledge as well as the local knowledge of CSO participants. These alliances have also worked in favor of the CSOs, especially when countries support their statements (as evidenced above). These alliances were strengthened through the development of side events, through meetings with country delegates and sharing positions in advance.

While alliance building and lobbying have been effective strategies, they are not strengths of CSO actors. CSOs need to find ways to increase lobbying efforts during the inter-sessional period. Resources permitting, CSOs would also benefit from attending bilateral meetings and lobbying in Rome and in capitals, however, as a former member of the CSM Coordination Committee noted:

> [this] is something the CSM does not do well. This moves to the impact beyond the CFS in Rome, to influencing policy at the national level in the capital. Civil society need to get much more organized in the capitals. And the CSM should be supporting CSOs at the national level to support the implementation of CFS outcomes. This is clearly stated in the CSM initiating document.
>
> (Interview, July 2014, Skype)

Through trial and error, CSOs have found key strategies that have served them well in their engagement with the CFS. These strategies do not represent a one-size-fits-all scenario and need to remain flexible and responsive to what is happening in the CFS. At the same time, they represent strategies that can be adapted and tested by CSOs working in other fora.

Challenges to effective CSO engagement

Effective and meaningful participation of civil society within the CSM and across the CFS has not been without challenges. Key challenges facing civil society actors include language, the scope of issues addressed, coherence, power politics and limitations inherent to food security as a concept.

While there is simultaneous translation into the six official languages of the FAO, when the CFS is negotiating text, the working language is English. Consequently participants who do not read English are unable to effectively participate. This issue extends beyond civil society and impacts many delegations. There is also the issue of becoming fluent in UN-speak: the technical language and communication style used in intergovernmental negotiations. Correspondingly, interventions made in non-UN-speak can be misunderstood and misinterpreted, and are often ignored. This disadvantages civil society actors.

Alongside different spoken languages and the technical language, CSOs communicate ideas in a variety of ways. Becoming conversant in these modes of communication takes a great deal of time and is best done outside of the formal meetings, which often juxtapose the informal, participatory environments more familiar to civil society actors. However, through their ongoing engagement, CSOs have become increasingly fluent in the processes and mode of speech that result in effective communication in the UN forum.

A major challenge facing the operation of the CFS, and CSO engagement therein, stems from challenges of other groups seeking leadership in food security at the global level. Since the food price crisis of 2007–2008, food security has consistently been on the agenda for G8 and G20 leaders' summits and new programs, initiatives, alliances and frameworks continue to be advanced through processes that lack the same level of participation, transparency and engagement. Given the political and diplomatic power of G20 countries, and the high-level political engagement in the activities of the G20, it is no surprise that the G20 agenda is advanced in the CFS: the CFS is, after all, striving for policy coherence. However, the implications of this are that the world's 20 most powerful nations are dictating the process for the remaining 106 member countries of the CFS: which hardly represents the democratic aspirations of the CFS or the UN more broadly.[1]

At the same time, CSOs and many country delegations lack the capacity and time to grapple with the ever-growing list of tasks required for engagement in the CFS, not to mention all of their other work related to the Rome-based food agencies, leaving wealthy countries and larger delegations at an advantage. The CFS must be careful to not fall victim to its own success by taking on an ever increasing workload. At the same time, the Committee needs to ensure that the argument just made is not given as an excuse to limit its functioning.

Implications for the future of global food security governance

The complexity of the way in which the discourse of food security is taken up across global food security governance raises more questions than it answers. Throughout this research the limitations of food security as a discourse and as a policy frame were consistently reinforced. First, food security employs a technocratic definition and approach: it has been highly negotiated and therefore does not necessarily reflect the best definition of the situation, but rather international consensus arrived at by diplomatic compromise. Food security is apolitical insofar as it fails to accept the political processes that contribute to food insecurity.

Food security is constructed as disembodied, non-located, absent from political, ecological, economic and sociocultural context. At the same time, food insecurity is constructed as embodied (normally a woman/mother), it is located (usually in Africa) and framed within a specific sociocultural context at the local or national scales. There is thus a disconnect between the way in which the end goal (food security) and the problem (food insecurity) are understood and framed. Food security as an approach, as a frame, as discourse and as a policy program, remains worthy of critique and scrutiny. At issue however is not the relevance or usefulness of the term, but rather the ways in which it is being redefined in a post-food price spike policy context. The amount of focus and attention being paid to food security at this moment illustrates the need for ongoing critical academic inquiry.

Food security, as a key policy frame, is an example of what James Ferguson (1994) calls an anti-political device. It turns a symptom of poverty into the ends of policy. Instead, hunger, and by extension poverty, must be situated within specific economic systems of production, modalities of representation and regimes of power (George 1984). Dominant discourses informing food security policy are marked by a reluctance to acknowledge hunger and malnutrition as a political problem linked to relations of power. Given the relationship between food security policy at the global level and broader neoliberal project, it is not surprising that international actors choose food security over trade or financial markets as the discourse to frame the fallout of the food price spikes. Food security has allowed actors to bypass difficult policy problems that make up the structural causes of hunger and malnutrition. In turn, governments can be seen to engage in seemingly urgent and earnest deliberations about food security with little threat to the status quo. In the global food security policy domain there is room for counter- and non-hegemonic actors to push for change (Holt-Giménez and Shattuck 2011), but all policy debates framed through food security will have a hard time escaping the history and trajectory of the term.

Does this mean that the term should be done away with? Despite the clear limitations and problems outlined above, at this moment, as the battle for leadership over the problem and solutions continues, the answer is, hesitatingly, no. This is in part because academic ponderings on discourses of food security remain removed from the fact that food security describes a very real, very troubling problem. Indeed there is a disconnect between policy and practice that demands stronger analysis and reflection. From this perspective, however flawed, food security provides a common language that governments, policy makers, field staff, NGOs, the private sector and social movements understand and, at least partly, agree on. They certainly do not agree on the adequacy of the definition. There is also no agreement on the path to achieving food security. Yet, importantly, there is clarity in what is meant by food security in international circles. This agreement is valuable. To begin to reimagine and reopen negotiations on another term to describe the same problem—a lack of adequate access and availability of appropriate foods to lead a healthy life—could take years and could shift attention away from the pressing issue: almost one sixth of the planet is hungry and industrial food production models are not sustainable. Attempts by the CFS to expand the term to "food and nutrition security" (CFS 2012) are illustrative of the challenges and tensions involved in reformulating terms in intergovernmental fora. At the same time, pushing to incorporate or embed language that provides a strategic critique of food security (i.e., food sovereignty) into these fora is also dangerous as critical aspects of these approaches are likely to be tempered through passive revolution (Gramsci 1971).

While the term remains useful (at least for now), food security programs and policies need to be reimagined and an alternative future developed in line with ecological principles that tackle distribution, consumption, injustice and that are effectively integrated at the local, national and regional (and global, if appropriate) levels in accordance with local realities. It is acknowledged that a catch-22 situation emerges when this statement is considered in the context of embedded neoliberalism. As a result, it is also recognized that change will need to extend far beyond food security to the core of systems of global governance. Until then, food security at the global level will continue to exist as a policy framework that claims to work towards the eradication of a structural problem without addressing the structural issues. As noted above, this approach simultaneously provides a way for governments to feign action without having to address difficult political decisions related to financial systems, justice and natural resources. This is the conundrum of late capitalism and extends across the key challenges of this century. Thinking ahead, a food policy approach (Lang et al. 2009), food sovereignty (Holt-Giménez and Altieri 2013; McMichael 2006; Mousseau and Mittal 2006) and emerging literature on resilience (Alinovi et al. 2010; De Schutter 2008) could prove useful in imaginations of a post-food security policy era.

Towards this end, it is imperative that action is taken around issues of international trade and the impacts on food security. The CFS will struggle to find authority in the area of trade, despite the clear links between trade policy and food (in)security. Indeed, the FAO faces similar challenges. Furthermore, a review by the Special Rapporteur on the Right to Food of key FAO reports on trade negotiations and agriculture unveiled that the conclusions of these reports are "unfortunately only partially and insufficiently reflected in the discourse promoted by the FAO at the global level, which does not systematically indicate the conditions under which trade can improve food security at the local, national and international levels" (De Schutter 2013: para 9). One way to build legitimacy would be for the FAO to:

> express its views more clearly on the question of trade and food security; building not only on its experience with a wide range of situations at country level, but also on its past attempts to ensure food security is always prioritised in the organization of trade in agricultural commodities.
>
> (De Schutter 2013: para 9)

At the same time, the role of the World Bank, the G8 and G20 in food security policy needs to be more carefully considered.

Since its reform, the CFS has addressed issues of climate change, gender, nutrition, protected crisis, land tenure, food price volatility and smallholder sensitive investment by developing negotiated policy recommendations facilitated through policy roundtables. It has also become a best practice in participation. This commitment to participation has meant that CSOs are participants on the Committee and in turn contribute to agenda setting. This is in line with, and reinforces, the reform vision of ensuring "strong linkages to the field to ensure the process is based on the reality on the ground" (CFS 2009: para 3) and ensures that these key themes, which are acknowledged as inadequately addressed by other actors, have been taken up by the CFS. That the CFS is tackling issues widely acknowledged as central to addressing food insecurity but largely ignored when it comes to formulating policy actions is in part what makes the CFS interesting, not only in terms of analysis but also with respect to the future of food security.

Lessons learned for global governance

The application of global governance theory to the reform of the CFS provides an opportunity to reflect on implications for global governance studies more broadly, specifically with respect to addressing key challenges and limitations as identified across the literature. What follows are insights into global governance as observable phenomenon and as political project, as informed by the CFS reform process.

Observable phenomenon

With respect to global governance as observable phenomenon, the CFS is positioned within the broader architecture of global food security governance and reflects the intersectional processes between the political, economic and sociocultural. In contrast to processes of multi-polarity of power and decentralization of power often associated with global governance, the CFS recentralizes authority in the hands of nation-states. At the same time, it is developing and supporting mechanisms to ensure that multiple stakeholders are involved in the processes. In this way, decision-making processes are pluralistic and decision making remains the authority of nations.

With respect to the variable geometry of political significance and regulatory capacity across systems of global governance, within and beyond the CFS, a shift in significance is evident. The CFS maintains limited regulatory capacity. Actors have sought to address this, in part, by anchoring policy recommendations in existing intergovernmental agreements—notably the right to food—and by starting work on monitoring and evaluation of their own policy proposals. These changes, alongside the consistent output of the Committee, have contributed to increased political significance. This comes at a potential risk insofar as the CFS has managed to advance comparatively progressive policies because the people negotiating them tend to fall below the ministerial level and hold diplomatic posts as permanent representatives to the Rome-based food agencies. Should the CFS become increasingly politically significant, it is likely that ministerial participation will increase. This will undoubtedly add a higher political dimension that has been relatively absent from the CFS thus far, but it could threaten existing procedures and flexibility that are in fact the strength and added value of the reformed CFS.

Global governance requires institutions to function as intermediaries to tie together different components of sociopolitical and economic systems. The CFS has been restructured to play such a role, and not only to bring components together but also to ensure that where they meet there is an interface space that constitutes "important terrains for confrontations between social movements and the defenders of the neoliberal agenda" (McKeon 2009:49).

Muldoon (2004:9) argues that "governance structures only survive if they promote stability in the system." As a participatory and inclusive platform for discussion, the CFS is in many ways addressing the issue of stability, in line with a broader participatory turn. Ignoring civil society in an era of networks and social media is increasingly challenging and problematic. Creating this interface space serves to focus and align actors who are often on opposing sides. While there are implications for resistance and the capacity for non-hegemonic action (Holt-Giménez and Shattuck 2011), that the confrontations take place within established parameters provides a level of enhanced stability. Where the CFS continues to struggle is in claiming authority to address political issues intimately tied to food security but addressed by other actors. Two key examples are trade (domain of the WTO) and climate change (domain of the UNFCCC).

With respect to shifts taking place at the level of global governance, the CFS exhibits an upward shift in authority as it seeks to coordinate national-level policies and ensure policy cohesion. Similarly, a downward shift is evident insofar as civil society participants have taken on a great deal of work in terms of research, coordination and planning. To date, this has not been perceived as the CFS unloading work and responsibilities to the civil society sector. Instead, this is understood as a meaningful opportunity for civil society actors to influence policy processes.

In terms of global governance as observable phenomena, there has been a rise in the popularity and usage of information comparison, such as benchmarking and best practices (van Kersbergen and Waarden 2004:55). The CFS reflects this trend but it is also acknowledged that such approaches are promoted within the CFS due to a lack of capacity to fund projects or to implement policies. Finally, as illustrated through the case studies, within the CFS, networks and alliances are being made and remade along key issues and not necessarily along ideological or historic lines.

Political project

Global governance as political project is taken up in several ways including: global governance as a way of solving the world's collective problems; global governance to re-democratize in the face of globalization; and global governance as advancement of a neoliberal project. Each of these forms of enactment can be seen in the reform of the CFS. The issue of coming together to solve a collective problem stems from the origins of the idea of food security and has continued to rationalize actions around food security as exemplified in part through the policy theme of relief. With respect to re-democratization in the face of globalization, the CFS has relied on transparency, participation and applicability of policy outcomes to secure greater legitimacy in the fight for authority over food security policy.

The political and social playing field—the transnational space—within which the CFS operates, is defined by embedded neoliberalism. The embedded nature of neoliberalism establishes the main boundaries of logic and operation, but the theory forwards that neoliberal hegemony is ever-changing, always contested and thus in a constant state of flux. It thus represents a hard—but not impassable—barrier for actors seeking to challenge its logic. At the same time, the CFS facilitates the advancement of a neoliberal project. Here, the understanding of embedded neoliberalism helps to make sense of why this is and how it functions. As Chapter 3 illustrated, the concept of food security in global policy debates has developed as part of a wider neoliberal project and as such, debates about food security necessarily take place within the boundaries of embedded neoliberalism. The neoliberal discourse is further strengthened by the CFS's principle of one vote per country, which is arguably democratic but fails to address inequalities in power, wealth and capacity. Furthermore, during CFS negotiations it is apparent that countries with greater power and influence—most notably G8 countries—remain better positioned and better able to block consensus than less powerful countries, although not always.

Whether previously "outside" actors prove more successful in their pursuits to change the system from the inside, as they continue to also work on the outside, remains to be seen. However, the research has shown that there is room for stronger democratic processes to emerge. Indeed, the real value of the reformed Committee is that it is an international forum that engages with the more difficult, even structural, issues and it is helped to do so through the participation of multiple actors. In this respect, the reformed CFS, as an actor in global governance, serves as a means to deal more effectively with the crisis-prone consequences of neoliberal social processes. The prevailing neoliberal logic, steering policy processes beyond the state, is deeply embedded in a broader political trend towards reregulation of the world economy in ways that obscure the negative tendencies of late capitalism. However, the logic of embedded neoliberalism, informed by neo-Gramscian understandings of hegemony, suggests that this is inevitable.

Related theories of change suggest that short of revolution, neoliberal hegemony will continue to be contested and in turn concessions will be granted to maintain relations of power in a slightly altered form. As such, while the CFS presents a space for confrontations between social movements and the defenders of the neoliberal agenda (McKeon 2009), the organizational structures within which it is embedded ensure that critical voices—the voices of those most affected by food insecurity—are engaged in counter-hegemonic action instead of non-hegemonic action.

Non-hegemonic action stands in contrast to counter-hegemonic action. A hegemonic arrangement is achieved when a population comes to be dominated partly through its own consent. However, hegemony is relational insofar as the processes of organizing consent may also create opportunities for constructing counter-hegemonic movements and resistance (Carroll 1990:393). Simplified: counter-hegemonic action potentially exists in relation to hegemony. When considered in the context of embedded neoliberalism, it is theorized that such counteractions serve to stretch boundaries but not deconstruct or rebuild them. Such actions remain vulnerable to co-option. Thus, counter-hegemony may present itself as transformative, but it remains tied to the agenda of the dominant hegemonic actors (Carroll 2007; Hall 1988). By contrast, anti-hegemonic action seeks to remove itself from the terrain of hegemony by moving beyond counter-hegemonic promotion of fragmentation and politics of difference and seeking solutions outside of the logic of embedded neoliberalism. Following from this, it is theorized that while the CFS presents opportunities for counter-hegemonic change, it skirts the possibility of anti-hegemonic change in so far as it remains tied to UN processes and the language of food security.

Addressing the limitations of global governance

Beyond the ideological barriers of embedded neoliberalism, global governance faces several challenges and critiques, notably with respect to questions of participation, accountability and legitimacy. These issues are now revisited to illustrate the way in they arise and are addressed within the CFS to contribute to the growing literature on global governance and global food security policy. First, however, it is important address the three weaknesses of global governance scholarship raised by Overbeek (in Overbeek et al. 2010: a historical analysis; blind pluralism; and apolitical analysis). First, ahistorical research been avoided by providing a review of the evolution of the discourse of food security policy in relation to wider political processes. Furthermore, the case studies are situated within the broader reform trajectory and build on one another to highlight the importance of process and history in policy making.

With respect to the challenge that analyses are necessarily pluralist in so far as they tend to take the plurality of actors, interests and structures as essential, it is here argued that this is a strength and not a weakness of this research. Of interest is how actors work together to achieve the reform objectives of the CFS. Finally, the concern that, in so much as power is often removed from analyses, inquiries into processes of global governance are apolitical, has been addressed by careful observation and reflection on relations of power within the CFS and outside, notably as they relate to language, capacity and perceived legitimacy, and by taking the standpoint of traditionally weaker actors—CSOs—through participant observation.

Participation

Through its recent reform process, the CFS has supported new mechanisms and structures that are reshaping the way food security policy is debated and developed by changing who is engaged in the debate (Duncan and Barling 2012). By including civil society actors as official participants on the Committee, the CFS is championing a model of enhanced participation at the level of international policy making and finding new ways to engage actors who have previously sat at the margins of official food security debates.

Through enhanced participation new opportunities to challenge the logic of embedded neoliberalism are being created. While this has the potential to expand the terms of debate, understandings of the problems and the scope of solutions, which are here deemed to be positive, the challenge for the CSM, moving forward, will be finding a way to balance insider status with outsider objectives (Duncan and Barling 2012).

How well the reformed CFS is able to put into practice the values and mechanisms it has developed and supported is an important test not only of the value of the Committee, but also of civil society participation in global policy-making processes, and global governance more broadly. Notably, how the CFS incorporates and manages the participation of civil society, and how CSOs manage their participation and retain a meaningful sense of agency, will be a litmus test for claims of legitimacy in the face of challenges from donor-based and wealthy country-led initiatives that seek to maintain neoliberal hegemony and continue to forward agro-industrial solutions to food security and nutrition.

Within the CFS, participation from research bodies, philanthropic foundations and to a lesser extent, the private sector, remains limited. The enthusiasm and diligent engagement of CSOs had helped propel the reformed Committee through its post-reform learning curve, but to increase the impact and influence of the CFS and to ensure that it upholds its mandate of inclusivity, it will need to find a way of engaging other participant groups in more meaningful ways. At the same time, greater participation from these actors could quickly shift the balance of power and strain the CFS's commitment to ensuring that the voices of those most affected by food security are heard. More research into ways of balancing increased buy-in without impacting the growing influence and engagement of civil society actors within the CFS would be valuable.

Accountability

One of the major critiques of multilateral policy processes relates to a lack of accountability. The likelihood of states agreeing to mechanisms to hold themselves to account, especially on non-binding issues, is minimal. Food security is a national responsibility: states are accountable for ensuring the right to food. In terms of policy making at the global level, states are being asked to monitor their own progress and to prioritize development. Yet states continue to prioritize economic values: food security remains framed as an outcome of a strong economy and not as a primary objective.

Of the dominant international policy initiatives targeting food security, explicit discussion of accountability is notably absent in most. By contrast, the CFS's GSF dedicates a section to monitoring and follow-up of food security policies. The CFS has been very clear on the issue of accountability: while the CFS's work and negotiations are participatory, states are accountable for decision making.

At the global level, the paucity of mechanisms to ensure accountability and follow-through by actors leads to unfulfilled commitments and a form of global-level policy amnesia wherein political leaders make declarations and commitments that are quickly forgotten or substituted for more appealing policies. While the CFS has initiated a process to monitor the uptake of its policy recommendations, it has no way of enforcing implementation and thus it becomes difficult to hold states accountable. That said, the outputs of the CFS, most notably the VGGT, can be used as tools to hold governments to account by donors and civil society actors. These inter-governmentally negotiated guidelines provide frameworks for assessment of national policies, practices and actions that contradict CFS outcomes.

Legitimacy

The CFS's reform document defines legitimate participants. The legitimacy of CFS member states is assumed. CSOs as a category of participant are understood to be legitimate in the CFS. The autonomous nature of the CSM means that legitimacy is defined within, by CSOs themselves. Social movement actors claim legitimacy based on their lived experience and insofar as they have been selected to engage in the CFS through the CSM (autonomously defined legitimacy). Social movements argue that they have internal legitimacy based on who they are and their work at the local level. Legitimacy, they note, is a problem of NGOs that speak on behalf of others. In turn, NGOs have tended to take on a supportive role to social movements and established networks. Internal perceptions of legitimacy may not transfer to external perception. Importantly, the legitimacy of CSOs in the CFS has been earned by way of active participation. Yet legitimacy is not a stable condition but something fluid that must be repeatedly created and recreated (Boström and Hallström 2010:15).

The CSM is continuously reflecting on and refining their participation processes (see Chapter 5) so as to enhance legitimacy. The autonomous nature of the Mechanism means that each constituency and sub-region is responsible for designing and following through with a process deemed legitimate to a range of related actors. This is an example of output legitimacy (Thomassen and Schmitt 1999:255). CSO participants in the CSM must be seen to be legitimate (as well as accountable) to their constituents and networks. If they are not, actors may raise complaints and undermine the broader participatory process.

When the CFS adopted the reform document, 123 countries agreed that it was the legitimate forum at the global level for coordination of actions related to food security. Despite this, actors undermine the Committee's legitimacy by coordinating actions and policies on food security outside of the CFS. This illustrates the challenges of legitimacy at the multilateral level, especially when the most legitimate platform operates below ministerial or head of state levels.

Conclusion

This book has provided a window onto the reorganization of a UN committee during a watershed period. It focused on the dynamics that took place within specific arrangements: the internal and external dynamics of the CFS. The data and analysis presented throughout this book illustrate how the reformed CFS has managed to achieve the majority of its reform objectives. It is clear that the CFS has emerged as an innovative, participatory and consultative body with the capacity to address challenges as they arise, while also producing progressive food security policies that move beyond business as usual and make a start at addressing the root causes of food insecurity. As such, the reformed CFS is the most legitimate and appropriate body to lead efforts towards improved global cohesion and best practices in food security policy. Yet challenges and obstacles remain.

As it moves forward, the Committee must refrain from overloading itself: a real risk as interest in the CFS grows. Already the CFS is receiving requests related to monitoring and evaluation of external programs. This type of work is beyond the scope and capacity of the Committee, at least at this time. The CFS should continue to reflect on its work plan and tackle issues within its mandate. Other challenges facing the CFS, and raised in this book, include: awareness and recognition; monitoring and evaluation; influence in terms of being able to achieve its mandate as the foremost international and intergovernmental platform; and the ability to address interconnected crises and associated challenges of depleting natural resources, further integration of food, financial and fuel markets, and climate change.

The Committee remains at the periphery of influence. It has been illustrated and argued in this book that this position is not inherently negative as it allows for, at times, greater freedom and flexibility with respect to policy processes and outcomes. The challenge becomes ensuring the uptake of the Committee's policy proposal. It is also acknowledged that it remains too early in the reform process to make declarations about the impact of the CFS.

What can be concluded at this stage is that despite its legitimacy, increasing recognition, deliberative mechanisms and wide rhetorical support, the CFS continues to be undermined by powerful economically driven actors. Policies and processes emerging from the CFS are in danger of being overlooked in favor of decisions made by competing international institutions and fora. Key multilateral actors have been identified as the G8, G20 and the World Bank. While all have expressed their support for the CFS, they have also pursued food security policy programs outside of the CFS. As illustrated throughout this book, the development of these initiatives present a threat to the mandate and legitimacy of the CFS. Furthermore, the initiatives often contradict policy recommendations developed and negotiated through the CFS, undermining calls for improved cohesion.

Theoretical assumptions of transnational neopluralism would suggest that within the architecture of global food security governance the ability of the CFS to fulfil its mandate is likely to remain limited. The CFS simply does not have the resources, power and influence of actors like the G8 and G20. Furthermore, the advancement of competing visions for the future of food security continues to move ahead, while the CFS is faced with the possibility of experiencing more challenges if it gains prominence and attracts actors who are not versed in the rules of operation or who are resistant to its participatory structure.

At the same time, to suggest that the G20 and G8 countries will disengage from food security, or that they even should, also fails to recognize the important role these actors could play. First, wealthy countries face pressing food security and nutrition challenges at the national level, notably related to issues of (over)consumption and malnutrition. Second, they have the responsibility of reforming financial and trade systems which currently negatively impact on food security. Not only do the G8 and G20 have technical capacity in this area, they also have a great deal of legitimacy in terms of regulating markets across the multilateral system.

Sophia Murphy (2013:4) has proposed important contributions the G20 could make towards global food security, all of which can also be applied to the G8:

> by reforming certain problematic domestic policies (for instance, the minimum-use biofuels mandates of the European Union and the United

States); by accepting greater transparency and predictability in the level and use of grain stocks; by accepting disciplines on the use of export restrictions and working with net-food importing developing countries to restore their confidence in international trade; and by improving the regulation of speculation and increasing transparency on commodity-futures markets; by making significant progress toward shifting their agricultural production systems toward less-polluting models.

In taking on such tasks, and "getting their houses in order," the G8 and G20 must avoid encroaching on wider intergovernmental processes wherein all countries participate, and especially processes where the voices of those most affected by food insecurity are given priority.

It is unlikely that the G8 and G20 will step back and they appear increasingly committed to strengthening trade liberalization and the role of the private sector. Consider for example that UK Prime Minister David Cameron declared that the G8's 2013 Lough Erne Summit would be "focused on three ways in which we can support the development of open economies, open governments and open societies to unleash the power of the private sector" (Cameron 2012). The G8's New Alliance appears to be doing just that in Africa, despite mounting evidence that these types of neoliberal policies have negative impacts on food security and the most vulnerable (Ben-David et al. 1999; De Schutter 2013; FAO 2000, 2012; Madeley 2000; Panda and Ganesh-Kumar 2009; Tyler and Dixie 2012; Wise 2009).

This book has argued that within a context of embedded neoliberalism, and amidst the competition for leadership, space has been made for maneuvering. CSOs have pushed the boundaries of status quo. In turn, the CFS has initiated discussions and processes to tackle some of the more pressing and structural issues impacting food insecurity and malnutrition. As such, the CFS is responding to calls to move away from "business as usual" (IAASTD 2009; UNCTAD 2013; UNEP 2012). However, it can also be concluded that so long as policy discussions revolve around food security, fundamental structural changes—non-hegemonic change—will remain impossible. This is the admittedly defeatist conundrum of social change in a neoliberal era. However, the theory predicts that resistance pushes the boundaries and forces change. Therefore while the neoliberal logic of food security will be hard to escape, changing the logic is inevitable and can be shaped by challenges to the status quo. This is best done through active engagement of civil society actors within the CFS and outside.

Looking forward: Opportunities for future research

There is more work to be done examining the use and implication of global governance and food security governance. As noted above, literature on global governance was used to frame the research project. However, global governance is also being enacted by policy makers and other actors to refer to processes of food security governance. The language of global food security governance is increasing in line with the G8 and G20's interest in the subject. As such there is a potential for reification between academic examinations of multilateral food security policies and a "real-world" discursive shift that more effectively aligns food security initiatives with the objectives and language of powerful economic actors.

Another interesting question is to understand at what stage of formalization (perhaps measured in terms of who participates) the CFS starts to become less effective. Or, framed positively, what is the ultimate level of formalization for impact? The question emerges out of concern that the success of the CFS will be its eventual downfall insofar as what makes it functional now is very much dependent on the negotiators and their distance from capitals and the (albeit varying) flexibility they have to operate. Thus, the balance between less formal, deliberate processes allowing for stronger outcomes and the power that comes from ministerial or leader-driven processes in terms of impact, is something worthy of more reflection and analysis.

There is also more work to be done on understanding the impact and influence of soft law on national and international action. As the case studies illustrated, soft law is being developed in ways that produce more legitimate products with higher degrees of buy-in from multiple stakeholders. It is possible that these could have more impact, influence and momentum then hard laws. Indeed, to suggest that the binding nature of an international agreement ensures action is naive. One need only reflect on the binding obligations set out in the Kyoto Protocol to the UNFCCC, or obligations of states to the right to food.

There is also a need for more research into the relationship between the FAO and the CFS. It appears that the FAO is keen to take up CFS-endorsed policies and to shift normally technical processes into political ones. The VGGT is a prime example of this. Research into whether this is an increasing trend, and if so, what the implications are for the FAO work plan is important.

In the context of this research, policy cohesion is assumed to be desirable. This can be seen as a limitation. Indeed, as discussed throughout, cohesion exists in the form of neoliberal hegemony. The CFS reformed to facilitate this cohesion but its authority is often undermined and its policies often continue to hold fast to a neoliberal trajectory. Questions of which and whose policies are to be cohered to are addressed but require further theoretical and analytical attention alongside the question of whether cohesion around global food security—in all its complexity and scope—is even desirable.

Opportunities for further research into global food security governance are varied, however it is essential that researchers responding to calls for increased research do not serve to support political stalling tactics aimed at avoiding having to make difficult policy decisions. Given the growing complexity of systems of global governance and the problems they seek to regulate, ongoing research into the ordering of global food security governance is needed, especially with respect to the roles, responsibilities and influence of the private sector and philanthropic foundations, as noted above. To better understand the impact of the CFS, careful mapping of the implementation and impact of CFS policies at the country level is needed. Here, energy must also be directed at developing rigorous methods to account for attribution of policy changes.

Research is needed to identify ways in which the CFS model of participation and the CSM approach to facilitation can be transferred to other policy and negotiation spaces. At the same time, more attention needs to be paid to the implications of having social activists move from the periphery to the center to understand if their engagement in counter-hegemonic action outweighs the benefits of non-hegemonic action.

Within the CSM there is a push by many social movement actors to engage in discussion and debate on food sovereignty. Deep reflection on the implications of allowing the CFS to potentially define a critical resistance discourse is needed to ensure that a strong resistance discourse does not become co-opted and redefined through multilateral negotiations.

Finally, there is a need to continue to map inconsistencies between food security research and policy. For example, calls for greater investment remain prominent and largely unchallenged within multilateral fora, especially outside of the CFS, yet research undertaken by the FAO (2012:7) argues that "investors are targeting countries with weak land tenure security" and that investors tend to focus on the "poorest countries, and those that are also less involved in world food exchanges." At a CFS side event hosted by the Inter-Agency Working Group discussing the impacts of investment and PRAI on developing country agriculture, the World Bank's Agribusiness Unit team leader presented a historical review of 179 agri-business investments in developing countries and noted that there was very little incentive to invest in food crops when investing in agriculture, and that most investors will opt for crops that provide high returns, such as palm oil or rubber.

The world is a messy place, overloaded with wicked problems. The interconnected nature of global food systems, the growing interconnectedness of food, fuel and financial markets and increasing competition for natural resources suggest that there is a need for meaningful global cooperation and cohesion so as to eradicate hunger and ensure the human right to adequate food. Despite the many challenges and limitations, the reformed CFS has emerged as the most legitimate and hopeful platform to lead the way on global food security governance.

Note

1   This is not to suggest that this is somehow a new phenomenon, but rather it highlights an ongoing limitation of multilateral negotiations, inside and outside the UN system.

References

Alinovi, L., M. D'Errico, E. Mane, and D. Romano. 2010. "Livelihoods strategies and household resilience to food insecurity: an empirical analysis to Kenya." Presented at

Promoting Resilience through Social Protection in Sub-Saharan Africa (June 28–30, 2010). Dakar, Senegal: European Report of Development. Retrieved (http://resilience.igadhost.com/attachments/article/244/Livelihoods%20Strategies%20and%20Household%20Resilience%20To%20Food%20Security.pdf).

Ben-David, D., H. Nordström, and A. Winters. 1999. *Trade, Income Disparity and Poverty.* Geneva. Retrieved (www.wto.org/english/news_e/pres00_e/pov1_e.pdf).

Boström, M. and K. T. Hallström. 2010. "The fragile authority of multi-stakeholder standard setting," in *Re-Discovering International Organizations* (9-11 September). Stockholm: Standing Group on International Relations.

Cameron, D. 2012. "A G8 Meeting That Goes Back to First Principles." *Eurobserver.com (opinion),* November. Retrieved (http://euobserver.com/opinion/118265).

Carroll, W. 2007. "Hegemony and Counter-Hegemony in a Global Field." *Studies in Social Justice* 1(1): 36–66.

Carroll, W.K. 1990. "Restructuring Capital, Reorganizing Consent: Gramsci, Political Economy and Canada." *Canadian Review of Sociology and Anthropology* 27: 390–416.

CFS. 2009. *Reform of the Committee on World Food Security Final Version.* Rome: FAO. Retrieved (www.fao.org/fileadmin/templates/cfs/Docs0910/ReformDoc/CFS_2009_2_Rev_2_E_K7197.pdf).

CFS. 2012. *Coming to Terms with Terminology (revised Draft 25 July).* Rome: FAO.

Charvet, J., and E. Kaczynska-Nay. 2008. *The Liberal Project and Human Right: The Theory and Practice of a New World Order.* Cambridge: Cambridge University Press.

Claeys, P. 2013. "From Food Sovereignty to Peasants' Rights: An Overview of La Via Campesina's Rights-Based Claims over the Last 20 Years," in *Food Sovereignty: A Critical Dialogue.* New Haven: Program in Agrarian Studies, Yale University, The Journal of Peasant Studies and Yale Sustainable Food Project. Retrieved (www.yale.edu/agrarianstudies/foodsovereignty/pprs/24_Claeys_2013-1.pdf).

De Schutter, O. 2008. *Building Resilience: A Human Rights Framework for World Food and Nutrition Security.* A/HRC/9/23. New York: UN.

De Schutter, O. 2013. *Mission to the Food and Agriculture Organization of the United Nations.* New York: UN.

Duncan, J., and D. Barling. 2012. "Renewal through Participation in Global Food Security Governance: Implementing the International Food Security and Nutrition Civil Society Mechanism to the Committee on World Food Security." *International Journal of Sociology of Agriculture and Food* 19:143–61.

FAO. 2000. *Agriculture, Trade and Food Security: Issues and Options in the WTO Negotiations from the Perspective of Developing Countries.* Rome: FAO. Retrieved (www.fao.org/DOCREP/003/X4829E/X4829E00.HTM).

FAO. 2012. *Trends and Impacts of Foreign Investment in Developing Country Agriculture: Evidence from Case Studies.* Rome: FAO.

Ferguson, J. 1994. *The Anti-Politics Machine.* Minneapolis: University of Minnesota Press. Retrieved (http://books.google.co.uk/books?id=hgXbebNQ918C&lpg=PP1&pg=PP1#v=onepage&q&f=false).

George, S. 1984. *Ill Fares the Land: Essays on Food, Hunger and Power.* New York: Penguin.

Gramsci, A. 1971. *Selections from the Prison Notebooks.* New York: International Publishers.

Hall, S. 1988. *The Hard Road to Renewal.* London: Verso.

Holt-Giménez, E., and M.A. Altieri. 2013. "Agroecology, Food Sovereignty and the New Green Revolution." *Journal of Sustainable Agriculture* 37(1):90–102. Retrieved (www.tandfonline.com/doi/abs/10.1080/10440046.2012.716388).

Holt-Giménez, E., and A. Shattuck. 2011. "Food Crises, Food Regimes and Food Movements: Rumblings of Reform or Tides of Transformation?" *The Journal of Peasant Studies* 38(1):109–44. Retrieved (www.ncbi.nlm.nih.gov/pubmed/21284237).

IAASTD. 2009. *Synthesis Report of the International Assessment of Agricultural Knowledge, Science and Technology for Development.* Washington DC: IAASTD. Retrieved (www.unep. org/dewa/agassessment/reports/IAASTD/EN/Agriculture%20at%20a%20Crossroads_ Synthesis%20Report%20(English).pdf).

Lang, T., D. Barling, and M. Caraher. 2009. *Food Policy: Integrating Health, Environment and Society.* Oxford: Oxford University Press.

Madeley, J. 2000. *The Impact of Trade Liberalisation on Food Security and Poverty.* Stockholm: IATP. Retrieved (www.iatp.org/files/Impact_of_Trade_Liberalisation_on_Food_ Securit.htm).

McKeon, N. 2009. "Who Speaks for Peasants ? Civil Society, Social Movements and the Global Governance of Food and Agriculture." *Interface* 1(2):48–82.

McMichael, P. 2006. "Food Sovereignty vs. the Corporate Food Regime." *Conference Papers—International Studies Association* 1. Retrieved (http://search.ebscohost.com/login. aspx?direct=true&AuthType=ip,cookie,url,uid&db=aph&AN=27205768&lang=es&sit e=ehost-live).

Mousseau, F., and A. Mittal. 2006. "Food Sovereignty: Ending World Hunger in Our Time." *Humanist* 66(2):24–26. Retrieved (http://search.ebscohost.com/login.aspx?direct=true& AuthType=ip,cookie,url,uid&db=aph&AN=19862072&lang=es&site=ehost-live).

Muldoon, J. P. 2004. *The Architecture of Global Governance: An Introduction to the Study of International Organizations.* Boulder: Westview Press.

Murphy, S. 2013. *The G-20 and Food Security: What Is the Right Agenda?* Muscatine, IA. Retrieved (www.stanleyfoundation.org/publications/pab/MurphyPAB313.pdf).

Overbeek, H., K. Dingwerth, P. Pattberg, and D. Compagnon. 2010. "Forum: Global Governance: Decline of Maturation of an Academic Concept?" *International Studies Review* 12(4):696–719.

Panda, M., and A. Ganesh-Kumar. 2009. *Trade Liberalization, Poverty, and Food Security in India.* Washington DC: IFPRI. Retrieved (www.ifpri.org/publication/ trade-liberalization-poverty-and-food-security-india).

Thomassen, J., and H. Schmitt. 1999. "In Conclusion: Political Representation and Legitimacy in the European Union," pp. 255–73 in *Political Representation and Legitimacy in the European Union* edited by Hermann Schmitt and Jacques Thomassen. Oxford: Oxford University Press.

Tyler, G., and G. Dixie. 2012. "Investments in Agribusiness: A Retrospective View of a Development Bank's Investment in Agribusiness in Africa and East Asia," in *Responsible Agricultural Investment: The Way Forward (Side event 39th Session of the CFS).* Washington DC: World Bank.

UNCTAD. 2013. *Trade and Environment Review 2013.* Geneva: UNCTAD. Retrieved (unctad.org/en/PublicationsLibrary/ditcted2012d3_en.pdf).

UNEP. 2012. *Avoiding Future Famines: Ecological Foundation Sustainable Food Systems.* Nairobi: UNEP.

Van Kersbergen, K., and F. Van Waarden. 2004. "'Governance' as a Bridge between Disciplines: Cross-Disciplinary Inspiration Regarding Shifts in Governance and Problems of Governability, Accountability and Legitimacy." *European Journal of Political Research* 43(2):143–71. Retrieved (http://search.ebscohost.com/login.aspx?direct=true&AuthT ype=ip,cookie,url,uid&db=aph&AN=12360014&site=ehost-live).

Wise, T. A. 2009. "Promise or Pitfall? The Limited Gains from Agricultural Trade Liberalisation for Developing Countries." *Journal of Peasant Studies* 36(4):855–70. Retrieved (www.tandfonline.com/doi/abs/10.1080/03066150903354056).

Index

For Product Safety Concerns and Information please contact our
EU representative GPSR@taylorandfrancis.com Taylor & Francis
Verlag GmbH, Kaufingerstraße 24, 80331 München, Germany